Lauren Johnson is not on... ...Z, she also holds a masters de... ...d with emotionally disturbed c... ...ng her patients in the therapeutic be... ...pursuit of personal development and the realization of dreams... ...dition to watching TV and writing trivia books, she's also a screenwriter and has really big dreams of her own. Born and raised in the western suburbs of Chicago, she now resides in Los Angeles. This is her second book.

Also available from
all good bookshops,
priced £14.99

F.R.I.E.N.D.S

The Official Trivia Quiz Book

Lauren Johnson

headline

The right of Lauren Johnson to be identified as the Author of
the Work has been asserted by her in accordance with the
Copyright, Designs and Patents Act 1988.

First published in 2003
by New American Library, a division of Penguin Group (USA) Inc.
as *Friends: The One About the #1 Sitcom*

First published in the United Kingdom in 2004
by HEADLINE BOOK PUBLISHING LTD
This edition published in the United Kingdom in 2005
by HEADLINE BOOK PUBLISHING LTD

10 9 8 7 6 5 4 3 2 1

ISBN 0 7553 1342 9

Typeset in Goudy
Designed by Jennifer Ann Daddio
Photography by Byron J. Cohen, Bonnie Colodzin, Danny Feld, Robert Isenberg,
Craig T. Matthew, Oliver Upton, Joseph Viles.

Printed and bound in Great Britain by Mackays of Chatham, Chatham, Kent

Headline's policy is to use papers that are natural, renewable and
recyclable products and made from wood grown in sustainable forests.
The logging and manufacturing processes are expected to conform
to the environmental regulations of the country of origin.

Headline Book Publishing
A division of Hodder Headline
338 Euston Road
London NW1 3BH

www.headline.co.uk

HEAD 2790

Contents

ACKNOWLEDGMENTS

So many people to thank, so little space.

Business first . . .

First and foremost, I want to thank Kevin Bright, Marta Kauffman, and David Crane for trusting me with this project and giving me such an incredible opportunity. I also want to thank Kevin's able assistant, Colleen Mahan, for being so wonderful and making it so easy to be persistent. Many, *many* thanks to Alicia Sky Varinaitis and Mark Kunerth for making sure I got my facts straight. And a *humongous* thanks to Skye Van Raalte-Herzog at Warner Bros. for helping me through the process, being so patient, and laughing *with* me and not at me!

And, of course, the incredibly talented cast of *Friends*, as well as the brilliant writers, without whom this book would be nothing but a bunch of blank pages (and not very funny at that).

I'd also like to thank my editor, Dan Slater, at New American Library for making this all happen and being so enthusiastic from the get-go to the let-go. And my attorney, Lisa Canon, for so wonderfully taking care of all the stuff I know nothing about.

And lastly, I want to thank Marty Krofft for making the call.

Now for the personal . . .

I want to thank my family (and self-appointed publicists): Lynn and Noel Johnson, Kirsten Johnson, Curt Johnson, Reid Johnson and Jean Scott. Thank you for all your love and support and love and support. And my babies: Buster, Mac and Spot. Thank you for keeping your demands to a minimum while I was writing this book.

And finally, *my Friends* and cheerleaders: Joy Quanruud, Wendi Conley, Alessa Carlino, Brooke Covington, Sherilyn Fenn, Alex Govostis, Maria Besso, Suzae Johnson, Alice Johnson, Amalia Stahowiak, Anne Askernese, Kevin McClure, Geraldine Caedo, Cathy Wozniak, Lydia Glass, Dani Minnick, Debbie Green, Catherine Milord, Linda Modaro and Jamal Kord, Kim and Mark Henderson, Roz and Richie Annenberg, and Dave and Eileen Diltz. You guys are the best!

FOREWORD

Gunther's World

I suppose it's only appropriate that I've been asked to write a foreword for a book about trivia. You might say that I'm a decaffeinated footnote in the lives of the people who come to Central Perk, the guy who takes their orders when they walk in the door. "Hey, Gunther—an East Timor half-roast, semi-nonfat, zuppa-blended, molé-sprinkled Arianna latte over here." Their experience is about the coffee, obviously, and it certainly isn't about me.

Don't get me wrong. I like the people who come here. Particularly the sextet that spends their time on the sofa, which somehow, magically, is unoccupied whenever they come through the door. Sometimes, with a little effort, I even *care* about Ross, Joey, Chandler, Phoebe, Monica, and Rachel.

Especially Rachel.

Their lives are so full of trivia that I can't expect them to waste time thinking about me—even though I *am* more interesting than the whole lot of them put together. Ross may know everything about dinosaurs, but unlike me, he can't speak Dutch. Joey has great looks, a stream of girlfriends, and a role on a soap opera. But I was working as Bryce on *All My Children* long before he was standing in for Al Pacino's butt. And I am SOOOOO much funnier than Chandler. I mean, how funny can you be if you're constantly trying to prove it? The way I see it, those that can, do. Those that do it too much . . . go blind.

It's true that I don't write songs or play an instrument, but it's also true that the world is a better place for it—no offense, Phoebe. (You too, Tesh.) I may not get the mugs as clean as Monica would like, but there are far more interesting things to obsess on.

Like Rachel.

I could write a whole trivia book about Rachel. Her hair. Her shoes. Her nose. Her insane on-again/off-again interest in Ross. I mean, the guy invested more passion in his relationship with a monkey than he ever did with her.

Not that my whole world revolves around Rachel. Just because I have her Slinky. And her cat. And her furniture. It's not as if I've dug through her garbage cans. Not today, at least.

Sometimes I feel that I'm an important part of that group, kind of like the fifth Beatle. Just call me the "Seventh Friend." I mean, they invite me to all their parties. Dinner parties. Birthday parties. Holiday parties. But they've never been to my place.

Not that they've asked...huh?

We've been together now for nearly ten years. We've all gone through a lot of changes. Jobs. Careers. Love. Marriage. Divorce. Lesbian marriage. Bracelet buddies. Birth. Multiple births, in Phoebe's case. Janice's whining. Richard's mustache. Chandler smoking. Muffins. Meatball sandwiches. Chandler not smoking. More meatball sandwiches. Alternating apartments. Alternating roommates. Twin Phoebes. Fake Monicas. Even Joey's supposedly fictional brain transplant.

Me, little has changed except my hair. There's less of it.

Maybe that's too personal. Forget that I mentioned it. Think about them instead.

Obviously, that's all I do.

—Gunther
aka James Michael Tyler

INTRODUCTION

Thank God It's Thursday

I *live* for Thursdays.

Every Thursday evening I curl up on my sofa, remote in hand, and join twenty-five million other Americans as we indulge ourselves in the lives of six of our favorite Friends as they watch free porn, play who-know-who-better, and reel at the sight of ugly naked guy. Sometimes they play foosball and sometimes they just sit around and drink coffee while working out life's problems. No matter what they do, they're there for us, every Thursday night, like clockwork, and I gotta tell you, there's nothing better in this world than spending time with good Friends. And unless you've had your head in the sand for the last nine years, for most of us, the word "Thursday" has become synonymous with *Friends*.

So what is it about these Friends that'll make me break all speed records just so I can get home to watch them in "real time" instead of VCR time?

Because missing *Friends* is like missing a party that all your friends have been invited to which you *know* they'll be laughing about for the next week. It means going to work the next morning and having to stand outside the circle with a neon "L" flashing on your forehead while all your coworkers stand around the water cooler bonding over their mutual make-believe Friends. And it's sad because we all just want to be a Friend.

As a kid, I wanted to be a Brady (Marcia, to be clear). But on September 24, 1994, I grew up and suddenly realized I wanted to be a Friend. I mean, *look* at them. Not only are they an attractive bunch with really cool careers who live in the greatest city in the world, but they're charming and funny and everything we could possibly want in *our* friends. They're loyal and honest and they all really love one another. They respect and accept one another, warts and all. We see ourselves in them and because of that, we know that if *they're* okay, *we're* okay.

And in these times of vast uncertainty and global change, we can count on our Friends to keep things in perspective and help us to not take it all so seriously. They inspire us to nurture *our* friendships as they have theirs for the last ten years.

Come May 2004, Thursdays will never be the same.

Thank God for reruns and home video.

—Lauren Johnson

The Part
WITH THE
Questions

Season One

1. Rachel: "And then I got really freaked out and that's when it hit me . . . how much Barry looks like _____."

2. To whom did Ross say, "Really? I don't remember you making any sperm"?

3. Why did Phoebe give away a thousand dollars to a street person?

4. What does Chandler's mother do for a living?

5. Roger the Psychiatrist Guy, on his take on the gang's dysfunctional group dynamic: "You know, this kind of codependent, emotionally stunted, sitting in your stupid coffeehouse with your stupid big cups, which, I'm sorry, might as well have _____ on them."

6. What was the significance of 55-JIMBO?

7. What's a WENUS?

8. What book did Susan read to Ross and Carol's baby while he was in utero?

9. What kind of cookie did Ross split with Rachel when he asked her if it would be okay to ask her out sometime?

10. Why did Joey say, "The way I see it, the guy's upset here, you know? I mean, his wife's dead, his brother's missing. I think his butt would be angry here"?

11. Which two Friends committed insurance fraud?

12. What was Rachel referring to when she told Chandler, "Well, you were not the only one there. Joey was there, too"?

13. To whom was Ross referring when he said, "We had our first fight this morning. I think it has to do with my working late. I said some things that I didn't mean and he threw some feces"?

14. How did Rachel meet Paolo?

15. What was Chandler referring to when he told Joey, "Well, it's just that it's a pretty big commitment. I mean, what if one of us wants to move out?"

16. What did Monica's aunt Iris teach the girls?

17. To whom was Rachel referring when she said, "He's Satan in a smock"?

18. To whom was Monica referring when she told Phoebe, "Okay. He's a lawyer who teaches sculpting on the side and he can dance"?

19. What was Chandler referring to when he said, "Hi, um, I'm account number 7143457 and, uh, I don't know if you got any of that, but I would really like a copy of the tape"?

20. Who went on Rachel's honeymoon with Barry?

21. Chandler: "Ew, ew, ew, ew, ew, ew, ew! _____ got a Thigh-Master."

22. What was the nurse referring to when she told the Geller family, "This almost never happens"?

23. What did the little candy hearts say that Janice gave Chandler for Valentine's Day?

24. Monica to Rachel: "You stay here. Just wait right by the phone. Spray Lysol in my _____ and wait for Ross to kill you."

25. To whom was Carl referring when he told Rachel, "Exactly! And you just know, I'm gonna be the guy caught behind this hammerhead in traffic!"?

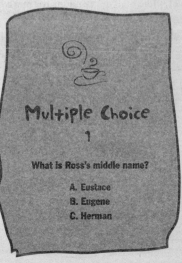

Multiple Choice
1

What is Ross's middle name?

A. Eustace
B. Eugene
C. Herman

26. Rachel to everyone: "Well, I just lost a _____ and I'd like to raise the bet five bucks. Does anyone have a problem with that?"

27. Who said, "You just start with half a dozen European cities, throw in thirty euphemisms for male genitalia and, BAM, you . . . got yourself a book!"?

28. Monica: "What? Are you nuts? We've got George Stephanopoulos's _____!"

29. What was Janice referring to when she told Chandler, "Well, I knew you had the Rockies. And so I figured, you know, you can wear Bullwinkle and Bullwinkle, or you can wear Rocky and Rocky, or you can mix and match, moose and squirrel"?

30. Ross to Paolo: "Do you know the word _____? 'Cause you're a huge _____."

31. To whom did Phoebe say, "You're going to Minsk?"

32. Chandler, on how he doesn't like his job: "I just don't want to be one of those guys that's in his office until twelve o'clock at night worrying about the _____."

33. What was Marcel wearing when Ross and Rachel found him in Mr. Heckles's apartment?

34. To whom was Monica referring when she said, "She buys tickets to plays that I want to see. She buys clothes at stores where I'm intimidated by the salespeople. She spent three hundred dollars on art supplies"?

35. Monica: "Oh, my God! I just had sex with someone who wasn't alive during the _____!"

36. What was the name on the jumpsuit Ross, Susan, and Phoebe found while locked in the broom closet as Carol gave birth?

37. To whom was Monica referring when she told Rachel, "How about the fact that he's engaged to a woman who happens to be your ex–best friend?"

38. To whom was Phoebe referring when she said, "In the cab on the way over, Steve blazed up a doobie"?

39. Who got hit in the face with a hockey puck?

40. To whom did Rachel say, "You got plugs!"?

41. Why did Monica tell Ross, "I'm thinking your new girlfriend wouldn't urinate on my new coffee table"?

42. What's Phoebe's twin's name?

43. Why did Phoebe say, "This is so intense. One side of my butt is totally asleep and the other side has no idea"?

44. What was Joey referring to when he said, "All right, come on, you guys. It's not that big of a deal, really. I mean, I just go down there every other day and make my contribution to the project"?

45. Chandler, to break the tension: "So, who's up for a big game of _____?"

46. Why did Rachel ask Monica, "Now, do you think his lovestick can be liberated from its denim prison?"

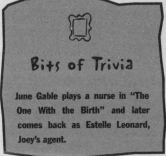

Bits of Trivia

June Gable plays a nurse in "The One With the Birth" and later comes back as Estelle Leonard, Joey's agent.

47. Joey: "Set another place for Thanksgiving. My entire family thinks I have _____."

48. Where was Ross when he announced, "All right, show's over. Nothin' to see here"?

49. What was Barry's profession?

50. Why did Rachel say, "It's like all my life, everyone has always told me, 'You're a shoe . . . you're a shoe, you're a shoe, you're a shoe,' and then today I just stopped and I said, 'What if I don't want to be a shoe? What if I want to be a purse . . . or a hat?'"

51. Phoebe: "You know those stupid soda people gave me seven thousand dollars for the _____."

52. To whom was Monica referring when she said, "I think he's shy. I think you have to draw him out. And then, when you do, he's a preppy animal"?

53. Chandler to Jill Goodacre: "You know, on second thought, gum would be _____ ."

54. What was Chandler referring to when he told everyone, "For me, this has been really great, you know. I think because it didn't involve divorce or projectile vomiting"?

55. What was Joey referring to when he told Ross, "You broke the code!"?

56. What did Joey buy Ursula, Phoebe's sister, for her birthday?

57. What is Barry's last name?

58. To whom did Ross say, "Oh, God, we didn't get into Scranton"?

59. To whom was Phoebe referring when she told Chandler, "No, I know. That's part of the whole them-not-liking-you *extravaganza*!"?

60. Monica: "No, it is me! You know, I'm not just the person who needs to fluff the pillows and pay the bills as soon as they come in! When I'm with her, I am so much more than that . . . I'm, I'm _____ !"

61. What was Chandler referring to when he said, "We think he was trying to spell 'monkey' "?

62. What did Phoebe say to Monica after she called Ross "competitive"?

63. What was Phoebe's twin sister doing for a living when Chandler and Joey first met her?

64. What happened when Joey's girlfriend set Chandler up on a blind date?

65. Who said, "Tartlets? Tartlets? Tartlets? The word has lost all meaning"?

66. What was Joey's dad's mistress's profession?

67. What did Joey wish for when he and Monica split a grilled cheese sandwich in lieu of the wishbone on Thanksgiving Day?

68. Who told Rachel, "You want to hear a freakish coincidence? Guess who's doing laundry there, too"?

69. What was Phoebe referring to when she said, "I know, I know. I opened it up and there it was, just floating in there like this tiny little hitchhiker"?

70. What did Monica's parents call her as a child?

71. To whom was Monica's coworker referring when she said, "You know, before me, there was no snap in his turtle for two years"?

72. What was Phoebe referring to when she shouted out the window to the apartment across the street, "Hey, that's not for you, bitch!"?

73. Why was Fun Bobby so bummed when he showed up at Monica's New Year's Eve party?

74. Who screamed, "What do you know? No one's going up to you and saying, 'Hi, is that your nostril? Mind if we push this pot roast through it?'"

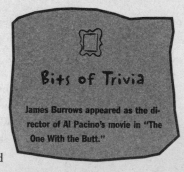

Bits of Trivia

James Burrows appeared as the director of Al Pacino's movie in "The One With the Butt."

75. To whom was Rachel referring when she said, "She loved me. She absolutely loved me. We talked for, like, two and a half hours. We have the same taste in clothes and . . . Oh! I went to camp with her cousin!"?

76. To whom did Rachel say, "Uh, we are here to break up with you"?

77. Who said, "Monica and I just crashed an embassy party"?

78. Ross to Rachel: "What happened to, uh, 'Forget relationships. I'm done with men'? The whole _____ embargo?"

79. Who said, "Oh, macaroni and cheese! We gotta make this!"?

80. To whom did Phoebe say, "Um, I have a question. Were you planning on kissing me ever?"

81. With whom did Chandler get trapped in an ATM vestibule during a blackout?

82. Joey: "I play _____'s butt."

83. Where was Ross when he was showered with Sweet'n Lows?

84. To whom was Phoebe's assistant referring when she said, "Oh, here comes your three o'clock. I don't mean to sound unprofessional, but yum"?

85. To whom was Chandler referring when he told Joey, "Oh, look, it's the woman we ordered," when encountering a strange woman sitting outside their door?

86. Why did Ross rush Marcel to the emergency room?

87. Rachel to Louisa: "All right. Well then, how about I call your supervisor and I tell her you shot my friend in the ass with a _____?"

88. How did Monica meet the woman who stole her credit card?

89. In which episode did Leah Remini appear?

90. Chandler: "Come on, Ross? Remember back in college when he fell in love with Carol and he bought her that ridiculously expensive crystal _____?"

91. What did all the Friends wind up eating for their first Thanksgiving dinner together?

92. What is Joey's mother's name?

93. Who said, "I could have cats"?

94. Phoebe: "Oh, and Debbie, my best friend from junior high, got struck dead on a miniature golf course. I always get this really strong Debbie vibe whenever I use one of those little _____ _____."

95. What was Monica referring to when she told Joey, "Hello? Were we at the same table? It's like cocktails in Appalachia!"?

96. Why did Rachel break up with Paolo?

97. Who played the two hot doctors that Rachel and Monica met while in the emergency room and consequently went out with?

98. Monica: "Oh, God! Oh, God! I'm like those women that you, you see with shiny guys named _____!"

99. Who saw whose boobies first?

100. Nora Bing to Jay Leno: "Occasionally after I've been intimate with a man, I just get this craving for _____."

101. What was Ross referring to when he told Carol, "Well, there is one way that seems to offer a certain acoustical advantage, but . . ."?

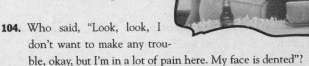

102. To whom did Phoebe say, "You have homosexual hair"?

103. Why did Rachel say, "God, I'm gonna look like a big Marshmallow Peep"?

104. Who said, "Look, look, I don't want to make any trouble, okay, but I'm in a lot of pain here. My face is dented"?

105. Rachel during a game of poker: "You know what? I think I'm going to make a little _____ pile."

106. Who was Louisa Gianetti?

107. Why did Rachel say, "Let's just say my Curious George doll is no longer curious"?

108. What did Ross give to Rachel for her birthday, the night she found out that he was in love with her?

109. What was Ross referring to when he told Phoebe, "You have to tell her. It's your moral obligation as a friend. As a woman, I think it's a feminist issue"?

110. To whom was Chandler referring when he told Ross, "This is basically the first time she's gonna see your underwear. Do you want her to see it dirty?"

111. Where did Rachel lose her engagement ring?

112. What was Ross referring to when he told Joey and Chandler, "Grab a spoon? Do you know how long it's been since I've grabbed a spoon? Do the words 'Billy, don't be a hero' mean anything to you?"

113. Rachel to Mindy: "If everything works out and you guys end up getting married and having kids and everything . . . I just hope they have his old _____ and your old nose."

114. Why were Ross and Carol asked never to return to the Magic Kingdom?

115. Why did Jack Geller yell out at Nana's funeral, "Now I'm depressed! Even more than I was"?

116. Phoebe to everyone: "Ugly Naked Guy is having Thanksgiving dinner with _____."

117. Why did Rachel say, "Ooh, I'm a man. Ooh, I have a penis. Ooh, I have to win money to exert my power over women"?

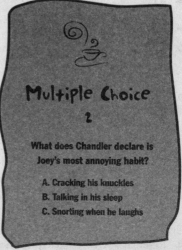

Multiple Choice

2

What does Chandler declare is Joey's most annoying habit?

A. Cracking his knuckles
B. Talking in his sleep
C. Snorting when he laughs

118. Who said, "Could we not go together? I wouldn't want to be the geek who invited the boss"?

119. Why did Ross go to China?

120. To whom and what was Chandler referring when

he said, "Well, I expect this from her. She's always been a Freudian nightmare"*!*

121. Who lived in the apartment below Monica and Rachel?

122. What was Joey's agent's name?

123. What was Rachel wearing when Monica first introduced her to the gang in Central Perk?

124. What was Susan's last name?

125. Who said, "All right, listen, missy! If you want this cart, you're gonna have to take me with it!"?

126. What happened to Ross at Nana's funeral?

127. Whom did Monica invite to their first New Year's party?

128. What was Phoebe referring to when she said, "Boy Scouts could have camped under there"?

129. Who said, "Mon, um, easy on those cookies, okay? Remember, they're just food. They're not love"?

130. What was Ross referring to when he said, "Yeah, the doctor got the K out. He also found an M and an O"?

131. What was Monica referring to when she said, "And you know what? We want a rematch"?

132. Why did Ross tell Rachel, "You had to be a bitch in high school. You couldn't have been fat"?

133. To whom was Monica referring when she asked, "You had sex in his chair?"

134. What was Chandler referring to when he told Ross, "I'm sorry. It was a onetime thing. I was very drunk and it was someone else's subconscious"?

135. To whom was Rachel referring when she said, "Look, all I know is that I cannot wait a week till I see him"?

136. What was Phoebe's response when Joey asked, "What do you think a good stage name for me would be?"

137. Phoebe to Monica and Rachel: "Now we need the _____ of a righteous man."

138. What was Ross referring to when he said, "Wasn't it supposed to be just a fling, huh? Shouldn't it be flung by now?"

139. How did Chandler find out his mother was coming to town?

140. What were Monica's last words to Rachel before they ran out the door on Thanksgiving Day to watch the Underdog balloon fly loose over the city?

141. Which Friend dated a married man or woman?

142. To whom did Ross say, "Hey, hey, hey. That's not the rule and you know it"?

143. What was George Stephanopoulos wearing when the girls spied on him in the apartment across the street?

144. Which Friend was an occasional smoker?

145. What number was on Monica and Rachel's door during the first season?

146. What is Chandler's mother's name?

147. Who told Chandler, "I wouldn't want to be there when the laughter stops"?

148. Chandler to his office crush: "Well, it throws my _____ out of whack."

149. Joey: "Whoa, whoa, whoa, whoa, Monica, what are you doing? This is a _____. You can't serve food with more than one syllable."

150. Which Friend was shot in the ass with a dart?

151. What zoo was Marcel accepted into?

152. Why did Monica say, "I'm Joan Collins!"?

153. What was Joey referring to when he said, "Yeah, well, I still got a week left to go in the program, and according to the rules, if I want to get the money, I'm not allowed to conduct any personal experiments, if you know what I mean"?

154. What was Janice's standard line?

155. What was the name of Joey's dad's mistress?

156. Which Friend dated Phoebe's twin sister?

157. Why did Rachel say, "He's a . . . he's a black capuchin monkey with a white face . . . with . . . with Russian dressing and pickles on the side"?

158. To whom was Rachel referring when she said, "Oh, she wants to see me tomorrow. Oh, she sounded really weird. I gotta call Barry"?

159. Joey to everyone: "You know there already *is* a Joseph _____."

160. To whom did Monica say, "I will always have gum"?

161. Carl to Rachel: "I'm just sayin', if I see one more picture of _____ in that stupid electric car, I'm gonna shoot myself."

162. Who was Chandler's roommate before Joey?

163. Who said, "Excuse me? You don't think I could get a Brian? Because I could get a Brian, believe you me"?

164. Chandler: "Oh, my God, I'm trapped in a _____ with Jill Goodacre."

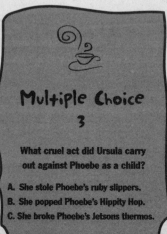

Multiple Choice 3

What cruel act did Ursula carry out against Phoebe as a child?

A. She stole Phoebe's ruby slippers.
B. She popped Phoebe's Hippity Hop.
C. She broke Phoebe's Jetsons thermos.

165. To whom did Chandler say, "We should always, always break up together"?

166. What was the significance of October twentieth for Ross?

167. To whom did Ross say, "Still, you say Minnie, you hear Mouse"?

168. What was Monica referring to when she asked Rachel, "So, are you going to tell us now or are we waiting for four wet bridesmaids?"

169. Who was the only Friend who didn't show up for Phoebe's surprise birthday party?

170. What was Ross referring to when he asked the girls, "Excuse me, but do any of you know how to play?"

171. Why did Monica tell Ethan that sex with him was "icky"?

172. Who said, "What am I supposed to do? Call Immigration? I could call Immigration"?

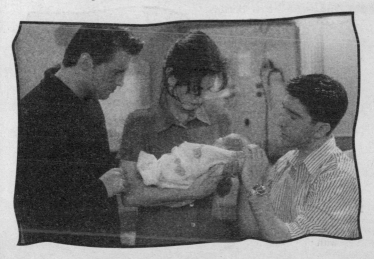

173. To whom was Ross referring when he said, "He keeps shutting me out. He's walking around all the time, dragging his hands"?

174. What was Chandler referring to when he said, "Right before he reached Macy's, he broke free and was spotted flying over Washington Square Park"?

175. To whom was Monica referring when she said, "This woman's living my life. She's living my life and she's doing it better than me"?

176. Who was locked in a broom closet while Carol was giving birth?

177. What was Chandler referring to when he asked, "Huh . . . did, uh, did any of the rest of you guys think that when you first met me?"

178. What did Chandler choke on while trapped in an ATM vestibule with Jill Goodacre?

179. What is Rachel's middle name?

180. Joey, on Al Pacino: "I'm his _____."

181. Who told Monica, "Ever since she left me, um, I haven't . . . I haven't been able to, uh, perform sexually"?

182. Who said, "Ross, that opens my cervix"?

Season Two

1. What was Phoebe referring to when she said, "That's when my mother would shut off the TV and say 'the end' "?

2. Joey to everyone: "The other day, I got this credit card application and I was _____. I've never been _____ for anything in my life."

3. Richard to Monica: "Oh, well, obviously you know that Barbara and I split up. Otherwise you wouldn't have done the head _____."

4. Rachel: "You have been in our lives for nearly two months now and we don't really know you. I mean, who is _____? I mean, what do you like? What don't you like? We want to know everything."

5. To whom was Joey referring when he said, "Monica, what are you doing? You can't go shopping with her. What about Rachel?"

6. Rachel to Ross: "Well, then I guess that's the difference between us. See, I'd never make a _____."

7. What is Rachel's mother's name?

8. Chandler to Eddie: "Good-bye, you _____-drying psycho-path."

9. Richard to Chandler: "Nice _____, by the way. When puberty hits, that thing's really gonna kick in."

10. Monica: "I don't want to have to wear flame-retardant _____."

11. What was Richard referring to when he said, "If I have to, I'll do it all again"?

12. Rachel on the telephone: "I am over you. And that, my friend, is what they call _____."

13. What was Phoebe's husband's name?

14. What happened to Phoebe's stepdad?

15. Who asked Rachel, "What's new in sex?"

16. To whom was Chandler referring when he said, "You know, he could have gotten me a VCR, he could have gotten me a set of golf clubs, but no, he has to get me the woman repeller"?

17. Joey to Chandler: "Can you believe this place? I was just in the bathroom and there's mirrors on both sides of you. So when you're in there, it's like you're peeing with _____."

18. What did Eddie's girlfriend come by to drop off at his and Chandler's apartment?

19. Where did Ross and Rachel first have sex?

20. What Barry Manilow song played over the montage of Ross and Marcel hanging out after Marcel finished shooting *Outbreak 2: The Virus Takes Manhattan*?

21. What was Ross referring to when he said, "Hey, I've been doing it since the ninth grade. I've gotten pretty damn good at it"?

22. What was Rachel referring to when she said, "Isn't that great! I mean, isn't that just kick-you-in-the-crotch, spit-on-your-neck fantastic?"

23. Ross to Phoebe: "Not even if Carol's _____ had a picture of a missing child on it."

24. Monica to Rachel, referring to the hickey on her neck: "That would be the work of a _____."

25. Chandler on the telephone: "Hello, Transit Authority? Yes, hello. I'm doing research for a book and I was wondering what somebody might do if they left a _____ on a city bus?"

26. To whom was Phoebe referring when she said, "Did you notice how he always starts his stories with, um, 'Okay, I was so wasted' or 'Oh, we were so bombed' or, um, ooh, ooh, ooh, 'So I wake up and I'm in this Dumpster in Connecticut' "?

27. To whom was Joey referring when he said, "Pheebs, how long do you think this lady will be with us?"

28. Why did Rachel say, "I have a Malibu Barbie who will no longer be wearing white to her wedding"?

29. A party guest at Jack Geller's birthday party, on Richard Burke: "Speaking of whom, I hear he's got some twenty-year-old _____ in the city."

30. Who said, "Oh, my God, am I an oat?"

31. Gunther to Joey: "I used to be _____ on *All My Children*."

32. Phoebe: "I don't want to meet my father over the phone. What am I gonna say? Like, 'Hi, I'm Phoebe, the daughter you abandoned, and by the way, I broke your _____.' "

33. Chandler: "If I'm gonna be an old, lonely man, I'm gonna need a thing, a hook, like that guy on the subway who eats his own face. So I figure I'll be Crazy Man With a _____. You know, Crazy _____ Man."

34. What fruit is Ross allergic to?

35. What happened to Phoebe's client, Mrs. Adelman?

36. What was Chandler referring to when he told Suzy Moss, "That was in the fourth grade! How could you still be upset about that?"

37. What was Mr. Heckles doing when he died?

Multiple Choice
4

Phoebe cuts Monica's hair to resemble the style of what celebrity?

A. Dudley Moore
B. Demi Moore
C. Mary Tyler Moore

38. To whom was Monica referring when she said, "No, if he doesn't like our cookies, too bad. I am not going to be blackmailed"?

39. What kind of doctor was Dr. Drake Ramoray?

40. Where were Joey and Chandler when Joey said, "I feel like Superman without my powers, you know? I have my cape and yet I cannot fly"?

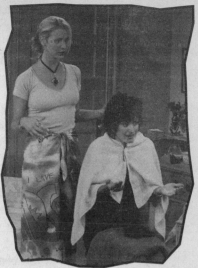

41. What was Chandler's response when Monica told everyone, "The camera adds ten pounds"?

42. Monica to Phoebe, on asking out Richard Burke: "Dr. Burke? I don't think so . . . I mean, like, he's a _____."

43. Who said, "With you it's like I've got two twenty-five-year-olds"?

44. Who played Mrs. Buffay?

45. To whom was Monica referring when she told Phoebe, "He's just going to be so glad you don't have barnacles on your butt"?

46. Chandler, shouting at the TV: "Run! Run, _____! Run like the wind!"

47. Rachel, crying to Monica: "I can't believe I don't get to go to my own prom. This is so _____."

48. To whom was Phoebe referring when she said, "I smell smoke. Maybe that's because someone's pants are on fire."

49. Chandler to Monica: "Come on, you're going to _____ with Julie? It's like cheating on Rachel in her house of worship."

50. What was Joey referring to when he said, "Why don't you go see Frankie? My family's been going to him forever"?

51. What did Phoebe's husband do for a living?

52. What was Ross and Monica's old cat's entire name?

53. To whom was Phoebe referring when she asked, "All right, so, what, he's not a famous tree surgeon? And then I guess, okay, he doesn't live in a hut in Burma where there's no phones?"

54. Mr. Adelman to Phoebe: "She always used to say that before she died. She wanted to see _____."

55. To whom was Ross referring when he said, "I guess I'm gonna call the beer company and find out where he is"?

56. Ross to Rachel on their first date: "It would really help when I'm kissing you if you didn't shout out my _____ name."

57. Joey to Ross: "Uh-oh. It's my _____. Envelope one of two."

58. How did Chandler and Ross become friends with the bullies?

59. To whose picture did Phoebe say, "Wish me luck, Grandpa"?

60. What was the name of the '50s diner where Monica worked as a waitress?

61. What was Phoebe referring to when she told Joey, "I'd recommend you to a friend"?

62. To whom was Phoebe referring when she said, "He doesn't have rabies. He has babies . . . That's what my mom said"?

Bits of Trivia

In "The One With Russ," David Schwimmer plays Russ, yet is credited as "Snaro," apparently as a tribute to a friend.

63. What was Monica referring to when she said, "Joey, promise me something. Never call me from that phone"?

64. What was Julie referring to when she said, "Yeah, we figured it would live with Ross half the time and me half the time"?

65. Ross to Phoebe: "How can you not believe in _____?"

66. Who told Rachel, "I'm pretty much totally intimidated by you"?

67. Why did Chandler answer the phone, "Bob here"?

68. Ross: "I get home, okay, and I see Julie's _____ on my night table and I think to myself, 'What the hell am I doin'?'"

69. Monica to Ross on Rachel's recent comment: "For the sixteenth time, no, I do not think you're _____!"

70. Who asked Joey, "How did you get here so fast? I just saw you in Salem"?

71. What was also on the prom video right after Monica and Rachel left for the prom?

72. Joey, on Carol: "Hey, if she were marrying a guy, she'd be, like, the worst _____ ever."

73. To whom was Chandler referring when he said, "Because he thinks I slept with his ex-girlfriend and killed his fish"?

74. What was Phoebe referring to when she said, "I never had it. I feel so left out"?

75. Rachel: "I cannot believe I have to walk down the aisle in front of two hundred people looking like something you drink when you're _____."

76. Monica to Fun Bobby: "You know, it seems like you've been making an awful lot of stuff _____ lately."

77. What was the name of the synthetic chocolate substitute Monica was hired to create recipes with?

78. What was Joey referring to when he said, "I can't believe you! You told me it was a nubbin!"?

79. Who said, "How do you expect me to grow if you don't let me blow?"

80. What was Chandler referring to when he told Rachel, "Well, I relied on a carefully regimented program of denial and wetting the bed"?

81. Joey to Chandler: "Check it out. We're _____ buddies!"

82. Rachel to Ross: "What the hell is a _____? Is that some stupid paleontology word that I wouldn't know, because I'm just a waitress?"

83. What was Joey referring to when he said, "There I am . . . there I am . . . there I am . . ."?

84. What was Joey referring to when he said, "You should see this guy, Chandler. He goes through, like, two bottles a day now"?

85. What was Rachel referring to when she said, "Phoebe, I'm so glad you made me do this"?

86. Rachel to Ross: "One minute I'm holding Ben like a football. The next thing I know, I've got two kids, I'm living in _____, complaining about the taxes."

87. Why did Chandler say, "Wow, that's some pretty powerful imaginary sperm you must have there"?

88. Richard to Monica: "I mean, hell, I'm a whole person who can _____ older than you."

89. To whom was Chandler referring when he said, "She's got me doing butt clenches at my desk"?

90. To whom was Chandler referring when he said, "Our trains are on the same track, okay? Yeah, sure I'm coming up thirty years behind him, but the stops are all the same. Bittertown! Aloneville! Hermit Junction!"?

91. Who hung up on Julie?

92. To whom was Ross referring when he asked, "Why does it say Property of Human Services on his butt?"

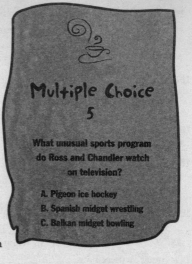

Multiple Choice 5

What unusual sports program do Ross and Chandler watch on television?

A. Pigeon ice hockey
B. Spanish midget wrestling
C. Balkan midget bowling

93. What was Phoebe's grandma referring to when she told Phoebe, "It was your mother's idea. You know she didn't want you to know your real father, because it hurt her so much when he left"?

94. To whom was Phoebe referring when she said, "You are so much the Smitten Kitten"?

95. What was Monica referring to when she said, "It's not going to happen. They're doing it tonight. We can do it tomorrow"?

96. What was Rachel's little sister's name?

97. What was Chandler referring to when he said, "Sometimes I like to hold stuff like this and pretend I'm a giant"?

98. What was Phoebe referring to when she said, "It's not like we can say anything about it 'cause, like, this is a birthday thing . . . you know, and it's for Ross"?

99. Joey to everyone: "When I first moved to the city, I went out a couple times with this girl, really hot, great kisser, but she had the biggest _____."

100. What was Eddie referring to when he shouted, "MAN ALIVE, THIS THING'S FANTASTIC!"?

101. Who said, "Ashley copies everything Brittany does"?

102. What was Phoebe referring to when she told Monica, "Would you relax? I know what I am doing. This is how he wears it"?

103. What was Phoebe's husband referring to when he said, "Now I know I don't have a choice about this. I was born this way"?

104. Who played the guy who threw the condom in Phoebe's guitar case as she played outside Central Perk?

105. Ross to Rachel, on why he never told her how he felt about her: "Things got in the way, you know, like, like _____ guys or ex-fiancés, or, or, or _____ guys."

106. To whom was Ross referring when he said, "I don't know what she sees in that goober. It takes him what, like, like, I don't know, uh, huh, hello? A week to get out a sentence"?

107. Rachel: "And then, _____ took me to that place Crossroads and that's where we hung out with Drew Barrymore."

108. What was Chandler referring to when he told Phoebe, "Oh, yeah, easy for you to say. You don't have to go around sporting some reject from the Mr. T collection"?

109. What was Ross referring to when he said, "I'll take it . . . my gift to you, man"?

110. Mr. Green to Ross at Rachel's birthday party: "You're wearing my _____."

111. According to Richard, why does he have to sleep on the west side of the bed?

112. To whom was Phoebe referring when she said, "I'm just . . . I'm nervous, so, you know what? Maybe if I just . . . if I picture them all in their underwear"?

113. What was Phoebe referring to when she said, "Okay, murder, cancer, soccer teams eating each other in the Andes"?

114. Mindy to Rachel, at Barry and Mindy's wedding: "Well, after you ran out on your wedding, Barry's parents told people you were sort of . . . insane . . . from the _____."

115. Who said, "That would be the work of a Blowfish"?

116. Chandler to Joey: "Okay, you have to stop the _____ when there's resistance."

117. What was Phoebe referring to when she told Ross, "Maybe the Overlords needed them to steer their spacecrafts"?

118. What was Eddie referring to when he said, "It's gonna make a hell of a conversation piece at our next cocktail party"?

119. What was Ross referring to when he said, "Yes, yes, it is . . . *in prison!*"?

120. Phoebe: "Okay, there is no top. All right? That's the beauty of _____."

121. Mr. Rastatter to Monica: "We're thinking, given the right marketing, we could make Thanksgiving the _____ holiday."

122. Phoebe to everyone, on Rachel kissing Ross: "See . . . he's her _____."

123. What was Phoebe referring to when she said, "Oh, my God . . . I sound amazing"?

124. Why did Phoebe say, "I just want to grab all these houses and rub them all over my body"?

125. How did Chandler's cybergirlfriend respond when asked what her current method of birth control was?

126. What was the name of the super in Monica's building?

127. To whom did Rachel say, "Okay, you're being a little weird about your phone"?

128. What was Ross referring to when he told Chandler, "Whip it out! Whip it out!"?

129. Joey, while watching a video of Ross during his freshman year of college: "Looking good, Mr. _____."

130. What was Richard referring to when he said to Monica, "You know, I don't need the actual number, just a ballpark"?

Bits of Trivia

In "The One With the Baby on the Bus," Lea Thompson crosses over in her role from *Caroline in the City*. The same night this episode aired, David Schwimmer appeared as Ross on *The Single Guy* and Matthew Perry appeared as Chandler on *Caroline in the City*.

131. To whom was Rachel referring when she told Monica, "What a jerk. I kept talking about you and he kept asking me out"?

132. Who yelled, "Oh, come on! Would you just grab my ass!"?

133. Phoebe: "Yeah, I talked to my grandma about the *Old Yeller* incident and she told me that my mom used to not show us the end of sad movies to protect us from the pain and sadness, you know, before she _____."

134. Frank Jr. to Phoebe, on Frank Sr.: "He just had this big smile on his face and he was waving 'cause he was always happiest when he was on his _____."

135. Rob Donen (Chris Isaak) to Phoebe: "I schedule performers for the children's _____ around the city, and I was just thinking, have you ever thought about playing your songs for kids?"

136. What was Ross referring to when he told Chandler: "Because she doesn't hate Yanni is not a real reason"?

137. Why did Monica say, "Hi, Jew!"

138. Chandler to Joey: "Yo, Paisan . . . can I talk to you for a sec? Your _____ is a very bad man."

139. To whom did Phoebe say, "So, how many chords do you know?"

140. Rachel to Ross: "I do not have chubby _____!"

141. Who said, "There are no hardware stores open past midnight in the Village"?

142. Who said, "Oh, my God. There's an unattractive nude man playing the cello"?

143. What was Chandler referring to when he said, "The eyesore from the Liberace House of Crap!"?

144. To whom did Monica say, "All right, I'll tell you what. I'll come get you in five minutes with some sort of, um, kabob emergency"?

145. To whom was Joey referring when he said, "All right, that's it! He just comes in here, Mr. Johnny New Eggs . . ."?

146. Why did *Days of Our Lives* kill off Joey's character?

147. What was Monica referring to when she said, "My boyfriend doesn't have a thing"?

148. Joey: "Come on, Chandler, I want this part so much. Just one _____. I won't tell anyone."

149. To whom was Rachel referring when she said, "And the chicken poops in her lap!"?

150. What was Monica referring to when she told Rachel, "We only did it once—it didn't mean anything to me!"?

151. Joey to Chandler: "What kind of scary-ass _____ came to your birthday?"

152. What was at the top of Ross's con list for Julie?

153. To whom did Ross say, "You're a doctor of gums. That's the smallest body part you can major in. It's like: day one, floss, day two, here's your diploma"?

154. Who said, "I know who it is you remind me of. Evelyn Dermer. 'Course that was before she got the lousy face-lift. Now she looks like Soupy Sales"?

155. Ross to Joey: "Check it out. I made Marcel's favorite dish—banana cake with _____."

156. What was Rachel referring to when she told Ross, "I know, I know, I know. I was just thinking about when they were there the last time. I'm sorry"?

157. Ross: "Joey, you owe eleven hundred dollars at I Love _____."

158. To whom was Chandler referring when he told Joey, "In fact, I have her panties right there in my drawer!"?

159. What did Rachel sing at Barry and Mindy's wedding?

160. To whom was Phoebe referring when she said, "Oh, I thought they were just watching me. You know, like at an aquarium"?

161. Ross: "I know this jacket . . . _____'s jacket! Where is he? He's here, isn't he?"

162. Rachel to Ross just hours before their Christmas party: "Did you just break the _____?"

163. What was Monica referring to when she said, "Would you look at this dump? He hated us! This was his final revenge!"?

164. What role did Joey play in a porno?

165. Ross: "Okay, can people stop drinking the _____!"

166. Ross to Julie: "One, two, three . . . well, you didn't _____ either!"

167. Why did Ross say, "Hey, hey, I got my S's back!"?

168. Who said, "You're over me? When, when were you under me?"

169. What did Joey call the acting method he often used to buy himself time to remember his lines while on *Days of Our Lives*?

Multiple Choice
6

What famous person does Phoebe believe is her grandfather?

A. Winston Churchill
B. Charles Lindbergh
C. Albert Einstein

170. Monica, reading Joey's first fan letter from a psychotic admirer: "P.S. Enclosed, please find fourteen of my _____."

171. Monica to Richard: "I'm dating a man whose _____ I once peed in."

172. Phoebe: "This is a _____ of the earth as seen from a great, great distance. It's the way my mother sees me from heaven."

173. Ross to Richard, while waiting for the girls to get condoms: "So were you in _____?"

174. Phoebe: "Okay, what kind of a sick doggie _____ film is this?"

175. Chandler to Monica, on marrying Richard: "Well, I think you should seriously consider the marriage thing. It'll give Rachel another chance to dress up like Princess _____."

176. Phoebe to Monica and Rachel: "You know what? If we were in prison, you guys would be, like, my _____."

177. Ross: "Yeah, but now that I think about it, I don't think I've ever seen _____ without a drink in his hand."

178. What was Rachel referring to when she told Ross, "You know what I'd do? I'd wait. Yes, absolutely. I would wait, and wait. Then I'd wait some more"?

179. What was Chandler referring to when he said, "Of course, the packaging does appeal to grown-ups"?

180. Jean-Claude Van Damme to Monica, on why he asked her out: "'Cause Rachel told me you were dying to have a threesome with me and _____ . . . who, by the way, has some ground rules."

181. What was Ross referring to when he said, "You know what, you guys, we don't have to watch this"?

182. What was Richard Burke's daughter's name?

183. What was Joey referring to when he told Rachel, "We, uh, we used it to, you know, fling water balloons off the roof"?

184. Joey: "Chandler gave me word-of-the-day _____."

185. Chandler: "Mean guys at the coffeehouse took my _____."

186. Monica: "Okay, we're not having a birthday cake—we're having a birthday _____."

187. Phoebe to Ryan (Charlie Sheen): "You have to stay back. I have the _____."

188. Rachel to Phoebe, on how she got her tattoo: "Really? You don't say? 'Cause mine was licked on by _____!"

Season Three

1. What was Phoebe referring to when she told Joey, "You keep the old ones in the back? That's so ageist"?

2. To whom did Ross say, "I think girls' night out is a great idea"?

3. Joey to Monica, on the kind of guy he thought she'd have babies with: "I always pictured you with one of those tall, smart, blond guys named, like, _____."

4. Phoebe, singing what she thought were the words to Elton John's "Tiny Dancer": "Hold me close, young _____."

5. What was Joey referring to when he said, "Maybe I should call this place and get them to put my *Days of Our Lives* gig on here. You know, juice this puppy up a little"?

6. To whom did Ross say, "See, we both have this list of five famous people. And you're one of mine, so I'm allowed to sleep with you"?

7. Who told Rachel, "I'm not supposed to drink coffee. It makes me gassy"?

8. Who told Rachel that Ross had slept with another woman?

9. Who was Rachel's officemate after Mark quit?

10. Phoebe's birth mother to Phoebe: "All right. The man in that picture is _____."

11. Rachel to Ross: "You do not bring a _____ to somebody's work . . . unless maybe they were a park ranger."

12. Who was Phoebe referring to when she screamed, "HE'S ALIVE! HE'S ALIVE!"?

13. What was the name of the product Joey advertised on the *Amazing Discoveries* infomercial?

14. Joey to Ross, on why he needs to wear underwear: "It's a rented tux. Okay? I'm not gonna go _____ in another man's fatigues."

15. What was Joey referring to when he said, "Awww, look at that. Every inch of this is glued down. It'd take forever to pry this off. You should just leave it"?

16. Chandler to everyone except Joey: "I can't remember which _____."

17. What was Joey referring to when he said, "God, it'd be weird if that situation presented itself tonight, huh?"

18. Who told Ross, "The girl who won last year sold four hundred seventy-five. So far I've sold seventy-five"?

19. What was Chandler referring to when he said, "She's dressed. She's a businesswoman, she's walking down the street window-shopping, and . . . oh, oh, oh, she's naked!"?

20. What did Phoebe's ex–singing partner leave her to do?

21. What did Joey use to unlock Phoebe's grandma's cab after they got locked out?

22. To whom was Rachel referring when she told her boss, "No, he's not married or involved with anyone"?

23. Who said, "Look, the only one who stands to get hurt is me and I'm okay with that"?

24. Ross to Chandler: "So, uh, did your _____ try to slap you again today?"

25. Ross to Rachel: "You _____ my girlfriend!"

26. Who said, "I'm gonna wear this all the time. I love this shirt!"?

27. What was Gunther's roommate's name?

28. Phoebe to Monica: "You *never* run on a _____."

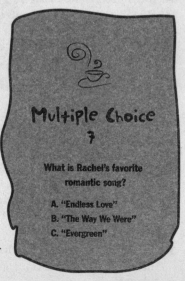

Multiple Choice 7

What is Rachel's favorite romantic song?

A. "Endless Love"
B. "The Way We Were"
C. "Evergreen"

29. To whom did Chandler say, "I was really drunk and you guys all look really similar"?

30. Janice to everyone: "I'm sorry. I find it hard to believe that a group of people who spends as much time together as you guys do has never bumped _____."

31. Monica to everyone: "Has anyone seen my left _____?"

32. What was Ross referring to when he told Rachel, "Okay. If that's what it takes to show you how much you mean to me and how much I want you there, then that's what I'll do"?

33. To whom was Joey referring when he told Chandler, "The good thing is, we spent the whole day together and I survived. And what's even more amazing is, so did she. It was bat day at Shea Stadium"?

34. Ross to Ben: "Give Daddy the _____. Ben, give . . . give me the _____. Okay, how about, don't you want to play with the monster truck?"

35. What was Ross referring to when he said, "That kind of thing requires some serious thought. First I'll divide my prospective candidates into categories"?

36. What was Joey's reason when he said, "You know how we save all those chopsticks when we get Chinese food? Well, uh, now we've got a reason"?

37. Joey: "Hey, everybody lies on their résumé, okay? I wasn't one of the _____ kids either."

38. Rachel to Joey: "Why do you have a copy of _____ in your freezer?"

39. What was Chandler referring to when he said, "The source of all my powers? Oh, dear God, what have I done?"

40. What did Monica order from an infomercial?

41. Rachel to Ross, on his getting hypnotized in Atlantic City: "Oh, right, 'cause you always pull your pants down on the count of three and play _____ on your butt cheeks."

42. What happened to Phoebe's dollhouse?

43. What was Monica referring to when she said, "Phoebe, it's been two days"?

44. What was the big news that Pete wanted to tell Monica when she thought he was going to ask her to marry him?

45. Where was Ross when he said, "Take Pinkie Tuscadero to Inspiration Point. Collect three cool points"?

46. What did Rachel shove up Monica's nose on Thanksgiving?

47. Who was Janice's husband?

48. Why did Monica make jam?

49. Joey, watching *Wheel of Fortune*: "This guy is so stupid. It's
_____ Rushmore!"

50. What was Chandler referring to when he said, "Oh, my God! That is so not the opposite of taking somebody's underwear!"?

51. Monica to Rachel, on something Ben just said: "Did he just say Monica _____? Oh, my God, he's gonna rat me out!"

52. What was Monica referring to when she said, "You've gotta help me out with a couple more boxes!"?

53. What was the title of Julio's poem about American women?

54. What was Richard referring to when he told Monica, "This will just be something we do . . . like racquetball"?

55. What was Ross referring to when he told Rachel, "Nobody likes change"?

56. To whom was Chandler referring when he said, "This guy invented MOSS-865. Every office in the world uses that program!"?

57. Chandler to Joey: "You notice that ever since we got this _____ we've been fighting a lot more than we used to?"

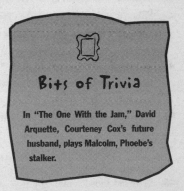

Bits of Trivia

In "The One With the Jam," David Arquette, Courteney Cox's future husband, plays Malcolm, Phoebe's stalker.

58. To whom was Joey referring when he said, "Wow, look at this. He wrote a check for fifty thousand dollars to Hugo Lingren's Ring Design"?

59. Who said, "It's more about the way you occasionally concentrate your enthusiasm on my buttocks"?

60. To whom was Phoebe referring when she said, "I found this picture on her fridge"?

61. To whom was Monica referring when she told Chandler, "Ten bucks says I'll never see that woman again in my life"?

62. Chandler: "Hey, Joe, I gotta ask. The girl from the Xerox place buck naked or a big tub of _____?"

63. What intimate detail did Chandler share with Ross about what happens to him sometimes while having sex with a woman?

64. To whom was Monica referring when she said, "Phoebe, why don't you just call her? You obviously want to"?

65. Monica: "You know, when I was younger, all I wanted to do was to play with this _____. But *noooo*, it was to be looked at, not played with."

66. Richard to Monica, after running into her in the video store: "You look great . . . no, you do . . . you just . . . you've got _____ stuck to your leg."

67. Who told Rachel, "I work at Bloomingdale's and I might know of a job possibility if you're interested"?

68. Ross to Rachel: "Yeah, well, missy, you better be glad that list is _____."

69. Phoebe, on Malcolm, her sister's stalker: "That's why he couldn't just come up and talk to me . . . because of the _____."

70. Monica's dad to Monica, on why he unexpectedly showed up at her apartment: "Well, it's your mother's bridge night, so I thought I'd come into the city for a little _____."

71. Who asked Ross, "You think I'm cheap?"

72. What was Joey referring to when he said, "Now remember, something this big and long is gonna be difficult to maneuver. Fortunately, I have a lot of experience in that area"?

73. What was Monica referring to when she told Ross, "When Mom and Dad drove you to the hospital to get your nose fixed, I swam into the lake and fished it out"?

74. What book was Rachel referring to when she said, "Joey? Do you want to put the book in the freezer?"

75. What happened after Chandler listened to the stop-smoking hypnosis tapes?

76. Chandler, rushing into Monica's apartment: "Do you guys know how to get a chick out of a _____?"

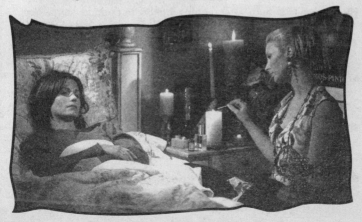

77. To whom was Ross referring when he said, "Tommy's in line for the bathroom and someone just cut in front of him. I think he's gonna snap"?

78. Chandler to Ross, whose doctor was reluctant to remove an unidentifiable skin abnormality on Ross's butt: "You should go to my guy 'cause when I went in there with my _____, he just lopped it right off."

79. Rachel: "You know, I don't. I don't understand guys. I mean I . . . I would never congratulate Monica on a great stew by, you know, grabbing her _____."

80. Rachel to Bonnie: "You know, I just have to tell you, I just loved your look when you were _____."

81. Monica to Rachel, on Pete the millionaire guy: "Can you believe he just offered me a _____?"

82. Rachel: "Why would you want to even come, Ross? You're a horrible _____."

83. What was Gunther refer-ring to when he told Ross, "I'm sorry. Was I not supposed to?"

84. Who said, "You're disturb-ing my oboe practice"?

85. Chandler to everyone: "Does anyone else think David _____ is cute?"

Multiple Choice 8

Name the stripper Chandler hires for his cousin's bachelor party.

A. Charity Knight
B. Chantilly Lace
C. Crystal Chandelier

86. Joey to Rachel: "You know, when you were a kid and your mom would drop you off at the movies with a jar of _____ and a little spoon?"

87. What did Phoebe get all over her dress the night of Ross's museum benefit?

88. Whom did Joey spot kissing at the mattress store?

89. Who said, "Hi, I'm an honorary Brown Bird"?

90. Who said, "I mean, you might as well have come in and peed all around my desk!"?

91. To whom did Monica say, "Getting over you was the hardest thing I ever had to do"?

92. Who said, "I know I'm no Jon Bon Jovi . . . or someone you find attractive"?

93. What was Ross referring to when he told Rachel, "Uh, sorry. Nothing you can do about it. It's one of my, uh, rights as the ex-boyfriend"?

94. Who said, "Good thing it's one of those 801 numbers, right?"

95. Pete to Monica: "I want to become the _____."

96. What was Chandler referring to when he told Ross, "Nine times. I had to put on lotion"?

97. Whom did Ross visualize while Rachel was wearing the Princess Leia costume?

98. What was Carol referring to when she said, "He picked it out at the toy store himself. He loves it"?

99. Who likes to "melt stuff"?

100. To whom was Joey referring when he said, "I say we poke him"?

101. What was Ross referring to when he said, "That's when it occurred to me, the key to my success, the munchies"?

102. Which of Joey's sisters did Chandler kiss?

103. Who said, "Hey, buddy, this is a family place. Put the mouse back in the house"?

104. Monica to Rachel, while stranded at a rest stop: "The _____ here are only a penny! Let's stock up!"

105. What was Frank Jr.'s wife's name?

106. Ross to Phoebe, on how her dollhouse burned down: "Well, we believe it originated here, in the _____ room."

107. Which of the girls dated two guys at once?

108. Who told Monica, "Well, if you're asking me to quit, you're asking me to be someone I'm not"?

109. What was Phoebe referring to when she said, "Oh, yeah, Bob said there might be flood damage"?

110. What was Rachel referring to when she said to Ross, "A mistake? What were you trying to put it in? Her purse?"

111. Monica to Phoebe: "It's a _____ . . . and a pencil sharpener."

112. What was Chandler referring to when he said, "Okay, is everybody else seeing a troll doll nailed to a two-by-four?"

113. Phoebe to Monica, after moving out in "The One With the Flashback": "I need to live in a land where people can _____."

114. While discussing Ross's list of celebrities he would sleep with, to whom was Chandler referring when he said, "Ehhh, you know what? She's too political. She probably wouldn't let you do it unless you donated four cans of food first"?

115. To whom was Joey referring when he said, "I'm telling you, he hasn't moved since this morning"?

116. What was Phoebe referring to when she said, "There's no such thing as an innocent burger"?

117. Monica: "Oh, my God. Joey, what did you do after you threw her _____ on the fire?"

118. Where did Pete take Monica on their first date?

119. To whom did Phoebe say, "Wow, that's exciting. You went to Japan, made up a woman"?

120. Rachel to Phoebe, on the girl she set up with Ross: "Yeah, I said it was okay when I thought she was some weird _____ chick."

☆ Star Sightings ☆

+ Jill Goodacre (Herself) "The One With the Blackout"

+ Elinor Donahue (Aunt Lillian) "The One Where Nana Dies Twice"

+ Hank Azaria (David the Scientist Guy) "The One With the Monkey"

+ Morgan Fairchild (Nora Bing) "The One With Mrs. Bing"

+ Jay Leno (himself) "The One With Mrs. Bing"

+ Fisher Stevens (Roger) "The One With the Boobies"

+ Brenda Vaccaro (Gloria Tribbiani) "The One With the Boobies"

+ Jon Lovitz (Steve) "The One With the Stoned Guy"

+ Helen Hunt (Jamie Buchman) "The One With Two Parts— Part 1"

+ Leila Kenzle (Fran Devanow) "The One With Two Parts— Part 1"

+ Noah Wyle (Dr. Jeffrey Rosen) "The One With Two Parts— Part 2"

- George Clooney (Dr. Michael Mitchell) "The One With Two Parts—Part 2"

- Beverly Garland (Aunt Iris) "The One With All the Poker"

- Megan Cavanagh (Louisa) "The One Where the Monkey Gets Away"

- Jennifer Grey (Mindy) "The One With the Evil Orthodontist"

- Claudia Shear (Fake Monica) "The One With Fake Monica"

- Leah Remini (Lydia) "The One With the Birth"

- Jonathan Silverman (Dr. Franzblau) "The One With the Birth"

- June Gable (nurse) "The One With the Birth"

- Lauren Tom (Julie) "The One Where Rachel Finds Out"

- Steve Zahn (Duncan) "The One With Phoebe's Husband"

- Lea Thompson (Caroline Duffy) "The One With the Baby on the Bus"

- Chrissie Hynde (Stephanie) "The One With the Baby on the Bus"

- Giovanni Ribisi (Condom Boy) "The One With the Baby on the Bus"

121. To whom did Ross say, "Good morning. Nice breasts, by the way"?

122. Monica to Phoebe: "Why is this _____ in my bedroom?"

123. To whom was Phoebe referring when she said, "Look, he gave me his night vision goggles and everything"?

124. Ross, to Chandler and Joey: "You know what? It doesn't matter. Because you both have to go _____ before the big vein in my head pops."

125. Ross to Rachel: "Do you tell people about the night of _____ times?"

126. To whom was Rachel referring when she told Ross, "You know what, honey? You go ahead. We'll call her an alternate"?

127. What was Joey referring to when he said, "Pheebs, you gotta stop doing this. I'm working on commission here"?

128. To whom was Ross referring when he asked Rachel, "So this guy is helping you for no apparent reason? He's a total stranger?"

129. To whom was Phoebe referring when she said, "Every time I see him it's like, *Is it on the loose? Is it watching me?*"

130. Chandler to Monica: "Hey, I like her. I don't want to stop seeing her. But every so often it's like, hey, you know what? Where's your _____?"

Bits of Trivia

During "The One With The Football," Phoebe wore a *That Girl* T-shirt, while Marlo Thomas had a recurring role as Rachel's mother, Sandra Green.

131. How did Frank Jr. meet Alice?

132. To whom was Chandler referring when he told Rachel, "She's really dull and she gets this gross mascara goop thing in the corner of her eye!"?

133. What was Monica referring to when she said, "You know what? I care about you too much to watch you hurt yourself like this. So if you have to do this, then you're going to have to do it without me"?

134. To whom was Ross referring when he said, "You can see the moonlight bouncing off her head"?

135. What did the shrunken T-shirt that Ross took back from Rachel after they broke up say?

136. What was wrong with the hypnosis tape Rachel gave Chandler to help him quit smoking?

137. What was the name of the hot girl at the copy store?

138. Who told Phoebe, "I was just thinking, and just hoping that . . . mmm . . . that maybe you'd want to get back together. . . ."?

139. To whom was Monica referring when she said, "Last night we were fooling around and he stops to write a poem"?

140. Ross to Monica, during the gang's Thanksgiving Day football game: "Cheater, cheater, _____ eater."

141. Joey: "Eeew. Ugly Naked Guy is using his new _____. It's like a Play-Doh Fat Factory."

142. To whom was Joey referring when he told Monica: "Wow, this guy's an astronaut? That would have been cool . . . for like a day"?

143. Rachel to Ross, on why she changed out of her formal dress into sweats: "I'm not going to go. No, I think I'm going to catch up on my _____."

144. To whom was Monica's dad referring when he told her, "The man is a mess"?

145. Where did Rachel work after Central Perk?

146. Rachel to Joey: "I will read *The Shining* and you will read _____."

147. What was Rachel referring to when she told Ross, "You think you're going to get out of this on a technicality?"

148. To whom did Monica say, "I so want to be attracted to you"?

149. Who played Rachel's date who screamed at everyone?

150. Rachel to everyone: "Monica's going to marry a _____!"

151. What was Phoebe referring to when she told Joey and Ross, "Please, you've got to talk him out of it"?

152. Ross to Rachel: "Can't a guy send a _____ to his girlfriend's office anymore?"

153. Joey, on an upcoming audition for *All My Children*: "It's this great part, this _____ named Nick."

154. What was Ross referring to when he told Rachel, "That was supposed to be a private, personal thing between us"?

155. Who left an answering machine message that said, "Hola, it's me. Yesterday was really fun. Call me about this weekend, okay?"

156. Phoebe: "All right, I'm going to play a song now that's really, really sad. Okay, it's called 'Magician Box _____.'"

157. To whom did Chandler keep repeating, "You're *our* age"?

158. What was Monica referring to when she said, "Joey, you had *the night*"?

159. What was Chandler referring to when he told Ross, "No, it's fancier than a pimple"?

160. Janice to everyone while watching TV: "I cannot believe he's using our divorce to sell _____."

Multiple Choice 9

What song reunites Phoebe and her old singing partner, Leslie?

A. "Sticky Shoes"
B. "Cross-eyed Dog"
C. "Calico Bat"

161. What was the name of the trophy Monica and Ross used to compete for every Thanksgiving as children?

162. Phoebe to Monica: "You know when you're on a date and you're getting along really great and the guy's _____ keeps getting in the way?"

163. Pete to Monica, on his supposed new girlfriend: "She asked me if she could finish off my _____. I thought she said something else. We had a big laugh."

164. What was Phoebe referring to when she said, "It's not about oral hygiene. I floss to save lives"?

165. What was Monica referring to when she said, "It was breezy. Oh, God, what if it wasn't breezy?"

166. Joey to the girls: "Whoever has the biggest boobs has the biggest bra, therefore has the biggest _____."

167. What was Phoebe referring to when she said, "Come, Dinosaur, we're not welcome in the house of no imagination"?

168. What was Rachel's boss's name at Fortunata Fashions?

Season Four

1. Why did Joey and Chandler pee on Monica's foot?

2. What can Rachel tie in a knot using just her tongue?

3. Who said, "So what if I like to go home, throw on some Kenny G, and take a bath?"

4. What did Rachel guess Chandler's job was during the Lightning Round of their who-knows-who-better game?

5. Chandler to Joey, while sitting on their new rusty old lawn furniture: "Could we be more _____?"

6. Where was Monica's first head chef job?

7. What did the singing man across the alley from Joey sing every morning?

8. What's "the sound"?

9. What was the name of Joey's girlfriend with whom Chandler fell in love?

10. After reclaiming her apartment while the guys were out, what was Rachel referring to when she told Joey and Chandler, "Okay. We figured you'd respond this way, so we have a backup offer"?

11. Who was the on-call eye doctor Monica went to see after getting ice in her eye?

12. Who said, "Hey, that's the day after I start menstruating"?

13. To whom was Ross referring when he told Rachel, "I can't stay here all night. And if I go in there, she's, she's gonna wanna . . . do stuff"?

14. What was wrong with Shelly, Ross's beautiful colleague he dated briefly?

15. What did Chandler buy for Joey's girlfriend on her birthday?

16. What did Joey buy Kathy for her birthday?

17. Who said, "It really creeps me out choosing other people's sex clothes"?

18. Who said, "Apparently to you people, I look like someone who's got a balloon full of cocaine stuffed up their bum"?

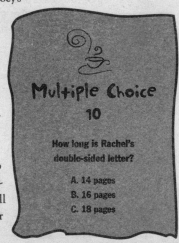

Multiple Choice
10

How long is Rachel's double-sided letter?

A. 14 pages
B. 16 pages
C. 18 pages

19. How did Joanna, Rachel's boss at Bloomingdale's, die?

20. Phoebe: "I just have this really strong feeling that this cat is _____."

21. Chandler: "Whenever I see a girl in fishnet stockings, it reminds me of my _____."

22. What was Monica describing when she said, "You could, uh, start out with a little one, a two, a one, two, three, a three, a five, a four, a three, two, two, a two, four, six, two, four, six, four, two, two, four, seven, five, seven, six, seven, seven, seven, seven, seven, seven, seven, seven, seven, seven . . ."?

23. What college did Phoebe's brother, Frank Jr., go to?

24. Who said, "Hey, and just so you know, it's not that common! It doesn't happen to every guy! And it is a big deal!"?

25. How did Ross meet Emily?

26. Rachel on the phone: "Monica, I'm quitting. I just helped an eighty-one-year-old woman put on a _____ and she didn't even buy it."

27. To whom did Phoebe say, "I think I can figure it out. I guess, you know, I was born and then everyone started lying their asses off"?

28. What was Ross referring to when he told Rachel, "It's five-thirty in the morning . . . so I'd better get cracking on this baby"?

29. What was Chandler referring to when he told Ross, "If you say that one more time, *I'm* going to break up with you!"?

30. Who said, "Ugh, turkey. Ugh, giving thanks. Ugh!"?

31. To whom was Joey referring when he said, "Smells like he went on a three-day fishing trip and then ate some licorice"?

32. Rachel to Phoebe, on Ross's hair: "His hair never bothered me that much. You know, it was always more _____ than it was _____."

33. Joey to everyone: "If I had to, I'd _____ on any one of you."

34. What name appears on the address label of Chandler and Joey's *TV Guide*?

35. What business did Monica and Phoebe join up to form?

36. Where was Joey when his and Chandler's apartment got robbed?

37. How long did Ross and Emily know each other before they decided to get married?

38. Rachel on her demotion at Bloomingdale's: "They stuck me in _____."

39. What was the name of Rachel's client at Bloomingdale's whom she had a crush on?

Bits of Trivia

Joey's address is 495 Grove St., Apt. 19, New York, NY 10001.

40. What was Rachel referring to when she told Chandler, "Last time I almost got fired. You must end it. You must end it now"?

41. What was Monica referring to when she said, "Oh, my God, it's in the quiche!"?

42. Who was Rachel referring to when she said to Monica: "It's like inviting a Greek tragedy over for dinner."

43. When, specifically, did Monica and Chandler first sleep together?

44. What was Ross referring to when he told Joey, "Fifteen? Your personal best"?

45. What is Monica's biggest pet peeve?

46. Who was Mike "Gandolf" Ganderson?

47. What profession did Maurice, Joey's childhood imaginary friend, have?

48. Who said, "I want a flabby gut and saggy man breasts"?

49. Why was Chandler made to spend time in a box?

50. Who said, "You should, you should think of, um, my work as word-less sound poems"?

51. How did Joey's girlfriend Kathy figure out that Chandler bought her her birthday present, and not Joey?

52. To whom did Ross's father say, "I'm not paying for your wine cellar, you thieving, would-be-speaking-German-if-it-weren't-for-us, cheap little man"?

53. What was Rachel's boss referring to when she told Chandler, "I want to show you something . . . just a little gag gift somebody gave me"?

54. How did Rachel's boss, Joanna, leave Chandler?

55. What is Rachel's favorite movie?

56. What did Joey and Chandler get for free on their television?

57. What was Phoebe referring to when she said, "I'm gonna be giving someone the greatest gift you can possibly give"?

58. Joey, on Chandler's depression: "Look, there's nothing I can do for him right now. He's still _____. That's only Phase One."

59. What color was the fingernail that Monica lost in the quiche?

60. To whom was Chandler referring when he said, "And now, I have seen her naked. I mean, at least when I'd see her with clothes on, I could imagine that her body was like covered in boils or something. But there are no boils. She's smooth. *Smooth!*"?

61. What was Monica referring to when she said, "I have not been picked on this much since I was in kindergarten and they had to bring in someone from junior high to do the seesaw with me"?

62. What is the name of Chandler's father's Las Vegas all-male burlesque?

63. What did Phoebe do to the client she was really attracted to?

64. Which encyclopedia volume did Joey buy?

65. Whose apartment did Monica sublet?

66. What was Chandler referring to when he said, "I got it—*Scotch Tape*"?

67. Emily: "Ross play _____? I don't think so."

68. Who said, "I'm just the oven. It's totally their bun"?

69. What were Chandler and Kathy doing when they first kissed?

70. Ross to Monica, who tried to entice everyone to come over to her new place after she and Rachel lost their apartment to the boys: "Cookies and _____? You're the best mom ever!"

71. Who told Rachel, "Farm birds really kind of freak me out!"?

72. Who asked Joey to be his dancing partner?

73. To whom was Chandler referring to when he told Joey, "His legs flail about as if independent of his body"?

74. To whom did Chandler say, "I think I know who the other guy is. It's me. I'm the other guy"?

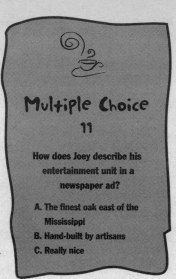

Multiple Choice
11

How does Joey describe his entertainment unit in a newspaper ad?

A. The finest oak east of the Mississippi
B. Hand-built by artisans
C. Really nice

75. Who did Phoebe think had addressed her invitation to Ross and Emily's wedding?

76. What was Monica's nickname when she played field hockey?

77. Where did Chandler tell Janice his company was transferring him to when he didn't want to start dating her again?

78. Joey, on what Monica's wearing: "She's mad because I know today's her laundry day and that means she's wearing her _____."

79. Who said, "I lost my sexy phlegm!"?

80. Phoebe to Monica: "I need your _____. I want my cold back!"

81. Monica to Phoebe: "I came up with a whole lot of businesses you can do with your _____."

82. Joey to Ross and Chandler: "What do you mean we never have fun anymore? You have fun with me. Remember that time we saw those strippers and you paid me fifty bucks to eat that _____?"

83. Why was Phoebe fired from Healing Hands?

84. What was Phoebe referring to when she said, "I knew it, I knew it! I felt really thick this morning"?

85. Why did Chandler refurnish the apartment after they'd been robbed?

86. What happened in the lunchroom at the museum on Joey's first day of work?

87. To whom was Rachel referring when she said, "They're in Vermont? How could this happen?"

88. Chandler to Monica, on how well he knows her: "You can only eat _____ in even numbers."

89. To whom was Monica referring when she said, "He had to go. There was a deer just outside eating fruit from the orchard."

90. Chandler to everyone, while in a box: "You can't tell, but I'm trying to break the tension by _____ you guys."

91. Monica to Rachel, after finishing a catering job: "The _____ wouldn't pay, so Phoebe yelled at her till she did."

92. What was the name of Rachel's boss's other assistant at Bloomingdale's?

93. What was Rachel referring to when she told Monica, "My lucky dress wasn't working out too well for me, but for four years this baby never missed"?

94. What was Nana's real name?

95. Who said, "No matter how badly you think you stink, you must never, ever bust into my dressing room and use my shower"?

96. What was Phoebe referring to when she told Monica, "Without you, it's just me driving up to people's houses with empty trays and asking for money"?

97. What was Joey referring to when he said, "It's kind of like chandelier, but it's not"?

98. What was Phoebe's birth mom referring to when she said, "I just think it would be something you would regret every single day for the rest of your life"?

Bits of Trivia

James Michael Tyler was actually working in a coffee shop in Hollywood when he got the part of Gunther. He kept the coffee gig for the first four seasons of *Friends*.

99. What was Monica referring to when she told Joey, "They wouldn't have put it there if it didn't do something. How can you not care?"

100. Alice (Phoebe's brother's wife) to Frank Jr. on why the doctor wouldn't put more than five embryos in Phoebe's uterus: "Sweetie, now, she's a woman, not a _____."

101. Why did Monica hire Joey to work at her restaurant?

102. Monica, trying to cheer up Ross, who had just said good-bye to Emily: "Hey, the guys have _____."

103. What was Phoebe referring to when she said, "I can't do this. I can't give him up"?

104. Rachel to everyone: "We have to have a surprise bon voyage party for Emily . . . but it's actually for _____."

105. What was Emily referring to when she told Ross, "I think it makes you look really dangerous"?

106. To whom did Joey say on video, "Okay, so say hi to my friend and tell him you like my hat"?

107. What was Frank Jr. referring to when he said, "I know, why doesn't she get drunk? That worked for a bunch of girls in my high school"?

108. Chandler: "If you win, we'll give up the _____. But if we win, we get your _____."

109. What was Monica referring to when she told Phoebe, "Don't mix those up. You could really ruin that lollypop"?

110. Why did Chandler and Kathy break up?

111. Phoebe: "So the baby is totally craving _____."

112. To whom did Rachel say, "Well, we should get started. Let me show you my underwear"?

113. What happened to interrupt Rachel from kissing Joshua during their game of spin the bottle?

114. Chandler to Ross, after seeing his newly pierced ear: "You do know that _____ broke up?"

115. What was Monica referring to when she said, "I talked to the guy with the shovel and found out what happened. They tore it down a few days early"?

116. What was Phoebe referring to when she said, "It's gonna be like one of those log rides when they just come shooting out"?

117. Frank Jr. on finding out he was having triplets: "I finally got my _____!"

118. Phoebe, referring to a name for Frank Jr. and Alice's third baby: "I want a name that's really, like, you know, strong and confident, you know, like _____."

119. What happened to Ross's dead grandmother's wedding ring?

120. Joey to Ross as he headed off to London: "If you're going to the airport, can you pick me up another one of those _____?"

121. What was Rachel wearing when she was having dinner with Joshua's parents?

122. What was Phoebe referring to when she said, "I went to a used clothes store and got, like, a bunch of maternity stuff. These are so comfortable"?

123. What was Rachel referring to when she told Joey and Chandler, "Do you guys want these? Oh well, you got 'em. Just give us our apartment back"?

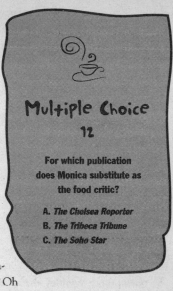

Multiple Choice 12

For which publication does Monica substitute as the food critic?

A. *The Chelsea Reporter*
B. *The Tribeca Tribune*
C. *The Soho Star*

124. What was Ross referring to when he told Emily, "Damn. I thought that was going to be romantic as hell"?

125. What was Phoebe referring to when she told Monica, "You know, about half of these are gonna end up getting divorced"?

126. To whom was Chandler referring when he said, "Well, what if we just, uh, called her, used a fake name, and had her come to my office"?

127. Ross to everyone: "Turns out that Emily is just crazy about _____. Yeah, they're going to the theater together. They're going to dinner. They're going horseback riding."

128. What did Emily say after Ross first told her he loved her?

Season Five

1. What was Emily's last name?

2. What was Rachel's childhood dog's name?

3. What was the name of the hot delivery girl Ross tried flirting with?

4. What was Joey referring to when he said, "It's not so much an underpant as it is a feat of engineering"?

5. To whom did Chandler say, "Oh, my God, *you* smoked. Yes, you did! You look happy and sick. . . . You smoked!"?

6. With whom did Ross hook up after finding out that Emily was getting married?

7. What gaffe did Ross commit as he was reciting his nuptials?

8. What was Ross referring to when he said, "Ironically, most of the boxes seem to be labeled CLOTHES"?

9. Where did Monica and Chandler spend their first anniversary?

10. What pseudonym did Phoebe use when speaking to Emily's stepmother on the telephone?

11. Who was Kip?

12. What were the Friends all about to do just as Phoebe went into labor?

13. To whom did Ross say, "Hey, lady! I don't care how much you want it. I'm not going to have sex with you in the bathroom!"?

14. What's "the moist-maker"?

15. What was Ross referring to when he told Joey over the phone, "They're still not comin' on, man, and the lotion and the powder made a paste!"?

16. To whom did Rachel say, "So there you go. You got courage. You got integrity. You got . . . courage again . . ."?

17. What was Chandler referring to when he told Monica, "Well, Ross and Emily aren't going to use it"?

18. What were the names of Frank Jr. and Alice's triplets?

19. Who told Ross, "We're very sad it didn't work out between you and Emily, Monkey. But I think you're absolutely delicious"?

20. To whom was Monica referring when she told Rachel, "So he's not inviting you to his party because he likes you"?

21. What did Monica call losing one's virginity?

22. Joey to Phoebe, referring to Chandler: "Show him your _____. He's afraid of them. Can't work them."

23. Joey: "Chandler! You are not going to believe this! I have found my identical _____."

24. To whom did Ross say, "I've been, been thinking about that thing you, you wanted me to do and, uh, I can do it"?

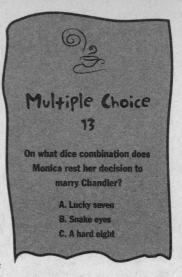

25. Joey to Chandler: "That hotel you stayed at called. Said someone left an _____ in your room."

26. Where did Phoebe meet her father?

27. To whom did Ross say, "Why don't you come? I mean, I have two tickets. Why not?"

28. What gift from her mother sent Phoebe into a moral conundrum?

29. Joey to Monica, referring to the dream he had about her the night before: "You were *my* girlfriend and *we* were doing the _____, you know, like you guys were doing last night."

30. What was Ross referring to when he said, "I can't believe someone just ate it"?

31. What is the policy Monica has about her belongings as they relate to Rachel?

32. Who was the first Friend to find out that Chandler was seeing Monica?

33. What was Chandler referring to when he said, "You know, technically, we're still over international waters"?

34. What was Ross referring to when he said, "How the hell am I supposed to make this kind of decision!"?

35. Phoebe's obstetrician: "I want you to know you're gonna be in good hands. I've been doing this for a long time. I'll be back in a minute to do your internal. In the meantime, just relax because everything here looks great. And also, I love _____."

36. Who bought all of Ross's old furniture?

37. What did Chandler say to Joey after he put on Phoebe's fur coat?

38. To whom did Rachel say, "My dad's a doctor and he would always tell me just horror stories . . . about, uh, ghosts and goblins who . . . totally supported . . . the princess's right to smoke"?

39. What was Ross's New Year's resolution?

40. What was Phoebe's New Year's resolution?

41. What was Chandler's New Year's resolution?

42. What was Joey's New Year's resolution?

43. What was Rachel's New Year's resolution?

44. What was Monica's New Year's resolution?

45. Joey about his new girlfriend: "I don't know. I mean I like her a lot and she's really nice, but . . . she keeps _____ me."

Bits of Trivia

Monica's address is 495 Grove St., Apt. 20, New York, NY 10001.

46. Who said, "I've been given the gift of time"?

47. What was Monica referring to when she asked Chandler, "What was that? What was that noise you just made?"

48. How much money did Condo President Steve suggest that Ross kick in on the day he moved into his new apartment, for a retirement gift for the building handyman?

49. What was the name of the retiring handyman in Ross's building?

50. Who did chip in for the retirement gift, and became the hit of the building party?

51. Where were Ross and Emily supposed to go on their honeymoon?

52. Why does Phoebe hate PBS?

53. What did Rachel name her Sphynx cat?

54. How much did Rachel pay for her cat?

55. Why was Joey jealous of Ross's son, Ben?

56. What was Phoebe referring to when she told Joey, "This is Bear Claw. Okay, um, Tricky Leg and Old Lady"?

57. What event did Rachel lie to Danny about having to attend, rather than go to his party?

58. To whom did Phoebe say, "Now, if after dinner you still really need to bust someone, I know a hot dog vendor who picks his nose"?

59. Ross: "I gotta cancel those five giant _____ I sent to Emily. My God, think of the massacre."

60. Rachel: "Phoebe, just because I'm alone doesn't mean I want to _____"

61. What did Phoebe hand out at her grandmother's funeral?

62. Ross: "I need a _____ that says, 'Kids welcome here,' but that also says, 'Come here to me.' "

63. What did Chandler claim Ross's occupation was when he was called as a reference during Ross's search for a new apartment?

64. What was Rachel referring to when she said, "All right, listen, um, I just bought something. I'm not sure she's gonna like it and it's gonna seem a little crazy but this is something I've wanted since I was a little girl"?

65. What was Monica referring to when she said, "Probably some, you know, European good-bye thing he picked up in London"?

66. Why did Joey say, "I'm Joey. I'm disgusting. I take my underwear off in other people's homes"?

67. To whom was Monica referring when she said, "She's obviously unstable. Okay, she's thinking about running out on her wedding day"?

68. What was Phoebe referring to when she said, "Or we could *not* tell them we know and have a little fun of our own"?

69. Joey to Rachel: "Hey, listen, is it obvious I'm wearing six _____?"

70. Chandler, apologizing to Monica for calling her fat when she was in high school: "I'm so sorry. I really am. But, come on, I was an idiot back then. I rushed the stage at a _____ concert, for crying out loud."

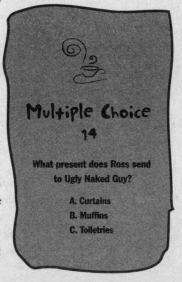

Multiple Choice
14

What present does Ross send
to Ugly Naked Guy?

A. Curtains
B. Muffins
C. Toiletries

71. What did Ross do to Rachel while she was sleeping on the way to Vegas?

72. What was Phoebe referring to when she said, "Does it look like a garbage can to you? Does it look like an ashtray? Does it look like a urinal?"

73. Phoebe, on Ross's comment about her wearing fur: "Okay, let's get some perspective, people. It's not like I'm wearing a _____ coat!"

74. Phoebe: "I thought you guys were doing it. I didn't know you guys were _____."

75. Phoebe: "Hi, um, I'm Phoebe Buffay and I have _____ coming out of me."

76. Why did Joey go to Vegas?

77. What kind of work did Joey do in Vegas while waiting for his movie to start up again?

78. Who screamed, "Chandler is a girl! Chandler is a girl!"?

79. What did Phoebe find in the seat cushions at Central Perk?

80. To whom did Joey say, "You and I have been given a gift. We have to do something with it. Like hand modeling . . . or magic"?

81. Emergency room doctor to Chandler (in a flashback): "This isn't your toe. This is a small, very cold piece of _____."

82. To whom was Joey referring when he said, "It's impossible to find her apartment. She lives in like some hot girl parallel universe or something"?

83. To whom was Chandler referring when he told Monica, "I think we should let them win the next game"?

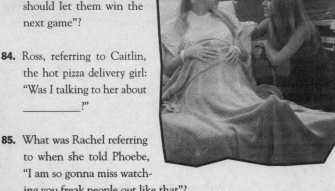

84. Ross, referring to Caitlin, the hot pizza delivery girl: "Was I talking to her about _____?"

85. What was Rachel referring to when she told Phoebe, "I am so gonna miss watching you freak people out like that"?

86. Jack to Rachel, referring to her nose job (in a flashback): "What? Dr. Wilson's an artist. He removed my _____. Wanna see?"

87. To whom did Ross say, "Not only did we go out—we did it two hundred and ninety-eight times"?

88. Phoebe to Rachel, who didn't read *Jane Eyre* for their literature class: "So, Jane Eyre? First of all, you'd think she's a woman but she's not. She's a _____."

89. To whom did Ross say, "You wet my pants!"?

90. What did they call Ross at work after he left a psychotic message about his stolen lunch?

91. Who went on the ride-along with Gary?

92. Rachel, on her job interview at Ralph Lauren: "I accidentally _____ during the interview."

93. What was Phoebe referring to when she told Rachel, "Can I tell you a secret? I want to keep one"?

94. To whom was Rachel referring when she said, "They were very, you know . . . wrestley. But I guess that's normal?"

95. What was Chandler referring to when he told Monica, "Did you see that, with the inappropriate . . . and the pinching"?

96. Why did Joey's grandmother come over to Monica's?

97. What was Phoebe referring to when she said, "Yeah, I better take it back. I'm totally drunk with power"?

98. What was Rachel referring to when she said, "Joey, look. Trust me. I tell you all the men are carrying them in the spring catalogue"?

99. What was Monica referring to when she told Chandler, "The only reason I didn't tell you was because I knew you'd get mad and I didn't want to spoil our anniversary"?

100. What directive did Ross continually shout while carrying his new couch up the stairs at his apartment building?

101. Why was Ross asked to take a leave of absence from the museum?

102. Why was Joey hospitalized while Phoebe was having her babies?

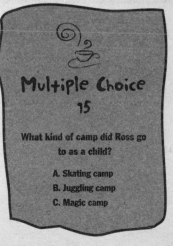

Multiple Choice 15

What kind of camp did Ross go to as a child?

A. Skating camp
B. Juggling camp
C. Magic camp

103. What prompted Rachel to tell Phoebe, "You've got to come with me. Wherever I go. We'll start a new group. We're the best ones"?

104. To whom was Phoebe referring when she said, "Oh, God, I really missed that fat bastard"?

105. Joey to Ben, trying to discourage him from an acting career: "One day you're Dr. Drake Ramoray, and the next day, you're eatin' _____ right out of the bottle."

106. What was Monica wearing when Chandler first told her he loved her?

107. Monica to Chandler: "We get to see Joey. Plus, we get to start our anniversary celebration on the plane. We can call it our _____!"

108. How did Rachel find out about Chandler and Monica?

109. Where were the remains of Ross's leftover Thanksgiving sandwich eventually found?

110. To whom did Phoebe say, "Lipstick and a daughter, big day for you"?

111. What was Monica referring to when she said, "I used to give them to Rachel all the time before she got allergic"?

112. What did Monica leave Phoebe in charge of for Rachel's surprise birthday party?

113. Ross: "I saw what you were doing through the window! I saw what you were doing to my _____! Now get out of here!"

114. Phoebe to a woman on the street: "Save it, Red. Unless you want to spend the night in the slammer, you apologize to the _____."

115. What was Ross referring to when he asked Rachel, "Why's it inside out?"

116. Who said, "I'm in Vice. Yeah, um, in fact, I'm undercover right now. I'm a whore"?

117. To whom did Ross say, "You've got ink on your lip"?

118. How did Phoebe violate Section 12, Paragraph 7 of the criminal code?

119. Who said, "Are you saying your kid eats soup better than my kid?"

120. What was Rachel referring to when she said, "Yeah, my tongue feels a little fuzzy and my fingers sort of smell"?

121. To whom was Chandler referring when he asked Joey, "If you'd said, 'Big lima bean bubbling up,' would she have understood the difference?"

122. Who said, "By the way, if it makes you feel any better, I happen to like eight-year-old boys"?

123. Who called Ross while Rachel went to his apartment to get margarita mix?

124. Joey to Chandler, who was upset that Joey risked his life for Ross instead of him: "I wasn't trying to save Ross. My _____ was next to Ross. All right? I was trying to save my _____."

125. To whom did Rachel sell her Sphynx cat?

126. Why did Phoebe break up with Gary the cop?

127. What was Ross referring to when he said, "She knows I'm home. She knows I can see her. What kind of game is she playing? I think someone's lonely tonight"?

128. Chandler to Monica: "You roll another hard eight and we get _____ here tonight."

Season Six

1. What were Rachel's sisters' names?

2. Monica to Phoebe: "What are you talking about? If you get married in _____, you're married everywhere."

3. What was Phoebe referring to when she said, "Ross, nobody cares about this thing except you. This embarrassment thing is all in your head"?

4. Who looked at himself in the mirror and said, "You're just a love machine"?

5. What did Ross do as a guest lecturer at NYU to make a good first impression?

6. Who played Janine, Joey's roommate after Chandler moved out?

7. What was Rachel referring to when she told Monica, "I guess I'm not upset because I don't actually see you actually going through with this"?

8. Who did Phoebe think she had kissed in the copy room at Rachel's office?

9. What was Joey's character's name in *Mac and* C.H.E.E.S.E.?

10. Why didn't Jack and Judy Geller like Chandler for so many years?

11. What was Monica referring to when she told Ross, "I think I shouldn't look directly at them"?

12. What was written on Ross's back when he woke up in Vegas?

13. How did Phoebe's apartment catch fire?

14. Joey, at Central Perk: "Oh, hey, someone left their keys. Ooh, and to a _____."

15. What did Chandler give Monica for Valentine's Day the year they promised to make their gifts?

16. What did Monica give Chandler for Valentine's Day the year they promised to make their gifts?

17. Who were the last two friends to know that Ross and Rachel got married in Vegas?

18. What was Joey referring to when he said, "I won! That was my guess! I guessed twenty thousand!"?

19. Ross, on hearing about Monica and Chandler moving in together: "Oh, my little sister and my best friend, _____."

20. Who was Phoebe's roommate before Rachel?

21. While he was teaching a class at NYU, what was the nickname Ross gave his student Elizabeth, whom he later dated?

22. Why did Ross say, "I've gotta go make a fake Ben"?

23. Rachel, about Phoebe: "You guys, I am telling you, when she _____, she looks like a cross between Kermit the Frog and the Six Million Dollar Man."

24. What does Chandler's father do for a living?

25. What was the name of the card game Chandler made up so that Joey could win his money back?

26. What was Rachel referring to when she said, "And the craziest thing is, now my boss likes me because I told her about it and she said it was the best gossip she's heard all year"?

27. What did Ross and Monica perform in order to get chosen to dance on the club's platform stage?

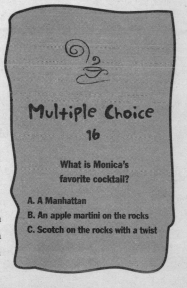

Multiple Choice 16

What is Monica's favorite cocktail?

A. A Manhattan
B. An apple martini on the rocks
C. Scotch on the rocks with a twist

28. What was Chandler referring to when he told Ross, "That is funny. It was also funny when I made it up"?

29. What's the significance of *Sex Toy Story 2*, *Inspect Her Gadget*, and *Lawrence of a Labia*?

30. With whom did Rachel want to have an affair in "The One That Could Have Been"?

31. Phoebe to Chandler, while ring shopping: "Can't you imagine getting down on one knee and handing her this gorgeous piece of _____?"

32. Drunken Phoebe in Vegas: "You love _____ so much, you're probably gonna marry it. And then it won't work out, so you're gonna have to divorce it, divorcing guy."

33. What did Chandler want to do with Rachel's room once she moved out and he moved in?

34. Whose health insurance lapsed?

35. Rachel to Ross: "I always thought if you and I got married that would be the one that stuck. And it wouldn't be a secret. And we wouldn't have our wedding dinner at _____."

36. To whom was Phoebe referring when she said, "I dreamed that he saved me from a burning building and he was so brave and so strong and it's making me look at him totally differently"?

37. Who told Ross, "Wow. Just hearing you describe it as forbidden . . . is really hot"?

38. What was Joey referring to when he told Phoebe, "It'll be great. We can talk and play games. This could be our chance to, like, renew our friendship"?

39. What was Gunther referring to when he told Joey, "Yeah, that's what I drive. I make four bucks an hour and I saved up for three hundred and fifty years"?

40. To whom did Monica say, "Call me when you get there. I'm really going to miss you"?

41. Chandler to Ross, on how they used to repel women: "Remember when we were back in college and went to that spring dance and you walked right up to that girl you liked and you could not stop talking about the _____?"

42. Rachel to Phoebe: "Check it out. For my dessert, I have chosen to make a traditional _____."

43. Ross to Joey, referring to Rachel's English trifle: "It tastes like _____!"

44. Who hates Pottery Barn?

45. What was the first song Ross learned on the keyboard?

46. Who said, "I don't cry. It's not a big deal"?

47. Monica to Joey: "You can't ask her out. She's your _____."

Bits of Trivia

In "The One After Vegas," the closing credits read: "To Courteney and David, who did get married."

48. Who lost thirteen million dollars in the stock market?

49. What happened just as Chandler was about to propose to Monica at dinner?

50. Phoebe to Rachel: "I was with Ross and _____ after you left and, um, I'm pretty sure I saw a little spark between them. Yeah, I mean, it's probably nothing, but I just wanted to warn you that there might be something there."

51. What was Rachel referring to when she said, "Ross, look, look. This is good for you. Okay? Let's face it. So far, the guy's not lovin' ya. But I can turn that around. I got the inside track"?

52. Ross, on a call with the head of the Paleontology Department at NYU: "Remember that paper I had published last year on _____? Huh? They loved it."

53. What was Rachel referring to when she said, "Hey, this is hollow. This bench is hollow! I can't believe I never knew that!"?

54. Chandler to Phoebe: "Joey's got a really bad _____, but it's nothing that a little laser eye surgery won't fix."

55. Which episode featured the name "Arquette" after every actor's name in the opening credits?

56. In "The One That Could Have Been," who became a high-powered Merrill Lynch stockbroker?

57. To whom did Monica say, "I am so glad you guys got together. Chandler and I are always looking for a couple to go out with and now we have one"?

58. Joey to Rachel: "Look, Rach, my parents bought this _____ just after I was born. Okay? Now, I have never had a problem with it and you show up and it breaks."

59. What was Monica referring to when she said, "Honey, we were at this beautiful place, and I-I-I just put our names down for fun. I mean, what's the harm in that?"

60. What was Joey referring to when he said, "Only an idiot would wear this stuff if he didn't have the car"?

61. What was Chandler referring to when he said, "Well, I think Ross already has one. Now this one's free, right, because you paid for the first two"?

62. To whom was Ross referring when he told Rachel, "Oh, so that's the only reason she could be here, huh? It couldn't have anything to do with the fact that . . . that maybe I'm a good listener and I, uh, I put on a great slide show?"

63. To whom did Rachel say, "Oh, my God! You're a thirty-year-old virgin!"?

64. Joey, on his audition for *Mac and C.H.E.E.S.E.*: "I'm a detective and I solve crimes with the help of my _____ partner."

65. To whom was Phoebe referring when she told Rachel, "Yeah, but then Jacques Cousteau came and kicked his ass for betraying me"?

☆ What's in a Name? ☆

- Monana—Pennsylvania Dutch for "Monica"

- "I'm the Twinkie"—Monica, referring to what a guest called Richard Burke's twenty-something girlfriend to her mother

- Dr. Philangie—Phoebe, who told Emily's stepmother that Ross had forgotten to take his medication and might involuntarily blurt out other women's names

- Regina Philangie—Phoebe's all-purpose alias

- Ken Adams—Joey's all-purpose alias

- Joseph Stalin—The stage name Chandler suggested for Joey

- Flame Boy—The stage name Phoebe suggested for Joey

- The Weenie from Tourini—Paolo

- The Yeti—The heavily bearded Danny

- Joseph the Processing Guy—Joey's character who worked at Chandler's office

- The Submarine Guy—Ryan, Phoebe's semiannual fling

- Scary Snake Man—Chandler, who decided he needed a hook

66. To whom was Rachel referring when she said, "He's a private guy. You know, I wish I could get him to open up a little bit, share some feelings"?

67. Why did Chandler tell Monica that Ross was in their apartment naked?

68. Ross: "This is crazy. I mean, yes, yes, Rachel is my good friend and I have loved her in the past, but now she is just my _____."

69. Who said sarcastically, "Yeah, nothing happened. You could cut the sexual tension in here with a knife"?

70. To whom did Monica say, "Yes, you're too late. Where was all this three years ago?"

71. What did Elizabeth do after Ross broke up with her?

72. What was Chandler referring to when he told Joey, "You took off your pants and climbed under the sheets"?

73. Who told Joey, "The money's good. Plus, you get to stare at Rachel all you want"?

74. Phoebe to Jill and Ross: "What about, what about what I said, you know, about the _____ pants. How dumb was I?"

75. What was Ross referring to when he told his attorney, "There's no way to do this without her? 'Cause I kinda already told her it, uh, it was, it was already taken care of"?

76. Rachel to Phoebe: "I mean, I don't really like it when Ross goes out with anyone, but my sister? Isn't that like _____ or something?"

77. Joey to the pretty woman at the medical research center: "I'm Joey Tribbiani, and with all due respect, I'd like to donate some _____."

78. Rachel, on what she won't miss about leaving Monica's: "Well, I guess I won't miss the fact that you're never allowed to move the _____."

79. To whom was Joey referring when he told Chandler and Monica, "She didn't want to hang out with you guys two nights in a row"?

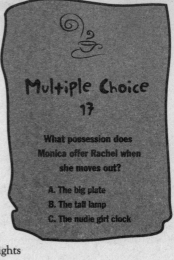

Multiple Choice 17

What possession does Monica offer Rachel when she moves out?

A. The big plate
B. The tall lamp
C. The nudie girl clock

80. Ross to Phoebe: "We're still _____. Don't tell Rachel. See you later."

81. What was Monica referring to when she told Chandler, "She picked Rachel. I mean, she tried to back out of it but it was obvious. She picked Rachel"?

82. What was Phoebe referring to when she told Rachel, "Ross invited us all to watch"?

83. Ross tattling to Jack and Judy: "Yeah, well Hurricane Gloria didn't break the _____. Monica did!"

84. What was Rachel referring to when she told Phoebe, "It's from yore, like the days of yore"?

85. Who said, "You know, I gotta tell you, if someone had told me a week ago that I'd be peeing in Joey Tribbiani's apartment . . ."?

86. Who told Rachel, "No, but I just walked by three sales and I didn't go in. How strong am I?"

87. Ross to everyone: "They would not let us _____ when we were that drunk."

88. Who said, "I'm not sick. I don't get sick"?

89. What was Phoebe referring to when she told Chandler, "Oh, wake up, Chandler. The one you picked is gone! It's over!"?

90. Joey to Monica and Chandler: "Carl is a guy I hired to be my _____ for a medical research project."

91. To whom was Ross referring when he told Joey, "Thank you for bringing her into our lives"?

92. Ross to Rachel and Phoebe: "Look, I studied karate for a long time. And there's a concept you should really be familiar with. It's what the Japanese call _____."

93. Why did everyone think Phoebe was a porn star?

94. Rachel: "Ross, come on! This is not a marriage. This is the world's worst _____!"

95. What was Monica referring to when she told Ross, "Why don't you just phase it out?"

96. How did Ross's date find out he'd bleached his teeth?

97. Which Friend was hospitalized with a heart attack?

98. Joey: "Pheebs, there you are. You broke my _____. You owe me four hundred bucks."

99. What was Chandler referring to when he said, "Richard was there, so I couldn't do it"?

100. To whom was Joey referring when he said, "I have to do something to . . . to repel this woman"?

101. Which Friend picked two backups? Who were they?

102. Who said, "Oh, my God, the three of us are going to have such a good time living together!"?

103. Phoebe to Rachel, on running: "Didn't you ever run so fast that you thought your legs were gonna fall off? You know, like when you were, like, running toward the swings or, or running away from _____?"

104. What was Ross referring to when he said, "It is frowned upon"?

105. Chandler to Joey, regarding a comment made about him by Janine: "And I am not _____. I am a _____!"

106. Where did Rachel buy her apothecary table?

107. To whom did Gunther say, "You are no longer authorized to distribute birthday muffins"?

108. Who told Ross, "Well, that makes sense since you're gay and addicted to heroin"?

109. To whom was Phoebe referring when she said, "Rachel, okay, look at him. Look at those strong hands. Oh what I wouldn't give to be that can of condensed milk"?

110. What was Joey referring to when he said, "When everyone eats that, that banana-meat thing, they're all gonna make fun of her"?

111. Which Friend was this said about: "She's very loud for such a small person"?

112. What was Rachel referring to when she told Phoebe, "It'll be like our, our first, you know, roommate bonding thing"?

113. Ross to Elizabeth and her friends: "Everybody put their _____ down! Now this is a nice suit!"

114. Who told Ross, "And you. I throw myself at you and you say no? How gay are you?"

115. What happened after Joey kissed Rachel in "The One That Could Have Been"?

116. To whom was Ross referring when he said, "Turns out she is going to Daytona for spring break"?

117. To whom did Ross say, "We could have a threesome"?

118. What was Ross referring to when he told Rachel, "And as my wife, I think you should grant me this favor"?

Season Seven

1. Which Friend is the youngest?

2. What is Chandler's mother's name?

3. Ross to his class: "And that should conclusively prove that I had the idea for _____ first."

4. What's Joey's middle name?

5. To whom did Monica say, "You kinda stole my thunder!"?

6. What was Phoebe referring to when she told Monica, "That was the one legacy my grandmother left me and I know you wanted it as an engagement present"?

7. What was Ross referring to when he told Monica, "So I finally heard back from Aunt Cheryl and apparently it wasn't a mistake"?

8. Joey to his movie costar: "Look, I know you're a great actor, okay, and you play all those Shakespeare guys and stuff, but you're _____ all over me, man."

9. Ross to Monica, on Chandler's deepest, darkest secrets: "Chandler entered a _____ look-alike contest and won."

10. Chandler to Monica, on Ross's deepest, darkest secrets: "In college, Ross used to wear _____."

11. Ross to Chandler, on Monica's deepest, darkest secrets: "Once Monica was sent to her room without dinner, so she ate the _____ off a jewelry box she made."

12. Why doesn't Ross like ice cream?

13. What was Joey referring to when he told Rachel, "Poor thing. Cut down in her prime"?

14. Who made Barry White play in the heads of others as she flipped her hair?

15. Phoebe to Ross: "Oh, my God, my first _____! Thank you for the best present I've ever gotten."

16. What was Rachel referring to when she said, "Chandler, this is not addressed to you. This is addressed to Mrs. Braverman downstairs"?

17. Who said, "S'up with the whack PlayStation, s'up?"

18. To whom was Rachel referring when she said, "She is so good at throwing drinks in people's faces. I mean, I don't think I've ever seen her finish a beverage"?

19. What was the name of Dr. Drake Ramoray's brother?

20. To whom was Rachel referring when she said, "Ooh, I could just spread him on a cracker"?

21. Who asked Chandler and Monica, "Do you want me to sing 'Careless Whisper' or 'Lady in Red'?"

22. Monica's dad on her childhood memories: "Well, I don't know what's in the boxes down here, but I do know there are six or seven _____ in the attic."

23. To whom was Phoebe referring when she told Ross, "She will paint a room a really bright color without even checking with you. And she uses sex as a weapon"?

24. What was Jack Geller referring to when he told Monica, "We have it. Only now we call it the beach house."

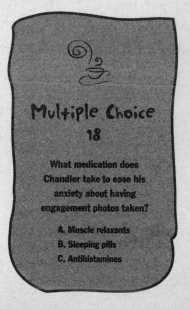

Multiple Choice 18

What medication does Chandler take to ease his anxiety about having engagement photos taken?

A. Muscle relaxants
B. Sleeping pills
C. Antihistamines

25. What did Phoebe find in the wastebasket in Monica's bathroom when she was looking for a tissue for Rachel?

26. What was Rachel referring to when she told Joey, "It's not a big deal. I do that, too, with my shampoo bottle"?

27. Ross to Rachel, whom he and Joey were giving a hard time for reading a trashy romance novel: "Dang, this coffee's cold. Hey, Rach, do you mind if I heat this up on your _____?"

28. Joey to Phoebe and Rachel: "We're going to give you hypothetical _____ situations and you'll be scored on a scale of one to ten."

29. Ross to Ben: "I'm the Holiday _____!"

30. How did Chandler develop his love of swing music?

31. Who told Ross, "Thanks for letting me stay at your place. I mean, Monica's place was nice, but her fiancé sure stares a lot"?

32. Joey to Ross, on wearing sunglasses: "I figure if I wear these in my scenes, I won't get _____ in my eyes."

33. To whom did Monica say, "You gave my father a lap dance"?

34. Phoebe to Ross: "My massage client Arthur? His daughter called and said that some guy that worked for me gave him a really weird massage this afternoon. He said you poked at him with _____."

35. What was Rachel referring to when she told Tag, "Oh, please, you're kidding, right? I wrote that one as a joke for you"?

36. Ross to Joey: "All right! All right! It was the best _____ ever! I said it, okay? But it's over, Joey!"

37. What was Monica referring to when she said, "Drunk enough that I know I want to do this. Not so drunk that you should feel guilty for taking advantage"?

38. To whom did Phoebe say, "So you hired yourself a little treat, did ya?"

39. What was Joey referring to when he said, "And the most important thing is, it won't be, like, some stranger up there who barely knows you. It'll be me"?

40. Chandler to Monica: "I don't know what it is. I just can't take a good _____."

41. What was Phoebe referring to when she said, "Okay, this is where you and I part ways—noisy bitch"?

42. What was Ross referring to when he said, "Oh, I thought it was just a kid yelling, 'I'm gay! I'm gay!' "?

43. Chandler to Monica, on what happened to Ross while on Space Mountain: "No, he visited a town a little south of _____."

44. To whom was Rachel referring when she told Joey and Ross, "Wait a minute. She just made a scene in the middle of the ceremony!"?

45. What door was Ross referring to when he said, "Joey, where's the pipe that was holding the door open?"

46. Judy Geller to Jack Geller, while reminiscing with Monica and Chandler about how Judy had gotten pregnant: "You don't know how that happened? Your dog thought my _____ was a chew toy."

47. What was Joey referring to when he told Rachel, "Hey, great, you're home. Guess what Phoebe got me for Christmas"?

48. Monica to Rachel, after she and Chandler got engaged: "I'm sorry I almost made you sleep with _____."

49. What was Ross referring to when he said, "I like this one. It seems to say 'I love you and that's why I have to kill you' "?

50. Ross to everyone: "Done. And with time to spare. You know I hate to lecture you guys, but it's kind of disgraceful that a group of well-educated adults, and Joey, can't name all the _____."

51. Why did Chandler tell Rachel, "I will give you a hundred dollars to whistle right now"?

52. What was Monica referring to when she said, "Limited seating, my ass. Let's see who made the cut"?

53. Phoebe to Monica: "Well, you know, I may have relatives in France who would know. My grandmother said she got the recipe from her grandmother, _____."

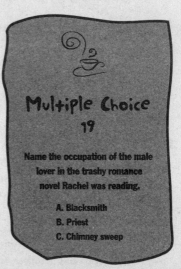

Multiple Choice 19

Name the occupation of the male lover in the trashy romance novel Rachel was reading.

A. Blacksmith
B. Priest
C. Chimney sweep

54. What was Joey referring to when he told Phoebe, "And things aren't as smashed down as I thought they were going to be"?

55. What happened on Monica's thirtieth birthday?

56. What happened on Phoebe's thirtieth birthday?

57. Why did Chandler say he was allergic to dogs?

58. What was Chandler referring to when he told Joey, "Okay, for the last time, it's not named after each individual man"?

59. To whom did Phoebe say, "You guys kissed? What does this mean?"

60. Why did Joey say to Rachel, "Where you goin'? The vicar won't be home for hours"?

61. What was Ross referring to when he said, "I think it means he freaked out and left!"?

62. Who asked Joey, "Wait a minute! Were you on a poster for gonorrhea?"

63. What was Phoebe referring to when she said, "Yeah, she used to put it out every Christmas to remind us that, even though it's Christmas, people still die. And you can put candy in it"?

64. What was Rachel referring to when she told Joey, "It's not a miracle, Joey. I'm sure there's some explanation"?

65. What was Joey referring to when he said, "It's a highly controversial procedure"?

66. To whom was Chandler referring when he told Monica, "What? Do you think she's just gonna sit there quietly? You don't think she's

gonna want to make a toast? You don't think she's gonna grab the microphone and sing 'Part-time Lover'?"

67. To whom was Monica referring when she told Rachel, "Would you look at him? I mean, he's obviously depressed. He's away from his family. He's spending Thanksgiving with strangers. What he needs right now is for you to be his friend"?

68. What was Ross referring to when he told Rachel, "What can I say? You missed your chance. From now on, the only person who's gonna enjoy these bad boys is me"?

69. Chandler to Phoebe and Ross, on why he can't marry Monica: "The Bings have horrible marriages. They yell, they fight, and they use the _____ as a pawn in their sexual games."

70. Phoebe to Rachel: "Oh, God, Rachel! I'm sorry. What was I thinking, giving Joey this big, gross, scary _____ in such a poorly constructed cage?"

71. Why did Ross say, "Delaware. Delaware. I want my turkey now"?

72. Rachel: "I don't know, Tag. How can your genitals make _____?"

73. Casting agent to Joey: "An Italian working immigrant at that time would not be _____."

74. Phoebe to everyone: "I did it! One mile on a _____! That's it! That's everything I wanted to do before I was thirty!"

75. What was Ross referring to when he said, "How hot do I look in this, huh?"

76. Who said, "When I think of the love that these two givers and receivers share, I cannot help but envy the lifetime ahead of having and loving and giving"?

77. Ross: "People are doing it in front of my _____!"

78. To whom was Chandler referring when he said, "Mustached bastard"?

79. To whom was Monica referring when she said, "He cannot play at our wedding. I mean, everyone will leave"?

80. What made Chandler flip out the night before his wedding?

81. Ross: "Phoebe, you can't _____ people in my apartment."

82. Joey to Phoebe: "Hey, you can cancel plans with friends if there's a possibility for _____."

83. Chandler to Monica, on his father: "Trust me, you don't want him there either. Okay. Nobody's gonna be staring at the bride when the father of the groom is wearing a _____."

84. To whom was Rachel referring when she said, "She said that since you get to keep the one-bedroom apartment you should give Rachel the purple chair"?

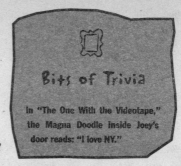

85. Ross: "Hey, you know what nickname never caught on? The _____."

86. To whom did Phoebe say, "Aren't you supposed to be in Russia?"

87. To whom was Joey referring when he said, "You get thrown from a horse into an electric fence"?

88. Who said, "Dearly beloved . . . I'm sorry I'm late"?

89. Chandler, as Santa, to Ben: "My favorite part was when _____ flew all the Jews out of Egypt."

90. Who said, "You know, I'm still twenty-nine in Guam"?

91. Chandler to Rachel: "This is _____ tux? Oh, I have to get married in _____ tux."

92. Phoebe: "Hi, Earl. This is Phoebe from Empire Office Supplies. I'd like to talk to you about your _____ needs."

93. Monica to Chandler, about the night they hooked up in London: "When I went to your room that night, I was actually looking for _____."

94. Ross to his dad: "W-w-wait a minute! I mean a couple of stupid boxes get wet and she gets a _____?"

95. What was Monica referring to when she said, "Unless . . . well, this might sound crazy, but there might be something we could fashion"?

96. Phoebe to Rachel's sorority sister (Winona Ryder), when asked if she'd ever been in a sorority: "Of course. Yes, I was a, um, thigh mega _____."

97. What was Chandler's dad's stage name in his Vegas drag show?

98. Who said, "I made a whole speech about how you do not cancel plans with friends"?

99. What was Ross referring to when he told Rachel, "Listen, I don't want you teaching my son that stuff anymore"?

100. What was Phoebe referring to when she told Rachel, "It just seems pretty wild. And you're, you know, so . . . vanilla"?

101. What was Chandler referring to when he told Ross and Joey, "I stole Monica's and changed the name"?

102. To whom was Phoebe referring when she told Rachel, "Can you believe that? We were waiting for a hot guy and then an even hotter one shows up"?

103. To whom was Joey referring when he said, "Oh, yeah. He looked like a real lumberjack in those pink lacies"?

104. To whom did Monica say, "I'm sorry. Apparently I've opened the door to the past"?

105. What was Monica referring to when she told Phoebe, "Why didn't you make a copy and keep it in a fireproof box and keep it at least a hundred yards away from the original?"

106. Why didn't Monica's cousin Franny invite Monica to her wedding?

107. To whom was Ross referring as he thought, "If she knew what was going on in your head, she'd think you were sick. Or would she? Let's back up for a second. She was the one who suggested opening a bottle of wine. She was the one who turned down the lights"?

108. What was Chandler referring to when he told Rachel, "I'm full. And yet I know if I stop eating this, I'll regret it"?

109. What was Cecilia Lockhart (Susan Sarandon) referring to when she told Monica, "I'd love to, but my lawyer said I can't do that anymore"?

110. What was Rachel referring to when she told Tag, "Sorry, it's for human resources. Everybody has to do it. Would you stand up please?"

111. Who said, "Chandler, you call me when this goes in the pooper"?

112. Jack Geller to Ross: "I think I accidentally used Monica's boxes to keep the water away from the _____."

113. What was Monica referring to when she said, "It's enough for wedding scenario A"?

114. What was the name of the soap opera award Joey was nominated for?

115. Monica to Rachel and Phoebe: "Well, um, I was thinking that maybe we could come up with a system where we trade off being _____ for each other."

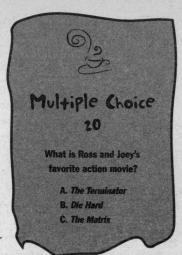

Multiple Choice
20

What is Ross and Joey's favorite action movie?

A. *The Terminator*
B. *Die Hard*
C. *The Matrix*

116. Ross to Joey, who wanted to wear sunglasses during his movie shoot because his costar kept spitting in his eyes: "And if I remember correctly, Ray•Ban was the official sponsor of _____."

117. What was Monica referring to when she told Chandler, "Listen, I'm sure that Dad doesn't care. He probably thought this was funny. He'll be telling this story for years"?

118. Why did Tag tell Rachel's boss, "I have a weird sense of humor and I'm kind of strangely proud of my butt"?

119. What was Monica referring to when she said, "You know what's weird? This doesn't feel weird"?

120. To whom did Rachel say, "All right, the first thing I need you to do is go downstairs and find a woman named Hilda and tell her to go home"?

121. Joey: "Wait, Internet _____ can still have sex, right?"

122. What was Phoebe referring to when she said, "Please don't be a spaceship. Please don't be a spaceship"?

123. Phoebe to Rachel: "I know you really want to do this. But I've never been _____ to anyone before. And I know you've done it at least twice."

124. Phoebe to Rachel: "So you like the _____. That, that's great. You know, I was worried that, you know, they might create an unbearable living situation. But, okay, apparently not, so yay!"

125. What was Ross referring to when he said, "I bet I can get all fifty before dinner"?

126. What did Ross do on his thirtieth birthday?

127. Phoebe to Monica: "I've had that _____ there for three days and Chandler had no idea. He's not so smart."

128. To whom was Rachel referring when she said, "I love him. He's so pretty I want to cry. I don't know what to do. Tell me what to do"?

129. To whom was Phoebe referring when she told Ross, "Oh, my God, why would you play hide-and-seek with someone you know is a flight risk?"

130. Joey to Ross, while in front of the young woman they were both dating: "Have you ever gotten stuck in a pair of your own _____?"

131. Cecilia (Susan Sarandon) to Joey: "Let's just say that if I'd left fifteen years ago, the landscape of _____ cinema would be very different today."

132. Phoebe to Monica: "You said I could sing at your wedding, so I'm just gonna need a small _____."

133. What was Nora Bing referring to when she told Chandler, "I thought we'd screwed you up so bad this day would never come"?

134. What was Monica referring to when she said, "Joey, this is not like learning to ride a horse. This is like learning to grow a turtle-neck"?

135. What was Ross referring to when he said, "Yes! My baby's free!"?

136. What was Chandler referring to when he said, "Hey, if you listen very carefully, I think it's 'Celebration' by Kool and the Gang"?

137. What was Chandler referring to when he told Monica, "Ross is Batman"?

138. What did Joey wear to an audition in which he was to appear naked with an uncircumcised penis?

139. Monica to Chandler: "And, honey, just so you know, now that you're marrying me, you don't get to _____ anymore."

140. To whom did Rachel say, "How could you not remember us kissing?"

141. What was Chandler referring to when he said, "So when I was in the gift shop, that's when I, uh, saw this. Yeah, you know, and I thought anything that could fit into this can't be scary"?

Season Eight

1. What was Joey referring to when he told Monica, "I'm sorry, okay? I went to the gift shop and it was either this or a bathrobe"?

2. What was Monica referring to when she told the cleaning woman, "I'm sorry. I've never had a maid before. Is this not okay?"

3. Why did Mona dump Ross?

4. Joey to the woman interviewing him for *Soap Opera Digest*: "In my spare time I read to the blind. And I'm also a _____, for kids."

5. Why did Chandler's boss take him to a strip club?

6. Rachel to Monica and Phoebe: "So my mother is not coming to my _____?"

7. Who caught Monica and Chandler having sex in a broom closet?

8. What was Phoebe referring to when she said, "Okay, okay. It's James Brolin"?

9. Who said, "I just slapped my future sister-in-law in the butt"?

10. What was Monica referring to when she told Rachel, "I thought it might be true. I thought you might cry, then show it to me"?

11. What was Chandler referring to when he told Monica, "You can wear 'em with shorts on the street corner and earn the money to pay for them"?

12. What was Monica referring to when she told Chandler, "Am I going in the Wife Hall of Fame or what?"

13. Monica: "No, really, any time Ross makes a _____, everyone cries and hugs him and pats him on the back."

14. Katie, the salesgirl at the baby store, to Ross: "A paleontologist who works out? You're like _____."

15. Why did Rachel tell Joey her boss wanted to buy her baby?

16. To whom was Ross referring when he asked Joey, "You're in love with her?"

17. Rachel's OB-GYN: "I know it's not my place, but please don't name your baby _____."

18. What was Chandler referring to when he told Monica, "Well, you know, they only give you three letters, so after A-S-S, it's a bit of a challenge"?

19. What was Rachel referring to when she told Phoebe, "Wow. This explains so much. Last weekend I went from store to store sitting on Santa's lap"?

20. To whom did Chandler say, "I'd shake your hand but I'm really into the game. Plus, I think it'd be better for my ego if we didn't stand right next to each other"?

21. Eric, Ursula's ex-fiancé, to Phoebe: "You're blurry, but you still look like Ursula. You're _____."

22. To whom did Chandler say, "Joey's gonna be thrilled. He was hoping you would come by as a slutty nurse"?

23. What was Ross referring to when he said, "Fine. But I want the record to show that I tried to take the high road. Because in about five minutes I'm gonna be saying *hahaaaaahaha . . .*"?

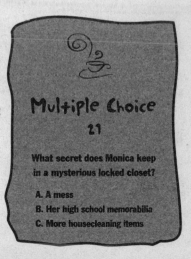

Multiple Choice
21

What secret does Monica keep in a mysterious locked closet?

A. A mess
B. Her high school memorabilia
C. More housecleaning items

24. What was Chandler referring to when he told Ross the day after his wedding, "So what? What? They're gone? Monica's gonna freak!"?

25. Who said, "It's not negative. It's positive"?

26. What was Rachel referring to when she told Joey, "Oh, no, I know. I couldn't see it either at first, but it's right, um, Ross, I lost it again"?

27. What was Phoebe referring to when she told Monica while running out the door, "Screw you! I'm going first!"?

28. To whom was Chandler referring when he told Monica, "Her ass print is still on your grandmother's quilt. Do you really want to talk about smoking?"

29. Who told Rachel, "I don't care about fashion. I'm pregnant and I know you are too, so you gotta help me"?

30. What was Ross referring to when he said, "Besides, I think I figured out a much faster route. I'm sure I can make it this time. I just can't be afraid to get a little bit hit by cars"?

31. Phoebe to Ross, on why she'd never had saltwater taffy: "I think my mother was too busy planning her _____ to provide saltwater treats."

32. Mr. Zelner to Rachel: "I want to make clear that I understand it's your _____, and it is not mine to purchase."

33. What was the name of the game show Joey auditioned for?

34. What was Rachel referring to when she told Ross, "Just think of me as, like, a ketchup bottle. You know, sometimes you have to bang on the end of it just to get something to come out"?

35. Ross, under his breath to Janice's husband while she was having contractions: "Sid, you lucky _____ bastard."

36. Chandler: "_____? Uh, I don't have a _____. I'm gonna go pack my regular long bathing suit."

37. What band did Monica and Chandler get to perform at their wedding ceremony?

38. To whom was Monica referring when she said, "Can we go call them? Is it too soon to call? I wanna call them"?

39. What did Gunther dress up as for Monica and Chandler's Halloween party?

40. Chandler to Rachel, on the rumor Ross and Will had started about her back in high school: "Everyone at my school heard it. You were the _____ cheerleader from Long Island."

41. What was Ross referring to when he said, "That's a really pretty name for an industrial solvent"?

42. What was Chandler referring to when he screamed, "Worst porn ever! Worst porn ever!"?

43. To whom did Phoebe say, "No, I am a positive person. You are like Santa Claus on Prozac . . . at Disneyland . . . getting laid!"?

44. Rachel to her mother: "He was a hamster! I am not going to vacuum up my _____!"

Bits of Trivia

In "The One With the Cheap Wedding Dress," Andrea Bendewald guest stars as a bride-to-be; in real life she is one of Jennifer Aniston's best friends and was a bridesmaid at her wedding.

45. What was a highly irritable and very pregnant Rachel referring to when she told Monica, "Well, there is one thing we didn't try but *someone thinks that that will open up a can of worms*"?

46. What was Chandler referring to when he said, "I got good. I played this game all day and now I rule at it"?

47. What was Ross referring to when he jokingly told Mona, "I thought it was best you heard it from Rachel's father"?

48. To whom was Monica referring when she said, "She stole my jeans!"?

49. To whom did Monica say, "You used the Europe story!"?

50. What was Joey referring to when he said, "These are my Thanksgiving pants!"?

51. Who told Phoebe, "I'm sure there's two sides to this story, but all I've heard is that Ben's a bit of a poopoo head"?

52. What was Chandler referring to when he said to himself, "All right, this isn't so bad. I like the flowery smell . . . which is okay 'cause I got my boat"?

53. After really enjoying Phoebe's massages, why did Monica suddenly stop enjoying them?

54. Ross to Chandler, referring to one of Chandler's coworkers: "Did that guy just call you _____?"

55. Monica: "I still don't get why Greg and Jenny would give us a fake _____."

56. To whom did Phoebe say, "You're just gonna knock on this guy's door and change his life forever"?

57. To whom was Chandler referring when he told Joey, "Okay, rock, paper, scissor for who has to tell the whore to leave"?

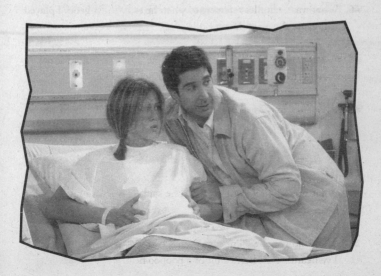

58. What was Chandler referring to when he said, "It was like *It's a Wonderful Life* with lap dances"?

59. Chandler to Monica: "Phoebe thinks you and Don are soul mates and I don't believe in that kind of stuff, but then you two totally get along. So look, I won't stand in your way if you want to run off with Don and live in a house of _____."

60. What was Rachel referring to when she said, "I know what this is . . . Wait a minute. That can't be right. Is that a beer bong for a baby?"

61. To whom was Ross referring when he asked Rachel, "What happened to the Disgustingtons?"

62. What was Rachel referring to when she said, "This is so stupid. How can I be upset over something I never had?"

63. Rachel, regarding the examination table at her OB-GYN's office: "Oh, man, if they sold these at _____ . . ."

64. Phoebe to Monica: "You can't _____ him today because I'm dumping him."

65. Who told Chandler, "Look, I know it must be hard that your wife is a lesbian. But it's wrong. You're married"?

66. What was Monica referring to when she said, "They hurt so much!"?

67. Chandler to Monica: "Honey, it's not the _____ I enjoy. It's the wet, naked lady."

68. What was Rachel referring to when she said, "Well, just ask Mona to give it back"?

69. Which Friends took a beginner's cooking class together?

70. What was Rachel referring to when she said, "It's not fair, Ross. I got here first"?

71. What was Ross referring to when he said, "No, just a key. I gave her the *only* key. I am now a homeless man in a very serious relationship"?

72. What was Phoebe referring to when she told Rachel, "How can you let him talk to your crotch like that?"

Multiple Choice 22

What hideous wedding gift do Chandler's aunt and uncle send?

A. A chirping clock
B. A punch bowl
C. A talking toilet paper roll

73. Where did Monica and Chandler first try to conceive?

74. Joey, after finishing off the Thanksgiving turkey: "Here come the _____ sweats."

75. What was Chandler doing when Monica said, "Oh, God, Chandler's making his sex face"?

76. What was Chandler referring to when he said, "Ross, it's got your wavy black lines"?

77. Why did Ross tell Rachel at the hospital, "Keep your legs together and cover the baby's ears"?

78. Chandler to Rachel, who asked for ribbon: "What do you need? We got lace, satin, sateen, raffia, gingham, felt . . . and I think my _____ may be in here, too."

79. Phoebe to Joey: "This is the happiest _____ in the world. So you can keep him till he cheers you up. And he will cheer you up."

80. Chandler to Joey, referring to the naked woman in the bedroom: "I can't believe there is a naked _____ in there."

81. What was Chandler referring to when he said, "Yeah, we're gonna need to see that tape"?

82. Ross to Chandler: "It's not just an 'M.' Your middle name is _____!"

83. To whom did Phoebe scream, "No! Don't tear out your eyes!"?

84. What was Monica referring to when she asked Chandler, "What is the matter with your hand?"

85. Where did everyone find out Ross and Rachel were having a baby girl?

86. Phoebe to Monica: "Why won't you let me _____ you?"

87. Monica to Joey, trying to lighten the mood after Joey told Rachel he loved her: "Tea gives Phoebe the _____."

88. To whom was Rachel referring when she said, "Oh, great. Only she sounds like a biblical whore"?

89. Phoebe: "Hey, Ross, doesn't Ben go to Smithfield Day School? _____ has a son that goes there, too."

90. Ross to Chandler, on why Chandler should let Ross win at arm wrestling: "I keep gettin' divorces and knockin' people up . . . and I'm dressed as _____."

91. Why did Rachel say to Ross, "Oh, I'm sorry. Are we having an eighty-nine-year-old?"

92. Chandler to Monica, after discovering the mess inside her closet: "I married _____!"

93. What was Rachel's initial reaction to Joey telling her he was in love with her?

94. Rachel to Joey: "And if you do the interview, you could mention, oh, I don't know, _____ Rachel Green."

95. What was Rachel referring to when she said, "You know that feeling when you're trying to blow a St. Bernard out your ass?"

96. Who said, "I just bamboozled Chandler!"?

97. To whom was Joey referring when he asked Rachel, "He wants to *buy* your baby?"

98. Who said, "In fact, when we were building houses in Uruguay, we were just two towns apart and we never met"?

99. Who is Ken Adams?

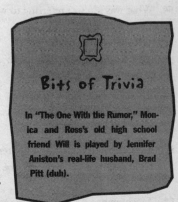

Bits of Trivia

In "The One With the Rumor," Monica and Ross's old high school friend Will is played by Jennifer Aniston's real-life husband, Brad Pitt (duh).

100. Monica to Ross and Rachel: "I'm so glad you guys got drunk and _____."

101. Ross to Rachel, who was highly irritable because she was eight days past her due date: "You know, we should probably ask the doctor if she even knows how to deliver a baby that's half human, half _____."

102. Chandler to Monica: "You know, I've been living here for a while and I've never seen what's inside that _____."

103. Ross to Rachel: "I want to talk to the president of the _____ company!"

104. What was Rachel referring to when she told Phoebe, "You said she was. I just didn't disagree with you"?

105. What was Phoebe referring to when she said, "You got fake-numbered!"?

106. What was Chandler referring to when he told Monica, "Shouldn't we give her the benefit of the doubt before we go snooping around her crotch?"

107. What was Mona referring to when she asked Ross, "How many did you want? I'm getting a hundred"?

108. What was Rachel referring to when she said, "You gotta light a fire up there and just smoke it out"?

109. Monica to Chandler: "Oh, I'm working on my _____ for the party. Or as I like to call it, Sobfest 2002."

110. What was Phoebe referring to when she said, "I got you a present! I got it for your wedding and I ordered it weeks ago and it finally got here!"?

111. Rachel's father to Rachel: "Young lady, don't you sit there and tell me my first grandchild's gonna be a _____."

112. Who said, "And now it's five years later, the doughnut's gone, and I'm still Toby"?

113. Joey to Rachel, on Monica and Chandler: "I still can't believe they took away my _____. You trust me with yours."

114. To whom did Phoebe say, "Rachel has something that she wants to tell you and, um, I believe that this is your red sweater"?

115. To whom did Joey say, "I think I'm falling in love with you"?

116. Chandler to Joey, who was testing Chandler after he fell asleep during Joey's movie's premiere: "I was surprised to see a _____ in a World War One epic."

117. What was Monica referring to when she said, "This is so embarrassing. Oh, my God, I'm never gonna get massaged again"?

118. Phoebe to Ross and Rachel on what to name their baby: "If it's a girl, Phoebe. And if it's a boy, _____."

119. What was Ross referring to when he said, "It's salmon"?

120. To whom did Ross say, "I'd like a Wicked Wango card"?

121. What was Joey referring to when he told Ross, "Whoa! Hey! Hold on! Are you serious? So, like three percent of the time they don't even work?"

122. Joey: "All right, _____ came as doody!"

123. Monica to Rachel: "Are you sure you _____ on the stick right?"

124. What was the rumor Ross and Will started back in high school while members of the I Hate Rachel Club?

125. What was Monica referring to when she said, "How cool is this? We know three down. I'm touching three down"?

126. What was Chandler referring to when he said to Monica, "Oh, no, it's gonna be named after some snack or baked good"?

127. Who said, "Hey, my sweater. I've been looking for this thing for like a month"?

Multiple Choice
23

Chandler has two copies of which movie soundtrack?

A. *Cabaret*
B. *Mission: Impossible*
C. *Annie*

Season Nine

1. What was Monica referring to when she told Chandler, "He didn't make it to one of my piano recitals, but this he sees!"?

2. What was Ross's recurring nightmare that brought him to see a therapist as a child?

3. Why did Chandler tell Monica, "The truth is, I soiled myself during some turbulence"?

4. What was Chandler referring to when he told Joey, "I'm gonna watch it. I mean, look, it's probably not even what I think it is. And even if it is, it can't possibly be as bad as what I'm picturing in my head . . . can it?"

5. What was Mike (Paul Rudd) referring to when he said to Phoebe, "Go back? To the land where time stands still?"

6. Chandler: "Am I sexy in _____?"

7. Rachel: "Ross still sees his _____!"

8. Ross to Rachel: "Please take your time. It's an important decision. Not like, say, I don't know, deciding to marry someone. This is about a _____."

9. Monica to Chandler: "I saw what you were doing in Tulsa. Angry _____ turn you on."

10. To whom did Ross say, "You gotta be at least bi"?

11. Rachel's sister Amy, on her disappointment that her boyfriend blew her off: "I was so looking forward to this. It was gonna be such a beautiful Thanksgiving. We were gonna have _____."

12. To whom was Joey referring when he told Chandler, "I'm gonna wait in the hall in case the dude comes out"?

13. To whom did Phoebe say, "You know, it's so surprising that you and Joey have known each other for so long and I've never heard about you"?

14. What was Joey referring to when he told Ross, "Can I just stop you right there for a second. When people do this"—he gestures—"I don't really know what that means"?

15. Phoebe to Ross: "If you hadn't just had a baby with my best friend, I swear to Lucifer a rabid dog would be feasting on your _____ right now."

16. Who asked Ross and Rachel, "Do you guys do random drug testing?"

17. Who told Phoebe, "Wow. You look like my mom"?

18. Rachel to her sister Amy: "Yeah, remember that time in high school and I died and didn't give you my _____?"

19. Wendy, a colleague in Tulsa, to Chandler: "Besides, I can't leave until that Christmas party downstairs clears out. There are some pissed-off insurance people looking for that _____."

20. What was Rachel referring to when she said, "I can't watch. It's like firing Elmo"?

21. What was Joey referring to when he said to himself, "I think I've been scared by that painting before"?

22. Chandler to Monica: "You know how people say Tulsa is the _____ of Oklahoma?"

23. To whom was Rachel referring when she said, "So what? He's smart, he's qualified. Give me one good reason we shouldn't try him out"?

24. Rachel: "Oh, Emma. This is your first Thanksgiving. What are you thankful for? Mommy's _____?"

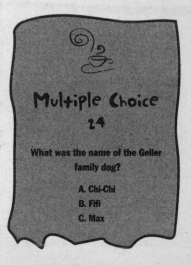

Multiple Choice
24

What was the name of the Geller family dog?

A. Chi-Chi
B. Fifi
C. Max

25. What was Chandler referring to when he told Monica, "I climb down the fire escape and you can't put *that* in the closet?"

26. To whom was Rachel referring when she said, "I wonder why Ross said that he died"?

27. Who said, "Oh, my God! She thinks we're engaged!"?

28. Who said, "I always wanted to play piano professionally, and I figured if I don't do this now, I never will"?

29. To whom was Ross referring when he told Phoebe, "He's a kite designer *and* he used to date Oprah"?

30. Chandler: "You got a man as a nanny? You got a _____?"

31. Monica to Chandler: "I think we should save our china for something really special. Like when the _____ comes over."

32. To whom was Rachel referring when she told Bill, a guy at a bar, "No sense of personal space . . . kinda smells like a kitchen . . . looks like a potato!"?

33. Chandler to Monica: "Willpower? I've watched home movies of you eating _____ without taking the tinfoil off!"

34. Mike to Phoebe, trying to convince her that he might be the right guy for her:

"And you don't have to worry about glue sniffing with me. Although I do smell the occasional _____."

35. Which Friend bruises like a peach?

36. What did Ross do to make Emma laugh her first laugh?

37. Ross to Rachel, on her wanting to invite her sister Amy for Thanksgiving: "You know, I think that's a great idea. It'll be like the Pilgrims bringing the Indians _____."

38. Phoebe, on Rachel's description of a "moment" between her and Ross: "Eye contact? I hope you were using _____."

39. To whom did Chandler say, "This is probably the wrong thing to be worrying about, but you're getting ham on my only tie"?

40. To whom was Chandler referring when he said, "I just hope the club doesn't slip out of my hand and beat the mustache off his face"?

41. Phoebe to Rachel: "And that's Judy over at the bar with _____?"

42. What was Rachel's pediatrician's name?

43. Ross to Phoebe: "Well, I didn't! I didn't _____! Unless . . . did I? I haven't slept in forty hours and it does sound like something I would do."

44. How did Joey meet Mike, the guy he met at the last minute to set up with Phoebe?

45. What was Monica referring to when she asked Chandler, "Then why were you watching them and giving yourself a treat?"

46. Joey, on how weird he thought it was that a guy would want to be a nanny: "That's like a woman wanting to be a . . . a _____."

47. Who asked, "So where does everyone summer?"

48. Phoebe to Joey, on a "bad" lie: "How about the whole man-walking-on-the-moon thing? You can see the _____, people!"

49. What was Mike (Paul Rudd) referring to when he told Ross, "Yeah. You know, I'm sorry. I don't really like to talk about it"?

50. Phoebe, at her birthday dinner: "Oh, for God's sake, Judy, pick up the _____! Pick up the _____! Pick up the _____!"

51. To what was Ross referring when he said, "Rach, I told you, you can't call him every time any little thing comes up"?

52. Who said, "I'm here to explain to the people who gave us our grant why it's a positive thing that we've spent all their money and accomplished nothing"?

53. Who asked Phoebe, "Did you just hit my dad?"

54. Monica to Chandler: "Emma is the product of a bottle of Merlot and a five-year-old _____."

55. Why did Joey call Chandler's cell phone and say, "Dude . . . come home. *Come home*"?

56. To whom did Chandler say, "Look, you're a really nice person . . . ham stealing and adultery aside"?

57. Why did Chandler commit to moving to Tulsa?

58. Who was Vikram?

59. To whom was Monica referring when she told Chandler, "He is without a doubt the funniest guy I ever met!"?

Bits of Trivia

Paul Rudd, who played Phoebe's pianist boyfriend in season nine, played Jennifer Aniston's gay roommate in the film *The Object of My Affection*.

60. What was Rachel referring to when she told Emma, "All right, sweetheart. This is only because I love you so much and I know that you're not going to tell anybody"?

61. What was Rachel referring to when she told Ross, "Okay, stop. Stop looking at me like that. Last time that happened, *that* happened"?

62. What was Chandler referring to when he said, "She's entitled to be a little paranoid or, in this case, right on the money"?

63. Joey: "I went out with this girl last night. Halfway through our date I realized I _____."

64. Monica to Chandler: "Are you trying to tell me that we're moving to Oklahoma or that you're _____?"

65. Chandler to Joey, on Ross: "And *you* did it first? This is gonna kill him. You know how much he loves to _____."

66. Ross to Rachel, who wanted him to knock the apartment door down after locking Emma inside: "I would, but I bruise like a _____."

67. What was Joey referring to when he said, "The producers are going to be so mad at me. They sat us down yesterday and said, 'Everyone has to be there at six a.m. sharp. That means you, Tribbiani' "?

68. Joey to Chandler: "It wasn't my _____. It fell out of Ross's jacket."

69. What did Chandler find while in Richard's apartment with Joey?

70. Joey to Chandler, on his beautiful colleague: "Oh, is Wendy the runner-up Miss _____?"

Multiple Choice 25

Which Friend enjoys a visit to the dry cleaner?

A. Monica
B. Phoebe
C. Joey

71. Rachel to Ross, after he told her he wasn't feeling well: "What do you mean you're not feeling well? What do you have? Is it _____? Because don't go near Emma. She has not had that shot."

72. What was Ross referring to when he said, "Dad, seriously! You know, you really should see someone about that!"?

73. Why didn't Monica go to Tulsa with Chandler?

74. Chandler to Joey, on why he wasn't helping Monica get ready for Rachel's birthday party: "I tried, but apparently singing 'I Will Survive' in a _____ voice . . . not helping."

75. Rachel to Monica, on why she changed her mind about Gavin: "Well, you know, honey, there is a thin line between love and hate and, uh, it turns out that line is a _____."

76. Who told Ross and Rachel, "I don't believe this! Hold on a second. You guys die, and I *don't* get your baby?"

77. Phoebe to Joey: "I learned never to borrow money from friends. That's why _____ and I don't speak anymore."

78. What was Monica and Chandler's dilemma while baby-sitting Emma?

79. Monica to Chandler: "Guys can _____? Unbelievable! The one thing that's ours!"

80. How did Joey create urgency during his audition with Leonard Hayes (Jeff Goldblum)?

81. What was the name of the mother of Phoebe's seven rat babies?

82. What was the first song Monica sang at Mike's piano bar?

83. What was Chandler referring to when he asked Joey, "Any chance you're trying to pick a fight to make all of this easier?"

84. Rachel: "If one more person says, 'What a cute little _____,' I'm gonna whip 'em with a car antenna."

85. To whom was Joey referring when he said, "Oh, man, what'd you have to go and say that for? Now that you told me I can't have her, it makes me want her even more"?

86. How did Chandler earn his allowance as a child?

87. Why did Phoebe and Mike break up?

88. What was Joey's favorite stuffed animal's name?

89. Who said, "Cheese . . . it's milk that you chew"?

90. What was Gavin's former profession?

91. To whom did Rachel say, "In fact, from now on, I'm going to take the high road and I'm going to be very, very nice to you, you mama's boy, starting right now"?

92. How did Phoebe and Joey try to get Ross and Rachel back together?

93. How did Joey cover after Chandler found out Monica had secretly borrowed money from him?

94. Why did Ross have Monica and Chandler throw him a memorial service?

Multiple Choice 26

In what context does Joey's name appear in an issue of *Soap Opera Digest*?

A. In a scandalous report
B. In a poor review
C. As a crossword answer

95. What was Chandler referring to when he said, "It's like a baby caterpillar chasing its mama"?

96. What was Chandler's first assignment as an intern?

97. Why did Joey tell Phoebe, "I think it might be time for my sponge bath"?

98. To whom was Ross referring when he told Rachel, "Do you realize that man has cried in our apartment three times?"

99. Rachel to Gavin, who asked about the photo of her and Ross: "Oh, he's dusting me with a _____. He thought it would be funny."

100. What happened the first time Phoebe encountered Ross?

101. Joey to Phoebe, paraphrasing the director on *Days of Our Lives*: "He said, if your _____ friend doesn't get her _____ act together, I am gonna fire her mother-_____ ass."

102. Ross, trying to hit on a couple of women: "Here's a question. Would you rather drown or be _____?"

103. Ross, on Phoebe's boyfriend, Mike: "He's been _____. I have some experience in that area."

104. What did Gavin give Rachel for her birthday?

105. Monica to Chandler: "So you stole that tape from _____?"

106. What did Phoebe sing at Mike's piano bar?

107. What was Phoebe referring to when she told Mike, "I haven't told you about that yet, have I?"

108. Why did Chandler say to his boss, "Farts, boobies, butt cracks!"?

109. Monica to everyone: "Joey is having a secret _____ party up on the roof!"

110. Monica to Chandler: "I still can't believe this. My _____ is an inhospitable environment? I always tried so hard to be a good hostess."

111. Who did Joey compare himself to when Rachel asked if he wasn't just a little bit curious as to what it would be like if the two of them got together?

112. To whom was Chandler referring when he said, "Look, he's intelligent. He's healthy. He's athletic. I mean, he's sperm-tastic"?

113. Which of the gang did not want to contribute to the Powerball fund?

114. Phoebe to Joey on their plan to set Ross and Rachel up on horrible blind dates: "You know what the best part is? I get to do my plan _____."

115. What was Emma's first word?

116. How did Rachel discover that it was really Phoebe who was giving her a massage at the corporate massage chain?

117. What was the name of the restaurant where Monica was head chef?

118. To whom did Phoebe say, "So we're both living in New York, not seeing anyone—that's so not like us"?

119. What did Joey threaten Monica and Chandler with if they didn't name their firstborn after him?

120. Phoebe, on the unfairness of being a vegetarian when it comes to wishbones: "Just because we don't eat the meat doesn't mean we don't like to play with the _____."

Multiple Choice 27

On which holiday did Chandler first meet Monica?

A. Thanksgiving
B. Christmas
C. Earth Day

121. To what was Rachel referring when she said, "Phoebe, come on, I don't want to waste it. It'd be like throwing away a hundred bucks!"?

122. How did Ross lose his keynote address at the convention in Barbados?

123. To whom was Ross referring when he said, "She only dates geniuses and Nobel Prize winners"?

124. Chandler, to the Vermont innkeeper, on why Ross was so agitated: "I'm sorry he's a little wound up. We had to stop at every _____ stand on the way up here."

125. Who told Rachel, "That's right. I have no money. I'm not funny. I live in a studio apartment with two other guys, and I'm pretty sure I'm infertile"?

126. To what was Chandler referring when he asked Monica, "What about the ones you have on the nightstand?"

127. To whom did Rachel shout, "You are having a party tonight!"?

128. How long was David the Scientist Guy in Minsk before he returned to New York?

129. Who scored the winning point at Ping-Pong in Barbados?

130. Rachel: "All right, I don't want to alarm anybody but Monica's _____ is twice as big as it was when we landed."

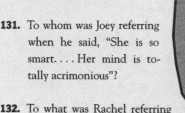

Bits of Trivia

The first line of dialogue uttered on the show was: "There's nothing to tell." Monica says those words as she sits on the Central Perk couch, defending her relationship with Paul the Wine Guy.

131. To whom was Joey referring when he said, "She is so smart. . . . Her mind is totally acrimonious"?

132. To what was Rachel referring when she suddenly woke up from a dream and said, "Well, that's new"?

133. Rachel, on the phone to her mother: "Mom, please. I know you love your new _____, but I can barely understand you."

134. To whom was Phoebe referring when she said, "You're ruining the plan! Joey, you've fixed him up with his perfect woman!"?

135. To what was Joey referring when he told Rachel, "It's up on the roof at eight"?

136. Monica to Chandler: "You can't just bring some random guy home and expect him to be our _____."

137. Monica: "Chandler, we have talked about this. You are not supposed to give people _____!"

138. With whom did Monica play Ping-Pong in Barbados?

Season Ten

1. Rachel, on Emma's impending eight-hour flight with Grandma Green: "Eight hours of my mother talking about _____? Good luck, Emma!"

2. What was Joey trying to say when he wrote of Monica and Chandler in his letter of recommendation to the adoption agency: "They're humid prepossessing Homo *sapiens* with full-sized aortic pumps"?

3. Joey to his *Pyramid* partner: "If I'm building a house, the plan isn't called a _____."

4. Why did Rachel think the French were going to hate her?

5. Ross to Chandler, who told him he went to the spray-on tanning salon too: "Really? Did you count _____?"

6. Why were Joey and Ross late for Thanksgiving dinner?

7. Mike: "I thought it'd be fun if the third groomsman was _____."

8. Why did Monica destroy the foosball table?

9. Benjamin Hobart (Greg Kinnear) to Ross: "I think I may have let my feelings for Charlie interfere with the _____ process."

10. To what was Chandler referring when he said, "What do you know? It's a treat for the eyes and the ears"?

11. What did Chandler compare Rachel's leaving to?

12. Phoebe, on Mike during their honeymoon: "He didn't _____ the whole time we were there."

13. Phoebe to Mike, after she tried proposing to him on-screen at the Knicks game: "That woman at the game didn't know what she was talking about. Mike, obviously you have _____."

14. To what was Monica referring when she asked Joey, "You hand-wrote it?"

15. Ross to Rachel, on his fear of spiders versus her irrational fear: "Oh, yeah, that's the same! I'm sure there are thirty different species of poisonous _____!"

16. Who said, "I've only ever been with two guys, but they sort of over-lapped"?

17. Joey: "Friends, family, dog . . . thank you all for being here to witness this blessed event. The cold has now spread to my _____, so I'm going to do the short version of this."

18. What instrument did Phoebe's friend Marjorie play at her wedding?

19. In which New York suburb did Monica and Chandler buy their first house?

20. To what was Frank Jr. referring when he told Phoebe, "I was thinking maybe you could take one"?

21. Why didn't Joey want to go on a second date with Phoebe's hot friend Sarah?

22. To what was Ross referring when he said, "It's been sixteen years but the air quotes still hurt"?

23. To what was Ross referring when he said, "Damn it, it's never off the table"?

24. To whom was Erica referring when she said, "He killed his father with a shovel"?

25. Who said, "Big surprise . . . the Hunk of Beef has feelings"?

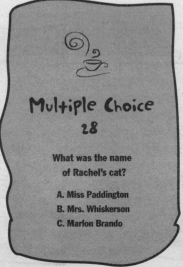

Multiple Choice 28

What was the name of Rachel's cat?

A. Miss Paddington
B. Mrs. Whiskerson
C. Marlon Brando

26. Charlie to Ross, on her ex-boyfriend Benjamin Hobart: "He does have a pretty serious _____ fetish."

27. To what was Phoebe referring when she told Monica, "Oh, this one is so cute. Get this one!"?

28. To whom was Phoebe referring when she said, "Oh, that tart, floozy . . . giant!"?

29. To whom was Rachel referring when she said, "He's a doctor. You don't expect doctors to get sick."

30. Ross: "Hi, Rachel. Here's your sister Amy. She thinks I need _____ implants."

31. Why were Phoebe and Rachel late for Thanksgiving dinner?

32. What was Joey referring to when he asked Mike, "How bad do you want to stick your tongue on that?"

33. What did Amy (Christina Applegate) do to Emma while baby-sitting her?

34. What did Phoebe put down Joey's pants while his head was stuck in Monica and Chandler's door?

35. Rachel: "Oh, my God! They put my baby's face on a _____!"

36. Ross to Joey: "Chandler and I have this stupid college alumni thing. I can't believe you get to meet _____."

37. Why did Joey say to Phoebe: "I can do a dramatic reading of one of her books"?

38. Ross to Rachel: "Some can sing. Some can dance. I apparently can turn phallic _____ into woodland creatures."

39. Rachel to Ross, who tried to convince her to get over her fear of swings: "I know what this is all about. You've always been jealous of my _____."

40. Rachel to Joey: "Ross and _____? Wow, she's really makin' her way through the group."

41. Why did Charlie break up with Ross?

42. Rachel to Joey: "And if it doesn't work, then we'll just be one of those couples that doesn't have _____."

43. Monica, outside Phoebe's wedding: "Okay! Who left the _____ on the steam grate?"

44. How did Ross try to sway Rachel's boss at Ralph Lauren into re-hiring her?

45. Who said, "And one more thing: There might be a picture of Precious on my coffee table"?

46. To what was Phoebe referring when she told Ross and Chandler, "If it helps, you were next in line. You just missed the cut"?

47. What is Rachel's bra size?

48. Who almost bought the house next door to Monica and Chandler's?

49. What was Rachel's traumatic swing incident when she was little?

50. According to Chandler, what's one of life's great unanswerable questions?

51. What was the name of the little girl Joey befriended while seeing the house Monica and Chandler had just bought?

52. To what was Monica referring when she said, "If only there were a smaller one to clean this one"?

53. Phoebe to Rachel: "You know, the strippers and the guys dancing and, you know, _____ flying about."

54. What product did Joey endorse in a commercial that only aired in Japan?

55. Who said, "If you two are happy, then I'm happy for you. I'm fine"?

Bits of Trivia

If you look carefully, you'll notice that after season one, the girls' apartment number changes from #5 to #20, as does their view. This was because after season one, *Friends* was shot on a different set.

56. Chandler to Monica: "I didn't get to the bathroom. I bumped into Owen on the way and he didn't know he was _____! And there's a slight chance I may have told him!"

57. Who told Ross, "When you put your feet on my bed, you tugged on my catheter"?

58. What did Monica and Chandler name their twins?

59. Who said, "Why couldn't I have been a reverend?"

60. Joey, on Monica and Chandler's empty apartment: "Has it always been _____?"

61. Chandler: "That fake _____ woman's a real bitch, but she sure can dance."

62. How did Chandler dissuade Janice from buying the house next door?

63. Chandler to Monica, on which twin was which: "Jack's going to have a tough time in high school with that _____."

64. What was the name of the band Ross and Chandler played for in college?

65. What did Joey buy for Monica and Chandler as a housewarming gift?

66. To what was Phoebe referring when she told Monica, "The good news is, Gladys is yours"?

67. Why was Rachel's airplane to Paris evacuated?

68. Why did Monica say, "Nana liked it rough"?

69. Ross to Joey, regarding Rachel: "We haven't been a couple in, like, _____ years. My God, is that right? Has it been that long?"

70. To whom was Rachel referring when she said, "Ross, please don't be so scared of him"?

71. Where did Rachel get the cowboy outfit Emma wore in the baby beauty pageant?

72. To what was Joey referring when he said, "What is wrong with me? It looked more delicious when it was a penis"?

73. To what was Phoebe referring when she said, "Mike was planning on proposing to me that same way last night"?

74. What was the name of Monica and Chandler's twins' birth mother?

75. To what was Ross referring when he said, "Oh, my God, it's like *Sophie's Choice*"?

76. Chandler to Ross, who went to a spray-on tanning salon and didn't turn around: "Oh, my God, you can do a duet of _____ all by yourself."

77. What game show did Joey appear on?

78. Ross to Rachel, who lied about where she had been: "You won an adult Thanksgiving Day _____?"

79. To what did Mike threaten to change his name after Phoebe changed hers?

80. Rachel: "You can't go away this weekend. It's _____'s birthday."

81. Precious to Phoebe: "He proposed to you? This is the worst _____ ever!"

82. To whom was Phoebe referring when she asked Mike, "All right now, is this guy gay or straight because one of us is going to have to start flirting?"

83. Who was Precious?

84. Why was Rachel fired from Ralph Lauren?

85. Who helped Rachel get a job with Louis Vuitton?

86. Which one of the gang spent a summer during college trying to make it as a dancer?

87. In what year did Ross and Chandler graduate from college?

88. To what did Phoebe change her name once she was married?

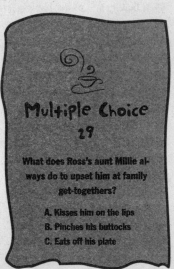

Multiple Choice 29

What does Ross's aunt Millie always do to upset him at family get-togethers?

A. Kisses him on the lips
B. Pinches his buttocks
C. Eats off his plate

89. What did Ross make for his first dinner party with Charlie and the newly coupled Joey and Rachel?

90. Who said, "Taking advantage? I am giving you the advantage. Enjoy!"?

91. Chandler to Monica: "See, here's the thing. The _____ were really a solution to your frizzy hair problem. And now that we're home, you don't have that problem anymore, so if you think about it, I hate them."

92. Who said, "It's enough that you're a doctor, but on top of it, you're married to a reverend"?

93. Rachel's sister Amy to Ross, whom she did not recognize: "Did I buy a _____ from you yesterday?"

94. To what was Rachel referring when she told Joey, "All right, fine. You can keep it . . . as long as you don't mind that she's haunted"?

95. Chandler: "I'm not having an affair. Nancy's our _____."

96. What was the name of Joey's Cabbage Patch Kid?

97. To whom was Ross referring when he asked Emma, "Did she give you a bottle of anti-depressants again to use as a rattle?"

98. Joey to Monica, after Rachel burst out in tears: "Why'd you have to say _____? Are you trying to push her buttons?"

99. Joey: "Joey doesn't share _____!"

100. What *For Dummies* book did one of Ross's coworkers give him as a joke?

101. Why did Joey say, "I want girls on bread"?

102. Ross: "Let's put _____ down Joey's pants and kick him!"

103. Chandler to Monica, regarding her decision to cook Thanksgiving dinner after all: "We are supposed to make these decisions together. Did you not watch the _____ I taped for you?"

104. What did Phoebe give Rachel as a going-away gift?

105. What was Chandler referring to when he told Joey, "I-I-I-I liked it. But my bosses didn't go for it. Stupid sons of bitches"?

106. Judy Geller to Monica: "I remember your first birthday. Ross was jealous of all the attention we were giving you. He pulled on his _____ so hard we had to take him to the emergency room."

107. What did Chandler find on the top shelf of the guest room closet?

The Part
WITH THE
Answers

Season One

1. Mr. Potato Head (Episode 1: "The Pilot")

2. Susan, after she referred to Ross and Carol's baby as hers. (Episode 2: "The One With the Sonogram at the End")

3. Her bank mistakenly credited her account and Phoebe couldn't in good conscience keep it. (Episode 3: "The One With the Thumb")

4. She's a trashy romance novelist. (Episode 11: "The One With Mrs. Bing")

5. nipples (Episode 13: "The One With the Boobies")

6. It was the pager number Ross used when Carol was pregnant. (Episode 22: "The One With the Ick Factor")

7. Weekly Estimated Net Use Statistics. (Episodes 16 and 17: "The One With Two Parts—Parts 1 and 2")

8. *Yertle the Turtle*. (Episode 9: "The One Where Underdog Gets Away")

9. An Oreo cookie. (Episode 1: "The Pilot")

10. He was explaining to the director of the Al Pacino movie why he was clenching his butt. (Joey was hired as a butt double.) (Episode 6: "The One With the Butt")

11. Monica and Rachel, after Rachel admitted she didn't have health insurance while at the emergency room. (Episodes 16 and 17: "The One With Two Parts—Parts 1 and 2")

12. Her sex dream. (Episode 22: "The One With the Ick Factor")

13. Marcel, his monkey. (Episode 10: "The One With the Monkey")

14. She found his lost cat during the blackout. (Episode 7: "The One With the Blackout")

15. Buying a new kitchen table together after the old one broke. (Episode 12: "The One With the Dozen Lasagnas")

16. To play poker. (Episode 18: "The One With All the Poker")

17. Barry. (Episode 20: "The One With the Evil Orthodontist")

18. The coma guy, who was hit by a car after Monica "woohooed" him. (Episode 11: "The One With Mrs. Bing")

19. The surveillance video of him and Jill Goodacre after being trapped in an ATM vestibule during a blackout. (Episode 7: "The One With the Blackout")

20. Mindy, her maid of honor. (Episode 2: "The One With the Sonogram at the End")

21. Ugly Naked Guy (Episode 2: "The One With the Sonogram at the End")

22. Nana's momentary rising from the dead. (Episode 8: "The One Where Nana Dies Twice")

23. Jan & Chan Forever. (Episode 14: "The One With the Candy Hearts")

24. shoe (Episode 19: "The One Where the Monkey Gets Away")

25. Ed Begley Jr. (Episode 24: "The One Where Rachel Finds Out")

26. job (Episode 18: "The One With All the Poker")

27. Nora Bing, Chandler's trashy romance novelist mother. (Episode 11: "The One With Mrs. Bing")

28. pizza (Episode 4: "The One With George Stephanopoulos")

29. Socks. (Episode 5: "The One With the East German Laundry Detergent")

30. crapweasle; crapweasle (Episode 7: "The One With the Blackout")

31. David the Scientist Guy. (Episode 10: "The One With the Monkey")

32. WENUS (Episode 15: "The One With the Stoned Guy")

33. A pink tutu. (Episode 19: "The One Where the Monkey Gets Away")

34. The woman who stole her credit card. (Episode 21: "The One With Fake Monica")

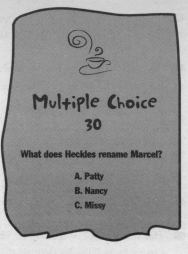

Multiple Choice 30

What does Heckles rename Marcel?

A. Patty
B. Nancy
C. Missy

35. Bicentennial (Episode 22: "The One With the Ick Factor")

36. Ben. (Episode 23: "The One With the Birth")

37. Barry. (Episode 20: "The One With the Evil Orthodontist")

38. Steve, the restaurant guy (Jon Lovitz) who went to Monica's to try her cooking. (Episode 15: "The One With the Stoned Guy")

39. Ross. (Episode 4: "The One With George Stephanopoulos")

40. Barry, after not seeing him since leaving him at the altar. (Episode 2: "The One With the Sonogram at the End")

41. Ross suggested that Monica wouldn't treat a new girlfriend the way she treats Marcel, his monkey. (Episode 10: "The One With the Monkey")

42. Ursula. (Episodes 16 and 17: "The One With Two Parts—Parts 1 and 2)

43. She had just been shot in the ass with a tranquilizer dart by Animal Control. (Episode 19: "The One Where the Monkey Gets Away")

44. His participation in a fertility study. (Episode 24: "The One Where Rachel Finds Out")

45. Kerplunk (Episode 13: "The One With the Boobies")

46. She was writing a trashy romance novel. (Episode 11: "The One With Mrs. Bing")

47. VD (Episode 9: "The One Where Underdog Gets Away")

48. The Laundromat with Rachel. (Episode 5: "The One With the East German Laundry Detergent")

49. He was an orthodontist. (Episode 2: "The One With the Sonogram at the End")

50. She was explaining why she decided not to marry Barry. (Episode 1: "The Pilot")

51. thumb (Episode 3: "The One With the Thumb")

52. George Stephanopoulos. (Episode 4: "The One With George Stephanopoulos")

53. perfection (Episode 7: "The One With the Blackout")

54. The gang's first Thanksgiving dinner together. (Episode 9: "The One Where Underdog Gets Away")

55. Ross's kissing Chandler's mom. (Episode 11: "The One With Mrs. Bing")

56. A sweater. (Episodes 16 and 17: "The One With Two Parts—Parts 1 and 2")

57. Farber. (Episode 20: "The One With the Evil Orthodontist")

58. Marcel, whom he was trying to place in a zoo. (Episode 21: "The One With Fake Monica")

59. His coworkers, who Phoebe found out, while temping at his office, didn't like Chandler after he was promoted. (Episode 22: "The One With the Ick Factor")

60. Monana (Episode 21: "The One With Fake Monica")

61. Marcel's eating the K, M, and O Scrabble tiles. (Episodes 16 and 17: "The One With Two Parts—Parts 1 and 2")

62. "Hello, Kettle? This is Monica. You're black." (Episode 18: "The One With All the Poker")

63. She was a waitress. (Episodes 16 and 17: "The One With Two Parts—Parts 1 and 2")

64. It turned out to be Janice. (Episode 14: "The One With the Candy Hearts")

65. The stoned restaurant guy (Jon Lovitz) who was at Monica's to try her cooking. (Episode 15: "The One With the Stoned Guy")

Bits of Trivia

"The Rachel," Jennifer Aniston's popular hairstyle, made its debut in "The One Where Nana Dies Twice."

66. She was a pet mortician. (Episode 13: "The One With the Boobies")

67. The bigger half. (Episode 9: "The One Where Underdog Gets Away")

68. Ross. (Episode 5: "The One With the East German Laundry Detergent")

69. The thumb she found inside her can of soda. (Episode 3: "The One With the Thumb")

70. Our Little Harmonica. (Episode 2: "The One With the Sonogram at the End")

71. Paul the Wine Guy. (Episode 1: "The Pilot")

72. The girls' pizza, which was mistakenly delivered to George Stephanopoulos and his girlfriend. (Episode 4: "The One With George Stephanopoulos")

73. His grandfather had just died. (Episode 10: "The One With the Monkey")

74. Carol, to Ross, when he tried to reassure her about the birthing process. (Episodes 16 and 17: "The One With Two Parts—Parts 1 and 2")

75. The woman who interviewed her at Saks Fifth Avenue. (Episode 18: "The One With All the Poker")

76. Barry, after she and Mindy (Barry's fiancée and Rachel's oldest friend) discovered that he was cheating on each of them with the other. (Episode 20: "The One With the Evil Orthodontist")

77. Monica, referring to the woman who stole her identity and credit card. (Episode 21: "The One With Fake Monica")

78. penis (Episode 19: "The One Where the Monkey Gets Away")

79. The stoned restaurant guy (Jon Lovitz), who was at Monica's to try her cooking. (Episode 15: "The One With the Stoned Guy")

80. David the Scientist Guy (Hank Azaria). (Episode 10: "The One With the Monkey")

81. Jill Goodacre. (Episode 7: "The One With the Blackout")

82. Al Pacino (Episode 6: "The One With the Butt")

83. Nana's closet. (Episode 8: "The One Where Nana Dies Twice")

84. Paolo. (Episode 12: "The One With the Dozen Lasagnas")

85. Ronnie, Joey's dad's mistress. (Episode 13: "The One With the Boobies")

86. He swallowed a Scrabble tile. (Episodes 16 and 17: "The One With Two Parts—Parts 1 and 2")

87. dart (Episode 19: "The One Where the Monkey Gets Away")

88. She went to the tap dancing class the woman paid for with Monica's credit card. (Episode 21: "The One With Fake Monica")

89. The one where Carol had the baby. Leah played another pregnant woman giving birth. (Episode 23: "The One With the Birth")

90. duck (Episode 24: "The One Where Rachel Finds Out")

91. Grilled cheese. (Episode 9: "The One Where Underdog Gets Away")

92. Gloria Tribbiani. (Episode 11: "The One With Mrs. Bing")

93. Mr. Heckles. (Episodes 16 and 17: "The One With Two Parts—Parts 1 and 2")

94. yellow pencils (Episode 8: "The One Where Nana Dies Twice")

95. The supposed brother and sister they went to dinner with who were actually boyfriend and girlfriend. (Episode 5: "The One With the East German Laundry Detergent")

96. He made a pass at Phoebe. (Episode 12: "The One With the Dozen Lasagnas")

97. George Clooney and Noah Wyle. (Episodes 16 and 17: "The One With Two Parts—Parts 1 and 2")

98. Chad (Episode 22: "The One With the Ick Factor")

99. Chandler saw Rachel's boobies first. (Episode 13: "The One With the Boobies")

100. kung pao chicken (Episode 11: "The One With Mrs. Bing")

Multiple Choice 31

What movie changed Fake Monica's life?

A. *Risky Business*
B. *Harry in Your Pocket*
C. *Dead Poets Society*

101. Talking to their baby while he was in utero. (Episode 9: "The One Where Underdog Gets Away")

102. Chandler, who wanted to know why people think he's gay. (Episode 8: "The One Where Nana Dies Twice")

103. She washed a red sock with all her whites the first time she did laundry. (Episode 5: "The One With the East German Laundry Detergent")

104. Ross, to the emergency room clerk after getting hit in the face with a hockey puck. (Episode 4: "The One With George Stephanopoulos")

105. Ross (Episode 18: "The One With All the Poker")

106. The animal control specialist who came to get Marcel after Rachel reported him missing. (She was also a high school student in Monica and Rachel's class.) (Episode 19: "The One Where the Monkey Gets Away")

107. Marcel was humping it. (Episode 21: "The One With Fake Monica")

108. An antique pin. (Episode 24: "The One Where Rachel Finds Out")

109. Telling Rachel that Paolo hit on Phoebe. (Episode 12: "The One With the Dozen Lasagnas")

110. Rachel, with whom Ross planned to do laundry. (Episode 5: "The One With the East German Laundry Detergent")

111. In Monica's lasagna. (Episode 2: "The One With the Sonogram at the End")

112. The last time he went for a girl. (Episode 1: "The Pilot")

113. hairline (Episode 2: "The One With the Sonogram at the End")

114. Because they were caught having sex while on the It's a Small World After All ride. (Episode 7: "The One With the Blackout")

115. The Giants lost. (Episode 8: "The One Where Nana Dies Twice")

116. Ugly Naked Gal (Episode 9: "The One Where Underdog Gets Away")

117. Ross was giving her a hard time for losing at poker. (Episode 18: "The One With All the Poker")

118. Phoebe, to Chandler, after she invited him to one of his work parties that she'd been invited to and he hadn't. (Episode 22: "The One With the Ick Factor")

119. To get a bone. (Episode 24: "The One Where Rachel Finds Out")

120. His mother kissing Ross. (Episode 11: "The One With Mrs. Bing")

121. Mr. Heckles. (Episode 7: "The One With the Blackout")

122. Estelle Leonard. (Episode 6: "The One With the Butt")

123. A wedding dress. (Episode 1: "The Pilot")

124. Bunch. (Episode 2: "The One With the Sonogram at the End")

125. Rachel, to the horrible woman at the Laundromat. (Episode 5: "The One With the East German Laundry Detergent")

126. He fell into an empty grave. (Episode 8: "The One Where Nana Dies Twice")

127. Fun Bobby, who wasn't so fun because his grandfather had just died. (Episode 10: "The One With the Monkey")

128. The sheet covering Paolo's "physical response" to her massage. (Episode 12: "The One With the Dozen Lasagnas")

129. Roger the Psychiatrist Guy. (Episode 13: "The One With the Boobies")

130. The Scrabble tiles Marcel ate. (Episodes 16 and 17: "The One With Two Parts—Parts 1 and 2")

131. Poker, which the girls lost to the guys. (Episode 18: "The One With All the Poker")

132. Because she was a bitch in high school to the Animal Control woman who came to take Marcel away. (Episode 19: "The One Where the Monkey Gets Away")

133. Rachel and Barry, after Rachel told Monica she had sex with him in his dental chair. (Episode 20: "The One With the Evil Orthodontist")

134. Rachel's having a sex dream about him. (Episode 22: "The One With the Ick Factor")

135. Ross, when she found out he was in love with her after he left for China. (Episode 24: "The One Where Rachel Finds Out")

136. Flame Boy. (Episode 21: "The One With Fake Monica")

Bits of Trivia

In "The One With Two Parts," Helen Hunt and Leila Kenzle cross over in their roles from *Mad About You*. Lisa Kudrow also plays the role of Phoebe's identical twin sister, *Mad About You*'s Ursula.

137. semen (Episode 14: "The One With the Candy Hearts")

138. Rachel's affair with Paolo. (Episode 12: "The One With the Dozen Lasagnas")

139. She announced it on *The Tonight Show with Jay Leno*. (Episode 11: "The One With Mrs. Bing")

140. "Got the keys?" (Episode 9: "The One Where Underdog Gets Away")

141. Chandler, who dated Aurora, the mysterious Italian woman with both a husband and a boyfriend. (Episode 6: "The One With the Butt")

142. The horrible lady at the Laundromat. (Episode 5: "The One With the East German Laundry Detergent")

143. A towel. (Episode 4: "The One With George Stephanopoulos")

144. Chandler. (Episode 3: "The One With the Thumb")

145. Five. (Episode 2: "The One With the Sonogram at the End")

146. Nora Tyler Bing. (Episode 11: "The One With Mrs. Bing")

147. Phoebe's new psychiatrist boyfriend, Roger. (Episode 13: "The One With the Boobies")

148. WENUS (Episodes 16 and 17: "The One With Two Parts—Parts 1 and 2")

149. poker game (Episode 18: "The One With All the Poker")

150. Phoebe, who was trying to protect Marcel from Animal Control. (Episode 19: "The One Where the Monkey Gets Away")

151. San Diego. (Episode 21: "The One With Fake Monica")

152. She just found out the guy she slept with was only seventeen. (Episode 22: "The One With the Ick Factor")

153. Having sex while participating in a fertility study. (Episode 24: "The One Where Rachel Finds Out")

154. "Oh. My. God." (Episode 14: "The One With the Candy Hearts")

155. Ronnie. (Episode 13: "The One With the Boobies")

156. Joey. (Episodes 16 and 17: "The One With Two Parts—Parts 1 and 2")

157. Ross walked in while she was on the phone with Animal Control after losing Marcel. (Episode 19: "The One Where the Monkey Gets Away")

158. Mindy, Barry's fiancée, who called after Rachel and Barry had just had sex. (Episode 20: "The One With the Evil Orthodontist")

159. Stalin (Episode 21: "The One With Fake Monica")

160. Ben, just minutes after he was born. (Episode 23: "The One With the Birth")

161. Ed Begley Jr. (Episode 24: "The One Where Rachel Finds Out")

162. Kip. (Episode 12: "The One With the Dozen Lasagnas")

163. Chandler, to a coworker who had thought he was gay. (Episode 8: "The One Where Nana Dies Twice")

164. ATM vestibule (Episode 7: "The One With the Blackout")

165. Phoebe, who broke up with Janice for him. (Episode 5: "The One With the East German Laundry Detergent")

166. It was the day that he and Carol first slept together. (Episode 4: "The One With George Stephanopoulos")

167. Carol, after she said she wanted to name their baby Minnie if it was a girl. (Episode 2: "The One With the Sonogram at the End")

168. Why she suddenly appeared at Central Perk wearing a wet wedding dress. (Episode 1: "The Pilot")

169. Joey, who was out with Ursula, Phoebe's twin sister, celebrating *her* birthday. (Episodes 16 and 17: "The One With Two Parts—Parts 1 and 2")

170. Poker. (Episode 18: "The One With All the Poker")

171. He was only seventeen. (Episode 22: "The One With the Ick Factor")

172. Ross, trying to figure out how to get Paolo out of the picture. (Episode 12: "The One With the Dozen Lasagnas")

173. Marcel. (Episode 10: "The One With the Monkey")

174. The Underdog balloon. (Episode 9: "The One Where Underdog Gets Away")

175. The woman who stole her credit card. (Episode 21: "The One With Fake Monica")

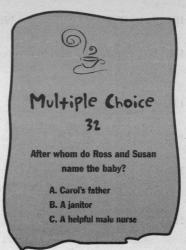

Multiple Choice
32

After whom do Ross and Susan name the baby?

A. Carol's father
B. A janitor
C. A helpful male nurse

176. Ross, Susan, and Phoebe. (Episode 23: "The One With the Birth")

177. If his coworkers thought that he was gay. (Episode 8: "The One Where Nana Dies Twice")

178. Someone's used gum. (Episode 7: "The One With the Blackout")

179. Karen. (Episode 4: "The One With George Stephanopoulos")

180. butt double (Episode 6: "The One With the Butt")

181. Paul the Wine Guy. (Episode 1: "The Pilot")

182. Carol, while she and Ross waited in her OB-GYN's office. (Episode 2: "The One With the Sonogram at the End")

Season Two

1. Her mother's turning off *Old Yeller* before Old Yeller died. (Episode 44: "The One Where Old Yeller Dies")

2. preapproved; preapproved (Episode 42: "The One Where Dr. Ramoray Dies")

3. tilt (Episode 39: "The One Where Ross and Rachel . . . You Know")

4. Julie (Episode 28: "The One With Phoebe's Husband")

5. Julie. (Episode 26: "The One With the Breast Milk")

6. list (Episode 32: "The One With the List")

7. Sandra Green. (Episode 35: "The One With the Lesbian Wedding")

8. fruit (Episode 43: "The One Where Eddie Won't Go")

9. mustache (Episode 44: "The One Where Old Yeller Dies")

10. boobs (Episode 45: "The One With the Bullies")

11. Having children with Monica. (Episode 48: "The One With Barry and Mindy's Wedding")

12. closure (Episode 31: "The One Where Ross Finds Out")

13. Duncan. (Episode 28: "The One With Phoebe's Husband")

14. He went to prison. (Episode 33: "The One With Phoebe's Dad")

15. Her mother, who was planning to leave her father. (Episode 35: "The One With the Lesbian Wedding")

16. Joey, who bought him an ugly gold bracelet. (Episode 38: "The One With the Prom Video")

17. the Rockettes (Episode 40: "The One Where Joey Moves Out")

18. A fish tank. (Episode 42: "The One Where Dr. Ramoray Dies")

19. The museum where Ross worked. (Episode 39: "The One Where Ross and Rachel . . . You Know")

20. "Looks Like We Made It." (Episodes 36 and 37: "The One After the Super Bowl—Parts 1 and 2")

21. Ignoring his feelings for Rachel. (Episode 31: "The One Where Ross Finds Out")

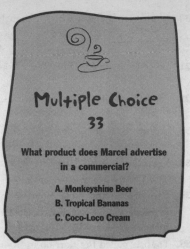

Multiple Choice
33

What product does Marcel advertise in a commercial?

A. Monkeyshine Beer
B. Tropical Bananas
C. Coco-Loco Cream

22. Ross's meeting Julie, an old college friend, as soon as he landed in China. (Episode 25: "The One With Ross's New Girlfriend")

23. breast (Episode 26: "The One With the Breast Milk")

24. Blowfish (Episode 29: "The One With Five Steaks and an Eggplant")

25. baby (Episode 30: "The One With the Baby on the Bus")

26. Fun Bobby. (Episode 34: "The One With Russ")

27. Mrs. Adelman, Phoebe's massage client who died on the table and then went on to inhabit Phoebe's body. (Episode 35: "The One With the Lesbian Wedding")

28. It had been humped by Marcel. (Episodes 36 and 37: "The One After the Super Bowl—Parts 1 and 2")

29. Twinkie (Episode 40: "The One Where Joey Moves Out")

30. Monica, to Richard, who she thought still needed to sow some wild oats. (Episode 42: "The One Where Dr. Ramoray Dies")

31. Bryce (Episode 43: "The One Where Eddie Won't Go")

32. dog (Episode 45: "The One With the Bullies")

33. Snake; Snake (Episode 27: "The One Where Heckles Dies")

34. Kiwi. (Episode 30: "The One With the Baby on the Bus")

35. She died on the table, then went on to inhabit Phoebe's body. (Episode 35: "The One With the Lesbian Wedding")

36. That he pulled her skirt up in front of the school during a school play. (Episodes 36 and 37: "The One After the Super Bowl—Parts 1 and 2")

37. Banging his broom on the ceiling. (Episode 27: "The One Where Heckles Dies")

38. The building super. (Episode 33: "The One With Phoebe's Dad")

39. A neurosurgeon. (Episode 34: "The One With Russ")

40. A lesbian wedding. (Episode 35: "The One With the Lesbian Wedding")

41. "So how many cameras are actually on you?" (Episode 38: "The One With the Prom Video")

42. grown-up (Episode 39: "The One Where Ross and Rachel . . . You Know")

43. Jack Geller to Judy, on why he wouldn't ever trade her in for a younger model. (Episode 40: "The One Where Joey Moves Out")

44. Laraine Newman. (Episode 45: "The One With the Bullies")

45. Ryan (Charlie Sheen), Phoebe's submarine guy, who was coming to see her while she had chicken pox. (Episode 47: "The One With the Chicken Pox")

46. Yasmine (Episode 41: "The One Where Eddie Moves In")

47. harsh (Episode 38: "The One With the Prom Video")

48. Her grandmother, who'd lied about her father. (Episode 33: "The One With Phoebe's Dad")

49. Bloomingdale's (Episode 26: "The One With the Breast Milk")

50. His tailor. (Episode 25: "The One With Ross's New Girlfriend")

51. He was an ice dancer. (Episode 28: "The One With Phoebe's Husband")

52. Fluffy Meowington. (Episode 31: "The One Where Ross Finds Out")

53. Her father, whom her mother and grandmother lied about to Phoebe all her life. (Episode 33: "The One With Phoebe's Dad")

54. everything (Episode 35: "The One With the Lesbian Wedding")

55. Marcel, who starred in a commercial for Monkey Shine Beer. (Episodes 36 and 37: "The One After the Super Bowl—Parts 1 and 2")

56. sister's (Episode 39: "The One Where Ross and Rachel . . . You Know")

57. Visa bill (Episode 43: "The One Where Eddie Won't Go")

58. They all bonded over beating up the guys who tried to steal their watches while they were about to fight each other. (Episode 45: "The One With the Bullies")

59. Albert Einstein's. Her grandmother told her he was her grandfather. (Episode 33: "The One With Phoebe's Dad")

60. The Moondance Diner. (Episode 46: "The One With Two Parties")

61. His kissing. (Episode 48: "The One With Barry and Mindy's Wedding")

62. Old Yeller. (Episode 44: "The One Where Old Yeller Dies")

Bits of Trivia

Gunther speaks his first line during Episode 33: "The One With Phoebe's Dad." His line: "Yeah."

63. The phone in the bathroom of his new apartment. (Episode 41: "The One Where Eddie Moves In")

64. The cat they planned to adopt together. (Episode 31: "The One Where Ross Finds Out")

65. evolution (Episode 27: "The One Where Heckles Dies")

66. Julie. (Episode 26: "The One With the Breast Milk")

67. There was a drunk, naked woman leaving a message for "Bob" on the answering machine. (Episode 29: "The One With Five Steaks and an Eggplant")

68. saline solution (Episode 32: "The One With the List")

69. obsessive (Episode 33: "The One With Phoebe's Dad")

70. Erica, his psychotic stalker, who thought he really was Dr. Drake Ramoray from *Days of Our Lives*. (Episodes 36 and 37: "The One After the Super Bowl—Parts 1 and 2")

71. Jack and Judy having sex. (Episode 38: "The One With the Prom Video")

72. lesbian (Episode 35: "The One With the Lesbian Wedding")

73. Eddie. (Episode 42: "The One Where Dr. Ramoray Dies")

74. Chicken pox. (Episode 47: "The One With the Chicken Pox")

75. nauseous (Episode 48: "The One With Barry and Mindy's Wedding")

76. Irish (Episode 34: "The One With Russ")

77. Mockolate. (Episode 32: "The One With the List")

78. Chandler's third nipple. (Episode 28: "The One With Phoebe's Husband")

79. Rachel, to Ross, after reading a new book called *Be Your Own Windkeeper*. (Episode 43: "The One Where Eddie Won't Go")

80. How he handled his parents' divorce. (Episode 46: "The One With Two Parties")

81. bracelet (Episode 38: "The One With the Prom Video")

82. Rachem (Episode 32: "The One With the List")

83. His part in the porno the gang was watching. (Episode 28: "The One With Phoebe's Husband")

84. The Hombré Man, Joey's rival in the Fragrance Department at work. (Episode 26: "The One With the Breast Milk")

85. Getting a tattoo. (Episode 40: "The One Where Joey Moves Out")

86. Scarsdale (Episode 44: "The One Where Old Yeller Dies")

87. Joey decided his character, Joseph the Processing Guy, and his wife just had another baby. (Episode 47: "The One With the Chicken Pox")

88. drink (Episode 39: "The One Where Ross and Rachel ... You Know")

89. Monica, who appointed herself Chandler's personal trainer after everyone thought he'd put on a little weight. (Episode 31: "The One Where Ross Finds Out")

90. Mr. Heckles, whose life was strikingly similar to Chandler's. (Episode 27: "The One Where Heckles Dies")

91. Rachel, when Ross wouldn't. (Episode 25: "The One With Ross's New Girlfriend")

92. Ben, who had to be retrieved from Human Services after Joey and Chandler left him on a bus. (Episode 30: "The One With the Baby on the Bus")

93. Telling Phoebe that her father was the guy who poses for all those picture-frame filler photos. (Episode 33: "The One With Phoebe's Dad")

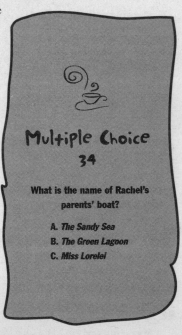

Multiple Choice 34

What is the name of Rachel's parents' boat?

A. *The Sandy Sea*

B. *The Green Lagoon*

C. *Miss Lorelei*

94. Monica, who had an obvious crush on Richard Burke while catering his party. (Episode 39: "The One Where Ross and Rachel . . . You Know")

95. Having sex with Richard, after Rachel got the last condom. (Episode 42: "The One Where Dr. Ramoray Dies")

96. Jill. (Episode 46: "The One With Two Parties")

97. A little airplane bottle of liquor. (Episode 34: "The One With Russ")

98. The fact that she, Rachel, and Joey can't afford to go out to nice places like the others can. (Episode 29: "The One With Five Steaks and an Eggplant")

99. Adam's apple (Episode 27: "The One Where Heckles Dies")

100. His new fruit dehydrator. (Episode 43: "The One Where Eddie Won't Go")

101. Joey, referring to his two fake daughters. (Episode 47: "The One With the Chicken Pox")

102. Dudley Moore's hair. (Episode 25: "The One With Ross's New Girlfriend")

103. Being straight. (Episode 28: "The One With Phoebe's Husband")

104. Giovanni Ribisi, who later played Phoebe's brother. (Episode 30: "The One With the Baby on the Bus")

105. Italian; Italian (Episode 31: "The One Where Ross Finds Out")

106. Russ, Rachel's date, who looked and acted just like Ross. (Episode 34: "The One With Russ")

107. Jean-Claude (Episodes 36 and 37: "The One After the Super Bowl—Parts 1 and 2")

108. The ugly gold bracelet Joey bought for him. (Episode 38: "The One With the Prom Video")

109. The ugly white ceramic dog. (Episode 43: "The One Where Eddie Won't Go")

110. glasses (Episode 46: "The One With Two Parties")

111. Because he grew up in California, and if he slept on the east side of the bed, the ocean would have been on the wrong side. (Episode 47: "The One With the Chicken Pox")

112. Her audience at the Children's Library, where she was asked to play children's songs. (Episodes 36 and 37: "The One After the Super Bowl—Parts 1 and 2")

113. The endings of all the movies her mother never let her see the endings to. (Episode 44: "The One Where Old Yeller Dies")

114. syphilis (Episode 48: "The One With Barry and Mindy's Wedding")

115. Monica, referring to the hickey on her neck. (Episode 29: "The One With Five Steaks and an Eggplant")

116. Q-tip (Episode 25: "The One With Ross's New Girlfriend")

117. Opposable thumbs, which Ross tried to convince Phoebe wouldn't exist without evolution. (Episode 27: "The One Where Heckles Dies")

118. A mannequin head he stole from the Junior Miss Department at Macy's. (Episode 43: "The One Where Eddie Won't Go")

119. How Joey's tailor measures pants. (Episode 25: "The One With Ross's New Girlfriend")

120. 'Smelly Cat' (Episode 30: "The One With the Baby on the Bus")

121. Mockolate (Episode 32: "The One With the List")

122. lobster (Episode 38: "The One With the Prom Video")

123. Her "Smelly Cat" music video, in which they used another voice. (Episode 41: "The One Where Eddie Moves In")

124. She was playing Monopoly with the chicken pox. (Episode 47: "The One With the Chicken Pox")

125. That her husband was sleeping with his secretary. (Episode 48: "The One With Barry and Mindy's Wedding")

126. Mr. Treeger. (Episode 33: "The One With Phoebe's Dad")

127. The stranger at the next table in a restaurant who was talking on his cell phone when a drunk Rachel asked to borrow it. (Episode 31: "The One Where Ross Finds Out")

128. His third nipple. (Episode 28: "The One With Phoebe's Husband")

129. Kotter (Episode 38: "The One With the Prom Video")

130. How many guys she'd slept with. (Episode 42: "The One Where Dr. Ramoray Dies")

131. Jean-Claude Van Damme. (Episodes 36 and 37: "The One After the Super Bowl—Parts 1 and 2")

132. Rachel, to Ross, who wouldn't put his hands on her butt after she laughed when he did it the first time. (Episode 39: "The One Where Ross and Rachel . . . You Know")

133. killed herself (Episode 44: "The One Where Old Yeller Dies")

134. stilts (Episode 45: "The One With the Bullies")

135. libraries (Episodes 36 and 37: "The One After the Super Bowl—Parts 1 and 2")

136. A real reason to break up with a girl. (Episode 27: "The One Where Heckles Dies")

137. She didn't want Rachel to know she was talking to Julie on the phone. (Episode 26: "The One With the Breast Milk")

Bits of Trivia

Giovanni Ribisi plays the guy who mistakenly tosses a condom in Phoebe's guitar case in "The One With the Baby on the Bus," then later comes back as her brother, Frank Jr.

138. tailor (Episode 25: "The One With Ross's New Girlfriend")

139. Stephanie (Chrissie Hynde), the woman Terry hired to play guitar at Central Perk. (Episode 30: "The One With the Baby on the Bus")

140. ankles (Episode 32: "The One With the List")

141. Fun Bobby, who was no longer fun after getting sober. (Episode 34: "The One With Russ")

142. Rachel's mother, referring to Ugly Naked Guy. (Episode 35: "The One With the Lesbian Wedding")

143. The ugly gold bracelet Joey bought for him. (Episode 38: "The One With the Prom Video")

144. Richard Burke, who wanted to stay in the kitchen with Monica instead of being with his party guests. (Episode 39: "The One Where Ross and Rachel . . . You Know")

145. Eddie, Chandler's new roommate, who had just fixed Chandler breakfast. (Episode 41: "The One Where Eddie Moves In")

146. He told *Soap Opera Digest* that he wrote most of his own lines. (Episode 42: "The One Where Dr. Ramoray Dies")

147. A weird obsessive thing like the many Monica has. (Episode 47: "The One With the Chicken Pox")

148. kiss (Episode 48: "The One With Barry and Mindy's Wedding")

149. Julie, as Rachel told the punch line of Julie's story before Julie had a chance to even tell it. (Episode 25: "The One With Ross's New Girlfriend")

150. Shopping with Julie, Ross's girlfriend. (Episode 26: "The One With the Breast Milk")

151. clowns (Episode 30: "The One With the Baby on the Bus")

152. "She's not Rachel." (Episode 32: "The One With the List")

153. Russ, Rachel's date, who looked and acted just like Ross. (Episode 34: "The One With Russ")

154. Phoebe, whose body was inhabited by an old lady who died on her massage table. (Episode 35: "The One With the Lesbian Wedding")

155. mealworms (Episodes 36 and 37: "The One After the Super Bowl—Parts 1 and 2")

156. Laughing at the thought of his hands being on her butt while they kissed on their first date. (Episode 39: "The One Where Ross and Rachel . . . You Know")

157. Lucite (Episode 43: "The One Where Eddie Won't Go")

158. Karen, the wife of Joseph the Processing Guy, Joey's character. (Episode 47: "The One With the Chicken Pox")

159. "Copacabana." (Episode 48: "The One With Barry and Mindy's Wedding")

160. Her backup singers as she was recording "Smelly Cat." (Episode 41: "The One Where Eddie Moves In")

161. Fun Bobby (Episode 34: "The One With Russ")

162. radiator (Episode 33: "The One With Phoebe's Dad")

163. Mr. Heckles's apartment and all his junk, which he left to Monica and Rachel in his will. (Episode 27: "The One Where Heckles Dies")

164. The guy who fixed the office copier. (Episode 28: "The One With Phoebe's Husband")

165. breast milk (Episode 26: "The One With the Breast Milk")

166. hang up (Episode 25: "The One With Ross's New Girlfriend")

Multiple Choice 35

From which Canadian province does Phoebe's husband hail?

A. Saskatchewan
B. Nova Scotia
C. New Brunswick

---

167. The swelling had gone down in his mouth after an allergic reaction to eating kiwi. (Episode 30: "The One With the Baby on the Bus")

168. Ross, to Rachel, who'd left him a drunken message on his answering machine saying she was over him. (Episode 31: "The One Where Ross Finds Out")

169. "Smell-the-fart" acting. (Episode 35: "The One With the Lesbian Wedding")

170. eyelashes (Episodes 36 and 37: "The One After the Super Bowl—Parts 1 and 2")

171. pool (Episode 39: "The One Where Ross and Rachel . . . You Know")

172. tattoo (Episode 40: "The One Where Joey Moves Out")

173. 'Nam (Episode 42: "The One Where Dr. Ramoray Dies")

174. snuff (Episode 44: "The One Where Old Yeller Dies")

175. Bubble Yum (Episode 48: "The One With Barry and Mindy's Wedding")

176. bitches (Episodes 36 and 37: "The One After the Super Bowl—Parts 1 and 2")

177. Fun Bobby (Episode 34: "The One With Russ")

178. Having sex with Julie. (Episode 28: "The One With Phoebe's Husband")

179. Carol's breast milk. (Episode 26: "The One With the Breast Milk")

180. Drew Barrymore (Episodes 36 and 37: "The One After the Super Bowl—Parts 1 and 2")

181. The prom video in which he got all dressed up to take Rachel to the prom after her date didn't show up. (Episode 38: "The One With the Prom Video")

182. Michelle. (Episode 39: "The One Where Ross and Rachel . . . You Know")

183. Her bra. (Episode 40: "The One Where Joey Moves Out")

184. toilet paper (Episode 43: "The One Where Eddie Won't Go")

185. hat (Episode 45: "The One With the Bullies")

186. flan (Episode 46: "The One With Two Parties")

187. pox (Episode 47: "The One With the Chicken Pox")

188. kittens (Episode 40: "The One Where Joey Moves Out")

Season Three

1. The dead Christmas trees at the lot where Joey worked. (Episode 58: "The One Where Rachel Quits")

2. Carol, in a flashback. (Episode 54: "The One With the Flashback")

3. Hoyt (Episode 51: "The One With the Jam")

4. Tony Danza (Episode 49: "The One With the Princess Leia Fantasy")

5. His sperm bank résumé. (Episode 51: "The One With the Jam")

6. Isabella Rossellini. (Episode 53: "The One With Frank Jr.")

7. Her boss, Mr. Kaplan, at Fortunata Fashions. (Episode 59: "The One Where Chandler Can't Remember Which Sister")

8. Gunther. (Episode 64: "The One With the Morning After")

9. Sophie. (Episode 68: "The One With the Dollhouse")

10. Chuck Mangione (Episode 73: "The One at the Beach")

11. picnic basket (Episode 63: "The One Where Ross and Rachel Take a Break")

12. Ugly Naked Guy, who they all thought was dead until they poked him. (Episode 56: "The One With the Giant Poking Device")

13. The Milkmaster 2000. (Episode 52: "The One With the Metaphorical Tunnel")

14. commando (Episode 50: "The One Where No One's Ready")

15. Monica's bathroom floor, after he pried a piece off to show her how easy it would be to replace. (Episode 53: "The One With Frank Jr.")

16. sister (Episode 59: "The One Where Chandler Can't Remember Which Sister")

17. A threesome between Joey, Chandler, and Chloe, the hot girl from the copy shop. (Episode 63: "The One Where Ross and Rachel Take a Break")

18. The little Brown Bird who was selling cookies door-to-door when Ross broke her leg. (Episode 58: "The One Where Rachel Quits")

19. The pen he got at a bachelor party. (Episode 60: "The One With All the Jealousy")

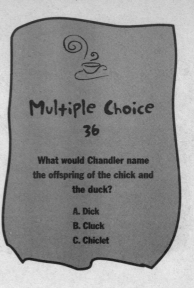

Multiple Choice 36

What would Chandler name the offspring of the chick and the duck?

A. Dick
B. Cluck
C. Chiclet

20. Write jingles. (Episode 62: "The One With Phoebe's Ex-Partner")

21. Phoebe's underwire from her bra. (Episode 65: "The One Without the Ski Trip")

22. Chandler, whom her boss had the hots for. (Episode 68: "The One With the Dollhouse")

23. Pete to Monica, who wanted to keep seeing her even after she told him she wasn't interested. (Episode 69: "The One With a Chick and a Duck")

24. boss (Episode 72: "The One With the Ultimate Fighting Champion")

25. balded (Episode 73: "The One at the Beach")

26. Ross, referring to the T-shirt he took back from Rachel after they broke up. (Episode 67: "The One With the Tiny T-shirt")

27. Jasmine, who worked with Phoebe. (Episode 64: "The One With the Morning After")

28. barge (Episode 62: "The One With Phoebe's Ex-Partner")

29. Joey's sisters, one of whom he kissed the night before. (Episode 59: "The One Where Chandler Can't Remember Which Sister")

30. uglies (Episode 54: "The One With the Flashback")

31. boob (Episode 52: "The One With the Metaphorical Tunnel")

32. Drinking Monica's glass of fat. (Episode 50: "The One Where No One's Ready")

33. Janice. (Episode 49: "The One With the Princess Leia Fantasy")

34. Barbie; Barbie (Episode 52: "The One With the Metaphorical Tunnel")

35. The list of five celebrities he's allowed to sleep with and Rachel can't get mad. (Episode 53: "The One With Frank Jr.")

36. They planned to make a long poking device so they could poke Ugly Naked Guy, who appeared to be dead. (Episode 56: "The One With the Giant Poking Device")

37. ZOOM (Episode 60: "The One With All the Jealousy")

38. *The Shining*. (Episode 61: "The One Where Monica and Richard Are Just Friends")

39. His nubbinectomy. (Episode 62: "The One With Phoebe's Ex-Partner")

40. Waxine leg wax. (Episode 64: "The One With the Morning After")

41. 'Wipeout' (Episode 66: "The One With the Hypnosis Tape")

42. It burned down. (Episode 68: "The One With the Dollhouse")

43. Phoebe's being on hold. (Episode 70: "The One With the Screamer")

44. That he wanted to be the Ultimate Fighting Champion. (Episode 72: "The One With the Ultimate Fighting Champion")

45. The beach house in Montauk, where they played the strip *Happy Days* game. (Episode 73: "The One at the Beach")

46. A marshmallow. (Episode 57: "The One With the Football")

47. The Mattress King. (Episode 55: "The One With the Race Car Bed")

48. To get over Richard. (Episode 51: "The One With the Jam")

49. Count (Episode 49: "The One With the Princess Leia Fantasy")

50. Joey's wearing all of Chandler's clothes. (Episode 50: "The One Where No One's Ready")

51. bang (Episode 56: "The One With the Giant Poking Device")

52. The Brown Bird cookies Ross was selling but withholding from Monica after she cleaned him out of Mint Treasures. (Episode 58: "The One Where Rachel Quits")

53. "The Empty Vase." (Episode 60: "The One With All the Jealousy")

54. Being friends who sleep together. (Episode 61: "The One Where Monica and Richard Are Just Friends")

55. Sleeping with Chloe, the girl from the copy store, after Rachel asked how it was. (Episode 64: "The One With the Morning After")

56. Pete Becker, the millionaire who was interested in Monica. (Episode 66: "The One With the Hypnosis Tape")

57. chick (Episode 69: "The One With a Chick and a Duck")

58. Pete, Monica's millionaire boyfriend. (Episode 71: "The One With Ross's Thing")

59. Chandler, to his boss, who kept slapping his butt. (Episode 72: "The One With the Ultimate Fighting Champion")

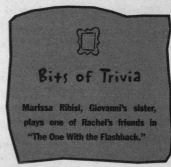

Bits of Trivia

Marissa Ribisi, Giovanni's sister, plays one of Rachel's friends in "The One With the Flashback."

60. Phoebe Abbott, the woman she thought had been her mother's best friend but who turned out to be her biological mother. (Episode 73: "The One at the Beach")

61. Rachel, in a flashback. (Episode 54: "The One With the Flashback")

62. jam (Episode 51: "The One With the Jam")

63. His mother's face pops into his head. (Episode 49: "The One With the Princess Leia Fantasy")

64. Leslie, her ex–singing partner. (Episode 62: "The One With Phoebe's Ex-Partner")

65. dollhouse (Episode 68: "The One With the Dollhouse")

66. panties (Episode 61: "The One Where Monica and Richard Are Just Friends")

67. Mark, the guy she met while having lunch at the diner where Monica worked. (Episode 59: "The One Where Chandler Can't Remember Which Sister")

68. laminated (Episode 53: "The One With Frank Jr.")

69. restraining order (Episode 51: "The One With the Jam")

70. Monicuddle (Episode 49: "The One With the Princess Leia Fantasy")

71. Rachel's dad, after Ross left an extra twenty for the waiter. (Episode 55: "The One With the Race Car Bed")

72. The poking device they used to poke Ugly Naked Guy. (Episode 56: "The One With the Giant Poking Device")

73. The Geller Cup. (Episode 57. "The One With the Football")

74. *Little Women*, because it was getting too sad. (Episode 61: "The One Where Monica and Richard Are Just Friends")

75. He began to act like a woman. (Episode 66: "The One With the Hypnosis Tape")

76. VCR (Episode 69: "The One With a Chick and a Duck")

77. Rachel's date, who had anger issues. (Episode 70: "The One With the Screamer")

78. third nipple (Episode 71: "The One With Ross's Thing")

79. boob (Episode 72: "The One With the Ultimate Fighting Champion")

80. bald (Episode 73: "The One at the Beach")

81. restaurant (Episode 69: "The One With a Chick and a Duck")

82. skier (Episode 65: "The One Without the Ski Trip")

83. Telling Rachel that Ross had slept with Chloe, the girl from the copy store. (Episode 64: "The One With the Morning After")

84. Mr. Heckles. (Episode 54: "The One With the Flashback")

85. Copperfield (Episode 53: "The One With Frank Jr.")

86. jam (Episode 51: "The One With the Jam")

87. hummus. (Episode 50: "The One Where No One's Ready")

88. Janice and her ex-husband. (Episode 55: "The One With the Race Car Bed")

89. Ross, who had to sell cookies door-to-door for the little girl whose leg he broke. (Episode 58: "The One Where Rachel Quits")

90. Rachel, to Ross, who she felt was trying to mark his territory after she started working with Mark at Bloomingdale's. (Episode 60: "The One With All the Jealousy")

91. Richard. (Episode 61: "The One Where Monica and Richard Are Friends")

92. Pete, the millionaire guy, to Monica, who just told him she wasn't attracted to him. (Episode 67: "The One With the Tiny T-shirt")

93. Picturing her naked. (Episode 69: "The One With a Chick and a Duck")

94. Phoebe, who'd been on hold for two days on what she thought was a toll-free number. (Episode 70: "The One With the Screamer")

95. Ultimate Fighting Champion (Episode 71: "The One With Ross's Thing")

96. How many times his boss slapped him on the ass. (Episode 72: "The One With the Ultimate Fighting Champion")

97. His mother, after Chandler told him that sometimes his own mother pops into his head while having sex. (Episode 49: "The One With the Princess Leia Fantasy")

98. Ben's Barbie doll. (Episode 52: "The One With the Metaphorical Tunnel")

99. Frank Jr. (Episode 53: "The One With Frank Jr.")

100. Ugly Naked Guy, who hadn't moved all day. (Episode 56: "The One With the Giant Poking Device")

101. Selling Brown Bird cookies for the little girl whose leg he broke. (Episode 58: "The One Where Rachel Quits")

102. Mary Angela. (Episode 59: "The One Where Chandler Can't Remember Which Sister")

103. Gunther, to Phoebe's boyfriend, Robert, who wore baggy shorts without underwear. (Episode 61: "The One Where Monica and Richard Are Just Friends")

104. tampons (Episode 65: "The One Without the Ski Trip")

105. Alice. (Episode 66: "The One With the Hypnosis Tape")

106. aroma (Episode 68: "The One With the Dollhouse")

107. Phoebe. A fireman named Vince and a kindergarten teacher named Jason. (Episode 71: "The One With Ross's Thing")

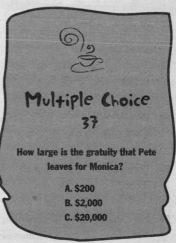

Multiple Choice
37

How large is the gratuity that Pete leaves for Monica?

A. $200

B. $2,000

C. $20,000

☆ More Star Sightings ☆

+ Michael McKean (Mr. Rastatter) "The One With the List"

+ Audra Lindley (Phoebe's grandma) "The One With Phoebe's Dad"

+ Marlo Thomas (Sandra Green) "The One With the Lesbian Wedding"

+ Candice Gingrich (the minister) "The One With the Lesbian Wedding"

+ Phil Leeds (Mr. Adelman) "The One With the Lesbian Wedding"

+ Brooke Shields (Erika Ford) "The One After the Super Bowl—Part 1"

+ Chris Isaak (Rob Donnen) "The One After the Super Bowl—Part 1"

+ Julia Roberts (Susie Moss) "The One After the Super Bowl—Part 2"

+ Jean-Claude Van Damme (himself) "The One After the Superbowl—Part 2"

+ Tom Selleck (Richard Burke) "The One Where Ross and Rachel . . . You Know"

- Adam Goldberg (Eddie) "The One Where Eddie Moves In"

- Giovanni Ribisi (Frank Jr.) "The One With the Bullies"

- Laraine Newman (Mrs. Buffay) "The One With the Bullies"

- Peter DeLuise (bully) "The One With the Bullies"

- Ron Leibman (Dr. Leonard Green) "The One With Two Parties"

- Charlie Sheen (Ryan) "The One With the Chicken Pox"

- David Arquette (Malcolm) "The One With the Jam"

- Isabella Rossellini (herself) "The One With Frank Jr."

- Alex Meneses (Cookie) "The One Where Chandler Can't Remember Which Sister"

- Sherilyn Fenn (Ginger) "The One With Phoebe's Ex-Partner"

- Jon Favreau (Pete) "The One With the Hypnosis Tape"

- Debra Jo Rupp (Alice) "The One With the Hypnosis Tape"

- Ben Stiller (Tommy) "The One With the Screamer"

- Billy Crystal [uncredited] (Tim) "The One With the Ultimate Fighting Champion"

108. Pete, the millionaire guy, who wanted to become the Ultimate Fighting Champion. (Episode 72: "The One With the Ultimate Fighting Champion")

109. Her friend's beach house floor covered in sand. (Episode 73: "The One at the Beach")

110. Ross's sleeping with Chloe, the girl from the copy store. (Episode 64: "The One With the Morning After")

111. globe (Episode 63: "The One Where Ross and Rachel Take a Break")

112. The Geller Cup. (Episode 57: "The One With the Football")

113. spill (Episode 54: "The One With the Flashback")

114. Susan Sarandon. (Episode 53: "The One With Frank Jr.")

115. Ugly Naked Guy. (Episode 56: "The One With the Giant Poking Device")

116. Monica's claim that she and Richard were just two friends having an innocent burger. (Episode 61: "The One Where Monica and Richard Are Just Friends")

117. leg (Episode 62: "The One With Phoebe's Ex-Partner")

118. To Italy for pizza. (Episode 66: "The One With the Hypnosis Tape")

119. Pete, who pretended to have met someone else so Monica would agree to work for him at his new restaurant. (Episode 69: "The One With a Chick and a Duck")

Bits of Trivia

Matthew Perry's dad, John Bennett Perry, plays Joshua's dad in "The One With Rachel's New Dress."

120. bald (Episode 72: "The One With the Ultimate Fighting Champion")

121. Joey, who woke up at the beach house covered in sand, shaped like a mermaid. (Episode 73: "The One at the Beach")

122. car (Episode 55: "The One With the Race Car Bed")

123. Malcolm, Ursula's stalker, whom *she* was now dating. (Episode 51: "The One With the Jam")

124. get dressed (Episode 50: "The One Where No One's Ready")

125. five (Episode 49: "The One With the Princess Leia Fantasy")

126. Isabella Rossellini, whom Ross took off his list of five celebrities he was allowed to sleep with. (Episode 53: "The One With Frank Jr.")

127. Phoebe was trying to get customers to buy the dead Christmas trees instead of the fresh ones. (Episode 58: "The One Where Rachel Quits")

128. Mark, the guy Rachel met who worked at Bloomingdale's and offered to help her get an interview. (Episode 59: "The One Where Chandler Can't Remember Which Sister")

129. Robert, her new boyfriend, who apparently didn't wear any underwear under his baggy shorts. (Episode 61: "The One Where Monica and Richard Are Just Friends")

130. leg (Episode 62: "The One With Phoebe's Ex-Partner")

131. He was in her home economics class. (Episode 66: "The One With the Hypnosis Tape")

132. Rachel's boss. (Episode 68: "The One With the Dollhouse")

133. Pete the millionaire guy's quest to become the Ultimate Fighting Champion. (Episode 72: "The One With the Ultimate Fighting Champion")

134. Bonnie, his new girlfriend, who had just shaved her head. (Episode 73: "The One at the Beach")

135. FRANKIE SAY RELAX (Episode 67: "The One With the Tiny T-shirt")

136. It was for women. (Episode 66: "The One With the Hypnosis Tape")

137. Chloe. (Episode 63: "The One Where Ross and Rachel Take a Break")

138. Leslie, her ex–singing partner. (Episode 62: "The One With Phoebe's Ex-Partner")

139. Julio, the busboy at the Moondance Diner, where Monica worked. (Episode 60: "The One With All the Jealousy")

140. compulsive (Episode 57: "The One With the Football")

141. hammock (Episode 56: "The One With the Giant Poking Device")

142. The sperm donor Monica almost used. (Episode 51: "The One With the Jam")

143. correspondence (Episode 50: "The One Where No One's Ready")

144. Richard, after the two broke up. (Episode 49: "The One With the Princess Leia Fantasy")

145. Fortunata Fashions. (Episode 58: "The One Where Rachel Quits")

146. *Little Women* (Episode 61: "The One Where Monica and Richard Are Just Friends")

147. His having sex with another woman while they were on a break. (Episode 64: "The One With the Morning After")

148. Pete, the millionaire guy. (Episode 67: "The One With the Tiny T-shirt")

149. Ben Stiller. (Episode 70: "The One With the Screamer")

150. millionaire (Episode 71: "The One With Ross's Thing")

151. Frank Jr. marrying Alice. (Episode 66: "The One With the Hypnosis Tape")

152. barbershop quartet (Episode 60: "The One With All the Jealousy")

Multiple Choice 38

What is Joey and Chandler's apartment number?

A. 18
B. 19
C. 20

153. boxer (Episode 55: "The One With the Race Car Bed")

154. His Princess Leia fantasy, which Rachel told Phoebe about. (Episode 49: "The One With the Princess Leia Fantasy")

155. Richard's daughter, whom Monica mistook as a new girlfriend after she checked his messages on his answering machine. (Episode 50: "The One Where No One's Ready")

156. Mix-up (Episode 62: "The One With Phoebe's Ex-Partner")

157. Pete, Monica's millionaire boyfriend. (Episode 67: "The One With the Tiny T-shirt")

158. Staying up and just talking all night with someone you really care about. (Episode 70: "The One With the Screamer")

159. The "thing" Ross discovered on his butt, but couldn't see, while in the shower. (Episode 71: "The One With Ross's Thing")

160. mattresses (Episode 55: "The One With the Race Car Bed")

161. The Geller Cup. (Episode 57: "The One With the Football")

162. translator (Episode 63: "The One Where Ross and Rachel Take a Break")

163. peanuts (Episode 69: "The One With a Chick and a Duck")

164. The fact that every time she goes to the dentist, someone she knows dies. (Episode 56: "The One With the Giant Poking Device")

165. The casual message she left for Richard after they'd broken up. (Episode 50: "The One Where No One's Ready")

166. wire (Episode 65: "The One Without the Ski Trip")

167. Monica's new dollhouse. (Episode 68: "The One With the Dollhouse")

168. Mr. Kaplan. (Episode 59: "The One Where Chandler Can't Remember Which Sister")

Season Four

1. She got stung by a jellyfish. "Don't blame me," Joey said. "I saw it on the Discovery Channel." (Episode 74: "The One With the Jellyfish")

2. A cherry stem. (Episode 89: "The One With the Fake Party")

3. Ross, justifying why he doesn't act like a twenty-one-year-old anymore. (Episode 82: "The One Where They Are Going to Party!")

4. Transpondster. (Episode 85: "The One With the Embryos")

5. white trash (Episode 76: "The One With the Cuffs")

6. Allesandro's. (Episode 82: "The One Where They Are Going to Party!")

7. "Morning's Here." (Episode 92: "The One With All the Haste")

8. Ross's musical style on the keyboard, which he developed in college. (Episode 80: "The One Where Chandler Crosses the Line")

9. Kathy. (Episode 78: "The One With Joey's New Girlfriend")

10. She and Monica would kiss for one minute. "If you had just done that right after the last contest, no one would have had to move at all," Phoebe had told them. (Episode 92: "The One With All the Haste")

11. Dr. Timothy Burke, Richard's son. (Episode 81: "The One With Chandler in a Box")

12. Joey, who was looking at someone else's calendar. (Episode 93: "The One With All the Wedding Dresses")

13. Bonnie, Ross's bald girlfriend. (Episode 74: "The One With the Jellyfish")

14. She was a slob. (Episode 79: "The One With the Dirty Girl")

15. An early edition of *The Velveteen Rabbit*. (Episode 79: "The One With the Dirty Girl")

16. A pen that's also a clock. (Episode 79: "The One With the Dirty Girl")

17. Monica, to Rachel, who had asked her which lingerie she should wear on her first time with Joshua. (Episode 91: "The One With Rachel's New Dress")

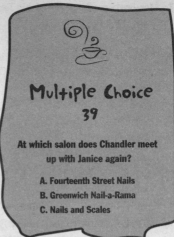

18. Emily, after a rough first day in the States. (Episode 87: "The One With Joey's Dirty Day")

19. She was leaving work and was hit by a cab. (Episode 82: "The One Where They Are Going to Party!")

20. my mother (Episode 75: "The One With the Cat")

21. father (Episode 78: "The One With Joey's New Girlfriend")

22. Foreplay. "Most guys will hit one, two, three, then go to seven and set up camp," she said. (Episode 84: "The One With Phoebe's Uterus")

23. Refrigerator College. (Episode 90: "The One With the Free Porn")

24. Rachel to Ross, after breaking up a second time. (Episode 74: "The One With the Jellyfish")

25. Rachel pawned Emily off on Ross after her boss (Emily's uncle) asked her to take his niece to the opera. (Episode 87: "The One With Joey's Dirty Day")

26. thong (Episode 86: "The One With Rachel's Crush")

27. Her birth mother (played by Teri Garr). (Episode 74: "The One With the Jellyfish")

28. The eighteen-page letter Rachel wanted him to read before getting back together. (Episode 74: "The One With the Jellyfish")

29. Ross's saying, *"We were on a break!"* (Episode 74: "The One With the Jellyfish")

30. Chandler, on Thanksgiving Day. (Episode 81: "The One With Chandler in a Box")

31. Charlton Heston, on whom Joey tried to blame his smell. (Episode 87: "The One With Joey's Dirty Day")

32. crunchy; greasy (Episodes 96 and 97: "The One With Ross's Wedding—Parts 1 and 2")

33. pee (Episode 74: "The One With the Jellyfish")

34. Miss Chanandelor Bong. (Episode 85: "The One With the Embryos")

35. A catering company. (Episode 79: "The One With the Dirty Girl")

36. Joey was locked in the entertainment center by the guy who was going to buy it. (Episode 75: "The One With the Cat")

37. Six weeks. (Episode 92: "The One With All the Haste")

38. personal shopping (Episode 86: "The One With Rachel's Crush")

39. Joshua Bergen (played by Tate Donovan). (Episode 86: "The One With Rachel's Crush")

40. His relationship with her boss. (Episode 76: "The One With the Cuffs")

41. Her fake fingernail. (Episode 76: "The One With the Cuffs")

42. Richard's son, Timothy. (Episode 81: "The One With Chandler in a Box")

43. The night of Ross and Emily's wedding rehearsal dinner. (Episodes 96 and 97: "The One With Ross's Wedding—Parts 1 and 2")

44. The number of Oreos Joey stuffed in his mouth at once. (Episode 83: "The One With the Girl from Poughkeepsie")

Bits of Trivia

According to the producers, a questionnaire regarding Monica's promiscuity was passed out to a test audience at the request of NBC before the pilot aired. Apparently NBC considered Monica a slut for sleeping with Paul the Wine Guy on their first date.

45. Animals dressed as humans. (Episode 85: "The One With the Embryos")

46. The funnest guy in the world according to Ross and Chandler. (Episode 82: "The One Where They Are Going to Party!")

47. Space cowboy. (Episode 85: "The One With the Embryos")

48. Chandler, to Ross, practicing to cancel his gym membership. (Episode 77: "The One With the Ballroom Dancing")

49. To prove to Joey how important their friendship was to him after stealing his girlfriend and to give him time to think about what he did. (Episode 81: "The One With Chandler in a Box")

50. Ross, referring to his music. (Episode 80: "The One Where Chandler Crosses the Line")

51. When Joey gave her the copy of *The Velveteen Rabbit*, he said, "This is 'cause I know you like rabbits and I know you like cheese." (Episode 79: "The One With the Dirty Girl")

52. Emily's father, who tried to tack on a couple other expenses to the cost of the wedding. (Episodes 96 and 97: "The One With Ross's Wedding Parts 1 and 2")

53. A pair of handcuffs. (Episode 76: "The One With the Cuffs")

54. His being handcuffed to the chair in her office. (Episode 76: "The One With the Cuffs")

55. *Weekend at Bernie's*. (Episode 85: "The One With the Embryos")

56. Porn. The two were very careful about not touching the TV or the remote to upset the transmission. "Imagine a protective porn bub-

ble if you will," Chandler said. (Episode 90: "The One With the Free Porn")

57. Being Frank Jr. and Alice's surrogate. (Episode 84: "The One With Phoebe's Uterus")

58. in his sweatpants (Episode 87: "The One With Joey's Dirty Day")

59. Blue. (Episode 76: "The One With the Cuffs")

60. Kathy, Joey's girlfriend, with whom Chandler was in love. (Episode 80: "The One Where Chandler Crosses the Line")

61. Being hated by all the employees at Allesandro's. (Episode 83: "The One With the Girl from Poughkeepsie")

62. Viva Las Gaygas. (Episode 85: "The One With the Embryos")

63. She bit his butt. (Episode 77: "The One With the Ballroom Dancing")

64. The "V." "Wow, there's a lot I didn't know about vomit," he said. (Episode 76: "The One With the Cuffs")

65. Her grandma's. (Episode 77: "The One With the Ballroom Dancing")

66. The last item in Rachel's grocery bag. (Episode 85: "The One With the Embryos")

67. rugby (Episode 88: "The One With All the Rugby")

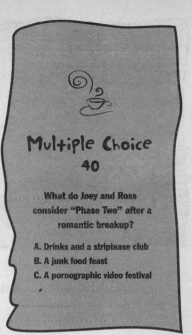

Multiple Choice 40

What do Joey and Ross consider "Phase Two" after a romantic breakup?

A. Drinks and a striptease club
B. A junk food feast
C. A pornographic video festival

68. Phoebe, referring to being the surrogate for Frank Jr. and Alice. (Episode 84: "The One With Phoebe's Uterus")

69. Kathy had just finished cutting his hair. (Episode 80: "The One Where Chandler Crosses the Line")

70. porn (Episode 86: "The One With Rachel's Crush")

71. Joshua, when he saw Chandler and Joey's birds. (Episode 91: "The One With Rachel's New Dress")

72. Mr. Treeger, the building super. (Episode 77: "The One With the Ballroom Dancing")

73. Michael Flatley, Lord of the Dance. (Episode 85: "The One With the Embryos")

74. Joey, referring to why Kathy broke up with Joey. (Episode 80: "The One Where Chandler Crosses the Line)

75. Ben. Ross's handwriting is apparently quite messy. (Episode 94: "The One With the Invitation")

76. Big Fat Goalie. (Episode 85: "The One With the Embryos")

77. Yemen. (Episode 88: "The One With All the Rugby")

78. old lady underpants (Episode 85: "The One With the Embryos")

79. Phoebe, who liked the way she sounded with a cold. (Episode 78: "The One With Joey's New Girlfriend")

80. germs (Episode 78: "The One With Joey's New Girlfriend")

81. van (Episode 82: "The One Where They Are Going to Party!")

82. book (Episode 82: "The One Where They Are Going to Party!")

83. For making out with a client. (Episode 77: "The One With the Ballroom Dancing")

84. That her uterus was ready for implantation. (Episode 85: "The One With the Embryos")

85. He felt guilty after kissing Kathy, Joey's girlfriend. (Episode 80: "The One Where Chandler Crosses the Line")

86. Ross wouldn't sit with him because of the color of his blazer. (Episode 84: "The One With Phoebe's Uterus")

87. Ross and Emily. (Episode 87: "The One With Joey's Dirty Day")

88. Tic Tacs (Episode 85: "The One With the Embryos")

89. Ross, who was at a bed-and-breakfast in Vermont with Emily. (Episode 87: "The One With Joey's Dirty Day")

90. mooning (Episode 81: "The One With Chandler in a Box")

91. widow (Episode 79: "The One With the Dirty Girl")

92. Sophie. (Episode 82: "The One Where They Are Going to Party!")

93. Her cheerleader uniform, which she put on to impress Joshua. (Episode 89: "The One With the Fake Party")

94. Althea. (Episode 85: "The One With the Embryos")

95. Charlton Heston, after he caught Joey taking a shower in his dressing room. (Episode 87: "The One With Joey's Dirty Day")

Bits of Trivia

Phoebe's address is 5 Morton St., Apt. 16.

96. Monica's backing out of their new catering business. (Episode 82: "The One Where They Are Going to Party!")

97. The name "Chandler." (Episode 91: "The One With Rachel's New Dress")

98. Being Frank Jr. and Alice's surrogate. (Episode 84: "The One With Phoebe's Uterus")

99. The light switch in her new apartment that didn't seem to do anything. (Episode 88: "The One With All the Rugby")

100. gumball machine. Referring to the number of embryos to be used in the implantation, Frank Jr. had said, "What are the odds like if, if you stuff, like, two hundred of them in there?" (Episode 85: "The One With the Embryos")

101. So she could fire him in front of her rebellious employees. (Episode 83: "The Girl from Poughkeepsie")

102. free porn (Episode 90: "The One With the Free Porn")

103. The puppy her mother gave her to prove how hard it would be to be a surrogate. (Episode 84: "The One With Phoebe's Uterus")

104. Joshua (Episode 89: "The One With the Fake Party")

105. His newly pierced ear. (Episode 92: "The One With All the Haste")

106. Sarah "Fergie" Ferguson, Duchess of York. (Episodes 96 and 97: "The One With Ross's Wedding—Parts 1 and 2")

107. How Phoebe could improve her chances of getting pregnant. (Episode 85: "The One With the Embryos")

108. birds; apartment (Episode 85: "The One With the Embryos")

109. The lollypop and pregnancy test Frank Jr. and Alice brought her. (Episode 85: "The One With the Embryos")

110. She slept with another guy. (Episode 86: "The One With Rachel's Crush")

111. meat (Episode 89: "The One With the Fake Party")

112. Joshua, her handsome client at Bloomingdale's. (Episode 86: "The One With Rachel's Crush")

113. Phoebe's baby began kicking. (Episode 89: "The One With the Fake Party")

114. Wham! (Episode 92: "The One With All the Haste")

115. The church in London where Ross and Emily were to be married. (Episodes 96 and 97: "The One With Ross's Wedding—Parts 1 and 2")

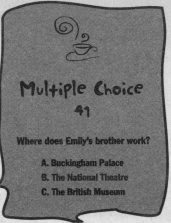

Multiple Choice

41

Where does Emily's brother work?

A. Buckingham Palace
B. The National Theatre
C. The British Museum

116. Giving birth to triplets. (Episode 90: "The One With the Free Porn")

117. band (Episode 90: "The One With the Free Porn")

118. Exxon (Episode 91: "The One With Rachel's New Dress")

119. The duck ate it. (Episode 95: "The One With the Worst Best Man Ever")

120. Toblerone chocolate bars (Episode 90: "The One With the Free Porn")

121. Her lingerie. "The best part though," Rachel said, "was when the, uh, waiter spilled water down my back. I jumped up and my boob popped out." (Episode 91: "The One With Rachel's New Dress")

122. Her new Santa pants. (Episode 92: "The One With All the Haste")

123. Season tickets for the Knicks. (Episode 92: "The One With All the Haste")

124. Using his earring as an engagement ring. (Episode 92: "The One With All the Haste")

125. The wedding dresses at the bridal shop where they went to pick up Emily's dress. (Episode 93: "The One With All the Wedding Dresses")

126. The stripper from Ross's bachelor party, who the guys thought stole his dead grandmother's wedding ring. (Episode 95: "The One With the Worst Best Man Ever")

127. Susan. He was worried about the time they were spending together, especially at the gym. "They take a steam together, things get a little playful. Didn't you see *Personal Best?*" Ross said. (Episode 91: "The One With Rachel's New Dress")

128. Thank you. (Episode 90: "The One With the Free Porn")

Season Five

1. Waltham. (Episode 98: "The One After Ross Says Rachel")

2. LaPooh. (Episode 102: "The One With the Kips")

3. Caitlin. (Episode 116: "The One Where Ross Can't Flirt")

4. Thong panties. (Episode 105: "The One With All the Thanksgivings")

5. Rachel, who smoked with her boss so she would fit in. (Episode 115: "The One Where Rachel Smokes")

6. Janice. (Episode 109: "The One With Chandler's Work Laugh")

7. He said Rachel's name instead of Emily's. (Episode 98: "The One After Ross Says Rachel")

8. Ugly Naked Guy's moving boxes. (Episode 111: "The One Where Everybody Finds Out")

9. Vegas. (Episodes 120 and 121: "The One in Vegas—Parts 1 and 2")

10. Dr. Philangie, Ross's personal physician. (Episode 98: "The One After Ross Says Rachel")

11. Chandler's old roommate. Rachel was scared that she was going to meet the same fate as Kip, thanks to Emily prohibiting Ross from being friends with Rachel. "[Kip] and Monica dated. When they broke up, they couldn't even be in the same room together, and you all promised you would stay his friend and what happened? He got phased out." (Episode 102: "The One With the Kips")

12. They were about to leave for Atlantic City. (Episode 99: "The One With All the Kissing")

13. Rachel, whom he was trying to embarrass while on their flight to Vegas. (Episodes 120 and 121: "The One in Vegas—Parts 1 and 2")

14. The extra slice of gravy-soaked bread Monica puts in the middle of her leftover Thanksgiving sandwiches. (Episode 106: "The One With Ross's Sandwich")

15. His leather pants, which he had pulled down to cool off while in the bathroom of his date's apartment, and had trouble putting back on. (Episode 108: "The One With All the Resolutions")

16. Mr. Zelner, during her interview at Ralph Lauren. (Episode 114: "The One With Rachel's Inadvertent Kiss")

17. The Honeymoon Suite. (Episode 98: "The One After Ross Says Rachel")

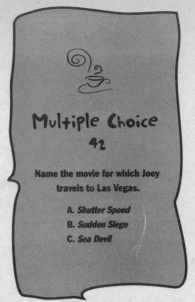

Multiple Choice

42

Name the movie for which Joey travels to Las Vegas.

A. *Shutter Speed*
B. *Sudden Siege*
C. *Sea Devil*

18. Chandler, Leslie, and Frank Jr. Jr. (Episode 100: "The One Hundredth")

19. Emily's stepmother. (Episode 98: "The One After Ross Says Rachel")

20. Danny, the Yeti, who hadn't asked Rachel out since taking her for pizza. (Episode 104: "The One Where Ross Moves In")

21. Giving away your flower. "If you keep calling it that, no one's ever gonna take it," Rachel told her. (Episode 105: "The One With All the Thanksgivings")

22. bra (Episode 111: "The One Where Everybody Finds Out")

23. hand twin (Episodes 120 and 121: "The One in Vegas—Parts 1 and 2")

24. Emily, who told him she'd move to New York if he stopped seeing Rachel. (Episode 101: "The One Where Phoebe Hates PBS")

25. eyelash curler (Episode 102: "The One With the Kips")

26. Her grandma's funeral. (Episode 110: "The One With Joey's Bag")

27. Rachel, referring to her coming with him on his honeymoon. (Episode 98: "The One After Ross Says Rachel")

28. A fur coat. (Episode 103: "The One With the Yeti")

29. crossword puzzle (Episode 113: "The One With the Cop")

30. His leftover Thanksgiving sandwich, which someone took at work. (Episode 106: "The One With Ross's Sandwich")

31. Rachel is not allowed to borrow Monica's stuff. (Episode 116: "The One Where Ross Can't Flirt")

32. Joey. (Episode 102: "The One With the Kips")

33. His and Monica's agreement that they wouldn't have sex after the London trip. "I'm still on London time. Does that count?" he later asks. (Episode 98: "The One After Ross Says Rachel")

34. Choosing between Rachel and Emily. (Episode 101: "The One Where Phoebe Hates PBS")

35. Fonzie (Episode 100: "The One Hundredth")

36. Gunther, after Monica called it a getting-rid-of-anything-Rachel-ever-touched sale. (Episode 103: "The One With the Yeti")

37. "You're on in five, Ms. Minnelli." (Episode 103: "The One With the Yeti")

38. Her new boss at Ralph Lauren, who asked her if she smoked. (Episode 115: "The One Where Rachel Smokes")

39. To do one new thing every day. (Episode 108: "The One With All the Resolutions")

40. To pilot a commercial jet. (Episode 108: "The One With All the Resolutions")

41. To not make fun of his friends. (Episode 108: "The One With All the Resolutions")

42. To learn to play the guitar. (Episode 108: "The One With All the Resolutions")

43. To gossip less. (Episode 108: "The One With All the Resolutions")

44. To take more pictures of everyone together. (Episode 108: "The One With All the Resolutions")

45. punching (Episode 112: "The One With the Girl Who Hits Joey")

46. Ross, about his commute, trying to convince himself that he didn't mind moving way uptown for Emily, who wanted Ross as far away from Rachel as possible. (Episode 103: "The One With the Yeti")

47. His work laugh. (Episode 109: "The One With Chandler's Work Laugh")

48. One hundred dollars. (Episode 112: "The One With the Girl Who Hits Joey")

49. Howard. (Episode 112: "The One With the Girl Who Hits Joey")

50. Phoebe. "This way I'm just, you know, the exotic generous stranger. That's always fun to be." (Episode 112: "The One With the Girl Who Hits Joey")

51. Athens, only Rachel went instead. (Episode 98: "The One After Ross Says Rachel")

52. She wrote to *Sesame Street* after her mother killed herself and all they sent her was a key chain. (Episode 101: "The One Where Phoebe Hates PBS")

53. Mrs. Whiskerson. (Episode 118: "The One With the Ball")

54. A thousand dollars. "I am out a thousand dollars, I'm

Multiple Choice
43

What does Joey declare that he's most thankful for at the Friends' fifth Thanksgiving together?

A. The woman he met while shopping
B. Being with the other Friends
C. A lovely autumn breeze

all scratched up, and I'm stuck with this stupid cat that looks like a hand," she later lamented. (Episode 118: "The One With the Ball")

55. "Ben takes one lousy walk in the park and gets an audition." (Episode 115: "The One Where Rachel Smokes")

56. The names of guitar chords she didn't know. (Episode 108: "The One With All the Resolutions")

57. A regatta gala. (Episode 104: "The One Where Ross Moves In")

58. Larry, her new health inspector boyfriend. (Episode 104: "The One Where Ross Moves In")

59. teddy bears (Episode 99: "The One With All the Kissing")

60. walk around naked (Episodes 120 and 121: "The One in Vegas—Parts 1 and 2")

61. 3-D glasses. (Episode 110: "The One With Joey's Bag")

62. couch (Episode 113: "The One With the Cop")

63. A big tap-dancing pimp. (Episode 104: "The One Where Ross Moves In")

64. A Sphynx cat. (Episode 118: "The One With the Ball")

65. Chandler's kissing all the girls good-bye to cover for getting busted kissing Monica. (Episode 99: "The One With All the Kissing")

66. He was trying to cover for Chandler, who left his underwear in the couch at Monica and Rachel's apartment. (Episode 106: "The One With Ross's Sandwich")

67. Emily, who had just left a message for Ross on his answering machine. (Episode 117: "The One With the Ride-along")

68. Telling Chandler and Monica that she and Rachel knew that they're a couple. (Episode 111: "The One Where Everybody Finds Out")

69. sweaters. He wore them as padding against his girlfriend's punches. (Episode 112: "The One With the Girl Who Hits Joey")

70. Wham! (Episode 105: "The One With All the Thanksgivings")

71. He drew on her face with permanent marker. (Episodes 120 and 121: "The One in Vegas—Parts 1 and 2")

72. The Christmas donation bucket. (Episode 107: "The One With the Inappropriate Sister")

73. seeing-eye dog (Episode 103: "The One With the Yeti")

74. in love (Episode 111: "The One Where Everybody Finds Out")

75. babies (Episode 100: "The One Hundredth")

76. To star in a movie that ended up never happening. (Episode 119: "The One With Joey's Big Break")

77. He was a Trojan at Caesar's Palace. (Episode 119: "The One With Joey's Big Break")

78. Frank Jr., referring to one of the triplets. (Episode 119: "The One With Joey's Big Break")

79. A police badge. (Episode 113: "The One With the Cop")

80. The blackjack dealer in Vegas, referring to their being identical hand twins. (Episodes 120 and 121: "The One in Vegas— Parts 1 and 2")

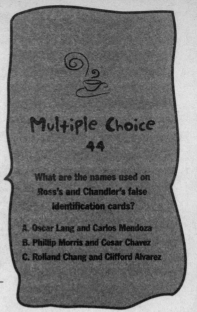

Multiple Choice
44

What are the names used on Ross's and Chandler's false identification cards?

A. Oscar Lang and Carlos Mendoza
B. Phillip Morris and Cesar Chavez
C. Rolland Chang and Clifford Alvarez

81. carrot (Episode 105: "The One With All the Thanksgivings")

82. The hot girl he spotted across the street in Ross's apartment building. (Episode 114: "The One With Rachel's Inadvertent Kiss")

83. His boss and his wife, with whom Chandler and Monica were playing tennis. (Episode 109: "The One With Chandler's Work Laugh")

84. gas (Episode 116: "The One Where Ross Can't Flirt")

85. Phoebe's telling people she was having her brother's babies. (Episode 100: "The One Hundredth")

86. mole cluster (Episode 105: "The One With All the Thanksgivings")

☆ What's in a Name? ☆

- ◆ Fruit Drying Psycho—Eddie Minowick, Chandler's short-term roommate

- ◆ Bryce—Gunther's character on *All My Children*

- ◆ Dr. Drake Ramoray—Joey's character on *Days of Our Lives*

- ◆ Hans Ramoray, Drake's evil twin—The character Ross came up with to help get rid of Joey's stalker

- ◆ Boss Man Bing—Chandler with a promotion

- ◆ Bingaling—Janice's nickname for Chandler

- ◆ Monica Faloola Geller—The name Phoebe signed when Monica's mattress was delivered

- ◆ Coma Guy—The hot guy in a coma

- ◆ Cookie Dude—What the NYU students called Ross when he sold Brown Bird cookies on campus

- ◆ The Dinosaur Guy—Copy Girl Chloe's nickname for Ross

- ◆ The Chan-Chan Man—Monica's term of endearment for Chandler in Vegas

- ◆ Chuckles—Chandler's nickname at work

87. The guy at the furniture store who didn't believe Ross and Rachel had dated. "You kept count? You are such a loser!" Rachel said. (Episode 113: "The One With the Cop")

88. cyborg (Episode 106: "The One With Ross's Sandwich")

89. Rachel, who poured a cup of water on his crotch while flying to Vegas. (Episodes 120 and 121: "The One in Vegas—Parts 1 and 2")

90. Mental Geller. (Episode 106: "The One With Ross's Sandwich")

91. Ross, Joey, and Chandler. (Episode 117: "The One With the Ride-along")

92. kissed him (Episode 114: "The One With Rachel's Inadvertent Kiss")

93. Keeping one of Frank Jr. and Alice's babies. (Episode 100: "The One Hundredth")

94. Danny and his inappropriate sister. (Episode 107: "The One With the Inappropriate Sister")

95. Phoebe's hitting on him. Of course, it was all in jest: "Phoebe knows and she's just trying to freak us out," Monica noted. Chandler and Monica then decided to mess back. (Episode 111: "The One Where Everybody Finds Out")

96. To watch him on *Law and Order*. (Episode 116: "The One Where Ross Can't Flirt")

97. The police badge she found at Central Perk. (Episode 113: "The One With the Cop")

98. A shoulder bag. "It is odd how a woman's purse looks so good on me, a man" and "You know what? Make fun all you want. This is a great bag, okay? And it's as handy as it is becoming" were some of Joey's later claims. (Episode 110: "The One With Joey's Bag")

99. That she had lunch with Richard the day before. (Episodes 120 and 121: "The One in Vegas—Parts 1 and 2")

100. *PIVOT!* (Episode 113: "The One With the Cop")

101. He yelled at his boss for taking his sandwich. (Episode 106: "The One With Ross's Sandwich")

102. Kidney stones. (Episode 100: "The One Hundredth")

103. She thought she was being phased out after Ross chose Emily over his friendship with Rachel. (Episode 102: "The One With the Kips")

104. Ugly Naked Guy, whom they hadn't seen for a while. (Episode 103: "The One With the Yeti")

105. ketchup (Episode 115: "The One Where Rachel Smokes")

106. A turkey on her head. (Episode 105: "The One With All the Thanksgivings")

107. plane-iversary (Episodes 120 and 121: "The One in Vegas—Parts 1 and 2")

108. She picked up the phone while they were talking. (Episode 108: "The One With All the Resolutions")

109. In his boss's trash can. (Episode 106: "The One With Ross's Sandwich")

110. Her father, whom she met earlier at her grandmother's funeral. (Episode 110: "The One With Joey's Bag")

111. Massages. (Episode 110: "The One With Joey's Bag")

112. Cups and ice. "Monica's gonna rue the day that she put me in charge of cups and ice," Phoebe vowed. (Episode 115: "The One Where Rachel Smokes")

113. sister (Episode 112: "The One With the Girl Who Hits Joey")

114. tree (Episode 113: "The One With the Cop")

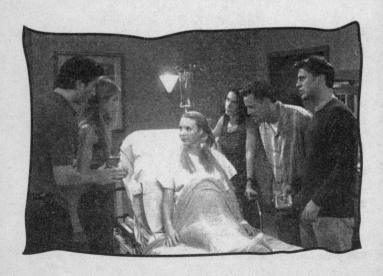

115. Her new Sphynx cat. (Episode 118: "The One With the Ball")

116. Phoebe, to Gary, the cute cop whose badge she found. "You're the prettiest fake undercover whore I've ever seen," Gary replied. (Episode 113: "The One With the Cop")

117. Rachel, who had just returned from an interview with a big blotch of ink on her lip. (Episode 114: "The One With Rachel's Inadvertent Kiss")

118. She and Gary, her cute cop boyfriend, had sex in the park. (Episode 114: "The One With Rachel's Inadvertent Kiss")

119. Joey, referring to the kid Joey was auditioning with for a soup commercial that Ben was also auditioning for. (Episode 115: "The One Where Rachel Smokes")

120. Smoking. (Episode 115: "The One Where Rachel Smokes")

121. Joey's grandma, who didn't speak English. (Episode 116: "The One Where Ross Can't Flirt")

122. Ross, to the hot pizza delivery girl, who thought her new haircut made her look like a little boy. (Episode 116: "The One Where Ross Can't Flirt")

123. Emily, who was going to get married the next day. (Episode 117: "The One With the Ride-along")

124. sandwich; sandwich (Episode 117: "The One With the Ride-along")

125. Gunther. (Episode 118: "The One With the Ball")

126. He shot a bird. (Episode 118: "The One With the Ball")

127. Rachel's walking around naked in her apartment. (Episodes 120 and 121: "The One in Vegas—Parts 1 and 2")

128. married (Episodes 120 and 121: "The One in Vegas—Parts 1 and 2")

Season Six

1. Jill and Amy. (Episode 134: "The One With Rachel's Sister")

2. Vegas (Episode 122: "The One After Vegas")

3. His complex over his three divorces. (Episode 123: "The One Where Ross Hugs Rachel")

4. Paul Stevens (Bruce Willis), Elizabeth's dad, while Ross hid under the bed and watched. Later in the episode, Ross said to Paul, "I

want you to know that you and I are not all that different. I mean, I, too, am a neat guy. And I, too, am just a love machine." (Episode 143: "The One Where Paul's the Man")

5. He spoke in a British accent. (Episode 125: "The One Where Joey Loses His Insurance")

6. Elle Macpherson. (Episode 128: "The One Where Phoebe Runs")

7. Monica and Chandler moving in together. (Episode 123: "The One Where Ross Hugs Rachel")

8. Ralph Lauren. "Oh, my God, Phoebe," Rachel said later, "that's not Ralph Lauren. That's Kenny the copy guy!" (Episode 129: "The One With Ross's Teeth")

9. Mac Machiavelli. (Episode 141: "The One With *Mac and* C.H.E.E.S.E.")

10. Ross had told them Chandler was the one smoking pot in Ross's bedroom back in college. (Episode 130: "The One Where Ross Got High")

11. His newly whitened teeth. (Episode 129: "The One With Ross's Teeth")

12. Just Married. (Episode 122: "The One After Vegas")

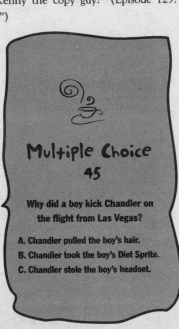

Multiple Choice 45

Why did a boy kick Chandler on the flight from Las Vegas?

A. Chandler pulled the boy's hair.
B. Chandler took the boy's Diet Sprite.
C. Chandler stole the boy's headset.

13. Rachel left her hair straightener on. (Episode 139: "The One Where Ross Dates a Student")

14. Porsche (Episode 126: "The One With Joey's Porsche")

15. A mix tape that Janice had made for him years before. (Episode 138: "The One With *Unagi*")

16. A sock bunny. (Episode 138: "The One With *Unagi*")

17. Ross and Rachel. (Episode 122: "The One After Vegas")

18. His unintentional bid on a sailboat at a silent auction. "I didn't know it was an auction. I figured I'd take a guess . . . free boat." (Episodes 145 and 146: "The One With the Proposal—Parts 1 and 2")

19. shackin' up (Episode 123: "The One Where Ross Hugs Rachel")

20. Denise. (Episode 126: "The One With Joey's Posche")

21. Cutie McPretty. (Episode 139: "The One Where Ross Dates a Student")

22. He told Monica that Ben was coming over to get out of helping Rachel pack. (Episode 127: "The One on the Last Night")

23. runs (Episode 128: "The One Where Phoebe Runs")

24. He's a headliner for a gay burlesque show in Vegas. (Episode 130: "The One Where Ross Got High")

25. Cups. Joey ended up losing $1500. (Episode 127: "The One on the Last Night")

26. Telling her she'd heard a rumor that Ralph Lauren had made out with someone in the copy room. (Episode 129: "The One With Ross's Teeth")

27. The Routine. (Episode 131: "The One With The Routine")

28. The joke Ross sent to *Playboy* magazine. (Episode 133: "The One With the Joke")

29. They were pornos Ursula starred in. (Episode 135: "The One Where Chandler Can't Cry")

30. Joey, who had a starring role on *Days of Our Lives*. (Episodes 136 and 137: "The One That Could Have Been—Parts 1 and 2")

31. weaponry (Episode 144: "The One With the Ring")

32. divorce (Episode 122: "The One After Vegas")

33. Turn it into a game room. (Episode 124: "The One With Ross's Denial")

34. Joey's, because he didn't work enough that year. (Episode 125: "The One Where Joey Loses His Insurance")

35. Pizza Hut (Episode 126: "The One With Joey's Porsche")

36. Jack Geller. (Episode 130: "The One Where Ross Got High")

37. Elizabeth, as Ross explained to her that he couldn't date a student. (Episode 139: "The One Where Ross Dates a Student")

38. Phoebe driving back from Vegas with him in her grandma's cab. (Episode 122: "The One After Vegas")

39. The Porsche to which Joey found the keys. (Episode 126: "The One With Joey's Porsche")

40. Rachel, who was moving out and into Phoebe's apartment. (Episode 127: "The One on the Last Night")

41. Irish Potato Famine (Episode 128: "The One Where Phoebe Runs")

42. English trifle. "Beef in a dessert?" exclaimed Ross. "There is *no* way." (Episode 130: "The One Where Ross Got High")

43. feet (Episode 130: "The One Where Ross Got High")

44. Phoebe. (Episode 132: "The One With the Apothecary Table")

45. Heart's "Barracuda." (Episode 133: "The One With the Joke")

46. Chandler. (Episode 135: "The One Where Chandler Can't Cry")

47. roommate (Episode 128: "The One Where Phoebe Runs")

48. Phoebe, the Merrill Lynch broker. "There was a little, little dip in the market . . ."

Bits of Trivia

In "The One That Could Have Been—Parts 1 and 2," during the theme song, the montage of clips featured scenes of what could have been, rather than the usual montage.

(Episodes 136 and 137: "The One That Could Have Been—Parts 1 and 2")

49. Richard and his date walked in and joined them. (Episodes 145 and 146: "The One With the Proposal—Parts 1 and 2")

50. Jill (Episode 134: "The One With Rachel's Sister")

51. Her dating Paul Stevens (Bruce Willis), Elizabeth's father. (Episode 142: "The One Where Ross Meets Elizabeth's Dad")

52. sediment flow rate (Episode 125: "The One Where Joey Loses His Insurance")

53. The bench along the window where Monica hid everyone's Christmas presents. (Episode 131: "The One With The Routine")

54. hernia (Episode 125: "The One Where Joey Loses His Insurance")

55. Episode 122: "The One After Vegas"

56. Phoebe. One of her great lines was: "I said sell when it hits fifty! Five-oh! It's a number! It comes after four-nine! No, it's okay, it's okay. You're allowed one mistake. Just kidding. You are, of course, fired." (Episodes 136 and 137: "The One That Could Have Been— Parts 1 and 2")

57. Joey and Janine. (Episode 132: "The One With the Apothecary Table)

58. fridge (Episode 140: "The One With Joey's Fridge")

59. Putting her and Chandler's names on a waiting list at the Morgan Chase Museum for their wedding. (Episode 143: "The One Where Paul's the Man")

60. The Porsche outfit he wore after the guy with the Porsche took his car back. Ross asks Joey, "Did a Porsche throw up on you?" (Episode 126: "The One With Joey's Porsche")

61. Ross's divorce lawyer. (Episode 122: "The One After Vegas")

62. Jill, Rachel's younger sister, who was using Ross to make Rachel jealous. (Episode 135: "The One Where Chandler Can't Cry")

63. Monica, who is still fat. (Episodes 136 and 137: "The One That Could Have Been—Parts 1 and 2")

64. robot. "If I don't get this part, I'm never gonna eat macaroni and cheese again," Joey said. (Episode 141: "The One With *Mac and C.H.E.E.S.E.*")

65. Jack Geller, who had cheated on her in her dream. (Episode 130: "The One Where Ross Got High")

66. Paul (Bruce Willis), Elizabeth's father. (Episode 144: "The One With the Ring")

67. So she wouldn't come in and see he'd moved everything around. (Episode 128: "The One Where Phoebe Runs")

68. wife (Episode 123: "The One Where Ross Hugs Rachel")

69. Rachel's boss, who thought Rachel and Ralph Lauren were having an affair. (Episode 129: "The One With Ross's Teeth")

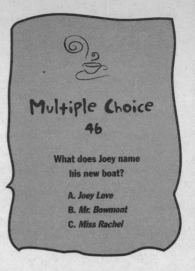

Multiple Choice 46

What does Joey name his new boat?

A. *Joey Love*
B. *Mr. Bowmont*
C. *Miss Rachel*

70. Richard, who told her he still loved her and wanted to marry her after seeing her at dinner with Chandler. (Episodes 145 and 146: "The One With the Proposal—Parts 1 and 2")

71. She threw water balloons at him. (Episodes 145 and 146: "The One With the Proposal—Parts 1 and 2")

72. Why Joey got kicked out of Pottery Barn. (Episode 132: "The One With the Apothecary Table")

73. Gunther, who offered Joey a job at Central Perk. (Episode 133: "The One With the Joke")

74. apartment (Episode 134: "The One With Rachel's Sister")

75. Getting an annulment. (Episode 123: "The One Where Ross Hugs Rachel")

76. incest (Episode 134: "The One With Rachel's Sister")

99. Proposing to Monica. (Episodes 145 and 146: "The One With the Proposal—Parts 1 and 2")

100. Janine, his hot new roommate. (Episode 128: "The One Where Phoebe Runs")

101. Phoebe. When selecting backups to marry in case they weren't married by the age of forty, Phoebe cheated and chose both Joey and Ross. "You can't have two backups!" exclaimed Rachel. (Episodes 145 and 146: "The One With the Proposal—Parts 1 and 2")

102. Rachel, who thought she was staying when Monica told her that Chandler was moving in. (Episode 123: "The One Where Ross Hugs Rachel")

103. Satan (Episode 128: "The One Where Phoebe Runs")

104. Dating a student. (Episode 139: "The One Where Ross Dates a Student")

105. blah; hoot (Episode 132: "The One With the Apothecary Table")

106. Pottery Barn. Rachel was buying so much from the retail store that Ross quipped, "Your place looks like page seventy-two of the catalogue." (Episode 132: "The One With the Apothecary Table")

107. Joey, who worked at Central Perk and kept giving away free muffins to all the pretty girls. (Episode 134: "The One With Rachel's Sister")

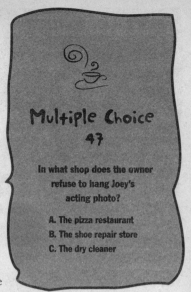

Multiple Choice 47

In what shop does the owner refuse to hang Joey's acting photo?

A. The pizza restaurant
B. The shoe repair store
C. The dry cleaner

108. The judge at Ross and Rachel's annulment hearing, referring to Rachel's claim that they were unable to consummate their marriage. (Episode 126: "The One With Joey's Porsche")

109. Jack Geller, whom she'd just had a dream about. (Episode 130: "The One Where Ross Got High")

110. The English trifle Rachel made for Thanksgiving. (Episode 130: "The One Where Ross Got High")

111. Monica. The comment was made by Joey's roommate Janine, who couldn't stand her. (Episode 132: "The One With the Apothecary Table")

112. Running in the park. (Episode 128: "The One Where Phoebe Runs")

113. balloons (Episodes 145 and 146: "The One With the Proposal—Parts 1 and 2")

114. Jill, Rachel's little sister. (Episode 135: "The One Where Chandler Can't Cry")

115. She threw up. (Episodes 136 and 137: "The One That Could Have Been—Parts 1 and 2")

116. Elizabeth, the ex-student he was dating. Ross had thought that she had asked him to go away with her to Florida. (Episode 140: "The One With Joey's Fridge")

117. Carol. (Episodes 136 and 137: "The One That Could Have Been—Parts 1 and 2")

118. Not divorcing him. (Episode 122: "The One After Vegas")

Season Seven

1. Rachel, as on her thirtieth birthday, the others reminisced about their thirtieth birthdays. (Episode 160: "The One Where They All Turn Thirty")

2. Nora Bing. (Episodes 169 and 170: "The One With Monica and Chandler's Wedding—Parts 1 and 2")

3. *Jurassic Park* (Episode 148: "The One With Rachel's Book")

4. Francis. (Episode 157: "The One With All the Cheesecakes")

5. Ross and Rachel, whom she caught kissing in the hallway the night she and Chandler got engaged. "Can I ask you just a little question?" Monica said. "Why tonight?" (Episode 147: "The One With Monica's Thunder")

6. Her grandmother's chocolate chip cookie recipe. Phoebe said that her "grandmother made me swear on her deathbed that I would never let it out of our family." (Episode 149: "The One With Phoebe's Cookies")

7. Monica's not being invited to her cousin Franny's wedding. (Episode 157: "The One With All the Cheesecakes")

8. spittin'. Joey's costar replied: "Enunciation is the mark of a good actor, and when you enunciate, you spit!" (Episodes 169 and 170: "The One With Monica and Chandler's Wedding—Parts 1 and 2")

9. Vanilla Ice (Episode 150; "The One With Rachel's Assistant")

10. leg warmers (Episode 150: "The One With Rachel's Assistant")

11. macaroni (Episode 150: "The One With Rachel's Assistant")

12. It's too cold. (Episode 154: "The One Where Chandler Doesn't Like Dogs")

13. Rosita, his Barcalounger. (Episode 159: "The One Where Rosita Dies")

14. Monica and Ross's hot cousin, Cassie (Denise Richards). (Episode 165: "The One With Ross and Monica's Cousin")

15. bike (Episode 155: "The One With All the Candy")

16. The cheesecake he was eating. (Episode 157: "The One With All the Cheesecakes")

17. Joey, who was trying to convince Chandler that he could play a nineteen year old. (Episode 147: "The One With Monica's Thunder")

18. Jessica, the character played by Cecilia Lockhart (Susan Sarandon) on *Days of Our Lives*. (Episode 161: "The One With Joey's New Brain")

19. Striker. (Episode 150: "The One With Rachel's Assistant")

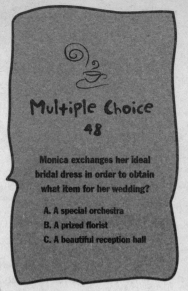

Multiple Choice 48

Monica exchanges her ideal bridal dress in order to obtain what item for her wedding?

A. A special orchestra
B. A prized florist
C. A beautiful reception hall

20. Tag, the hot new assistant she just hired. (Episode 151: "The One With the Engagement Picture")

21. Janice, referring to singing at their wedding reception. (Episode 153: "The One With Ross's Library Book")

22. Easy-Bake Ovens (Episode 159: "The One Where Rosita Dies")

23. Whitney, the soon-to-be ex-wife of Phoebe's new boyfriend, who's now dating Ross. (Episode 151: "The One With the Engagement Picture")

24. The Monica wedding fund. (Episode 148: "The One With Rachel's Book")

25. A used pregnancy test. (Episodes 169 and 170: "The One With Monica and Chandler's Wedding—Parts 1 and 2")

26. Practicing getting a Grammy. (Episode 164: "The One With Joey's Award")

27. loins (Episode 148: "The One With Rachel's Book")

28. maid of honor (Episode 152: "The One With the Nap Partners")

29. armadillo. Ben later whines, "Why can't the armadillo leave? I want Santa." (Episode 156: "The One With the Holiday Armadillo")

30. From a Gap commercial. (Episode 163: "The One With the Cheap Wedding Dress")

31. His hot cousin, Cassie (Denise Richards). (Episode 165: "The One With Ross and Monica's Cousin")

32. silt (Episodes 169 and 170: "The One With Monica and Chandler's Wedding—Parts 1 and 2")

33. Chandler, who sat on Jack's lap in the steam room. (Episode 149: "The One With Phoebe's Cookies")

34. wooden spoons (Episode 148: "The One With Rachel's Book")

35. The performance evaluation she wrote for Tag's eyes only in which she evaluated his sexual performance. Rachel said: "When asked if you take initiative, I wrote, 'Yes, he was able to unhook my bra with minimal supervision.'" (Episode 155: "The One With All the Candy")

36. nap (Episode 152: "The One With the Nap Partners")

37. Sleeping with Chandler. (Episode 162: "The One With the Truth About London")

38. Rachel, who hired Tag, the hot guy, over Hilda, the qualified assistant. Tag didn't exactly have appropriate work experience for the position, as Rachel noted during his interview: "You got three years painting houses, two whole summers at T.G.I. Fridays." (Episode 150: "The One With Rachel's Assistant")

39. Performing Monica and Chandler's wedding ceremony. (Episode 162: "The One With the Truth About London")

40. picture (Episode 151: "The One With the Engagement Picture")

41. Her smoke detector, which she'd just thrown down the garbage chute. (Episode 158: "The One Where They're Up All Night")

42. Monica screaming from her balcony that she was engaged. (Episode 147: "The One With Monica's Thunder")

43. throw-up (Episode 150: "The One With Rachel's Assistant")

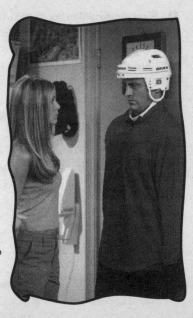

44. Phoebe, against whom Rachel was competing to see who would make a better maid of honor for Monica. (Episode 152: "The One With the Nap Partners")

45. The door to the rooftop, where they were locked out after Joey took the pipe to use it as a telescope. (Episode 158: "The One Where They're Up All Night")

46. diaphragm (Episode 148: "The One With Rachel's Book")

47. The drum set he was playing when she walked in. (Episode 156: "The One With the Holiday Armadillo")

48. Ross (Episode 147: "The One With Monica's Thunder")

49. One of Monica and Chandler's engagement photo proofs. Chandler couldn't smile like a normal person in any of them. (Episode 151: "The One With the Engagement Picture")

50. states (Episode 154: "The One Where Chandler Doesn't Like Dogs")

51. To prove that she'd been eating their stolen cheesecake without him. (Episode 157: "The One With All the Cheesecakes")

52. Who got invited to her cousin's wedding after she wasn't. (Episode 157: "The One With All the Cheesecakes")

53. Nesslay Toolouse (Nestlé Tollhouse) (Episode 149: "The One With Phoebe's Cookies")

54. Wearing women's panties. (Episode 168: "The One With Chandler's Dad")

55. She showed up drunk at her surprise party. (Episode 160: "The One Where They All Turn Thirty")

56. She found out from her sister, Ursula, that she was really thirty-one. "I just lost a whole year of my life!" (Episode 160: "The One Where They All Turn Thirty")

57. Because he really hates dogs and was embarrassed to admit it. (Episode 154: "The One Where Chandler Doesn't Like Dogs")

58. Joey's Adam's apple. (Episode 160: "The One Where They All Turn Thirty")

59. Ross and Rachel, who kissed the night Monica and Chandler got engaged. (Episode 147: "The One With Monica's Thunder")

60. He was mocking her for reading a trashy romance novel. (Episode 148: "The One With Rachel's Book")

61. The note Chandler left for Monica the night before their wedding. Phoebe told Ross, "If you don't find him and bring him back, I am gonna hunt you down and kick *your* ass!" (Episodes 169 and 170: "The One With Monica and Chandler's Wedding—Parts 1 and 2")

62. Ross, who was pissed at Joey for showing up in the middle of Ross's date with the woman they were competing for. (Episode 163: "The One With the Cheap Wedding Dress")

63. Her mother's holiday skull. (Episode 156: "The One With the Holiday Armadillo")

64. Rosita, his broken Barcalounger, mysteriously healing itself. Rachel's suggestion was: "Maybe somebody came in here and fixed it, or something." (Episode 159: "The One Where Rosita Dies")

65. The brain transplant his character on *Days of Our Lives* was about to get. (Episode 161: "The One With Joey's New Brain")

66. Janice, who invited herself to their wedding after finding out about their engagement. (Episode 153: "The One With Ross's Library Book")

67. Tag, who had just broken up with his girlfriend and took Rachel up on her offer to have Thanksgiving with the gang. (Episode 154: "The One Where Chandler Doesn't Like Dogs")

68. His hands, which Rachel had commented on earlier as being very "talented." (Episode 147: "The One With Monica's Thunder")

69. pool boy (Episodes 169 and 170: "The One With Monica and Chandler's Wedding—Parts 1 and 2")

70. spider (Episode 156: "The One With the Holiday Armadillo")

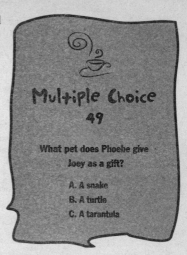

Multiple Choice 49

What pet does Phoebe give Joey as a gift?

A. A snake
B. A turtle
C. A tarantula

71. He agreed not to eat Thanksgiving dinner until he named all fifty states. (Episode 154: "The One Where Chandler Doesn't Like Dogs")

72. phone calls (Episode 158: "The One Where They're Up All Night")

73. circumcised (Episode 165: "The One With Ross and Monica's Cousin")

74. Hippity Hop (Episode 160: "The One Where They All Turn Thirty")

75. The little red sports car he bought on his thirtieth birthday. (Episode 160: "The One Where They All Turn Thirty")

76. Joey, reading what he planned to say while performing the ceremony at Monica and Chandler's wedding. (Episode 162: "The One With the Truth About London")

77. book (Episode 153: "The One With Ross's Library Book")

78. Richard. (Episode 156: "The One With the Holiday Armadillo")

79. Ross, who was teaching himself to play the bagpipes so he could play at their wedding. Chandler would later break the news to him: "While we appreciate the gesture, we just don't feel that bagpipes are appropriate for our wedding." (Episode 161: "The One With Joey's New Brain")

80. Listening to Monica's new outgoing message on their answering machine, which referred to them as "the Bings." (Episodes 169 and 170: "The One With Monica and Chandler's Wedding—Parts 1 and 2")

81. massage (Episode 148: "The One With Rachel's Book")

82. sex (Episode 157: "The One With All the Cheesecakes")

83. backless dress. Later in the episode, Chandler reveals: "When I was in high school, he used to come to all of my swim meets dressed as a different Hollywood starlet." (Episode 168: "The One With Chandler's Dad")

84. Phoebe's dead grandmother. (Episode 156: "The One With the Holiday Armadillo")

85. Rossatron (Episode 157: "The One With All the Cheesecakes")

86. David the Scientist Guy (Hank Azaria), who was in town for a conference. (Episode 157: "The One With All the Cheesecakes")

87. Cecilia Lockhart's character on *Days of Our Lives*, whose brain goes to Joey's character. (Episode 161: "The One With Joey's New Brain")

88. Joey, who was late in getting to Monica and Chandler's wedding, where he was about to officiate at the ceremony. (Episodes 169 and 170: "The One With Monica and Chandler's Wedding—Parts 1 and 2")

89. Superman (Episode 156: "The One With the Holiday Armadillo")

90. Rachel, who was having issues about turning thirty. (Episode 160: "The One Where They All Turn Thirty")

91. James Bond's; James Bond's. Rachel had shown Chandler a tuxedo that Pierce Brosnan had once worn to an awards show. (Episode 166: "The One With Rachel's Big Kiss")

92. toner. Earl (Jason Alexander) replied to Phoebe: "I don't need any toner because I'm going to kill myself." (Episode 159: "The One Where Rosita Dies")

93. Joey (Episode 162: "The One With the Truth About London")

94. Porsche. Jack Geller gave Monica his Porsche out of guilt for ruining the boxes that contained her childhood memories. (Episode 159: "The One Where Rosita Dies")

95. Making Joey a fake uncircumcised penis. "Off the top of my head, I'm thinking double-sided tape and some kind of luncheon meat," she continued. (Episode 165: "The One With Ross and Monica's Cousin")

96. tampon (Episode 166: "The One With Rachel's Big Kiss")

97. Helena Handbasket. (Episode 168: "The One With Chandler's Dad")

98. Phoebe, who had been upset with Joey for blowing her off to go on a date. (Episode 157: "The One With All the Cheesecakes")

Multiple Choice 50

Which Friend is half Scottish?

A. Chandler
B. Ross
C. Rachel

99. Practical jokes. (Episode 162: "The One With the Truth About London")

100. Rachel's claim to making out with a sorority sister while drunk. (Episode 166: "The One With Rachel's Big Kiss")

101. How he wrote his wedding vows. (Episode 167: "The One With the Vows")

102. The older man who came to pick up his lost cell phone, which Phoebe and Rachel found at Central Perk. Rachel, clearly not enamored, took advantage of the situation: "All right, Phoebe. I will let you have him. But you owe me. You owe me big." (Episode 161: "The One With Joey's New Brain")

103. Jake, Phoebe's boyfriend, whom Joey spotted wearing Phoebe's underwear while he was bending over. (Episode 168: "The One With Chandler's Dad")

104. Ross and Rachel, who were out in the hall kissing the night she and Chandler got engaged. (Episode 147: "The One With Monica's Thunder")

105. Phoebe's grandma's chocolate chip cookie recipe. (Episode 149: "The One With Phoebe's Cookies")

106. Monica had slept with the groom. (Episode 157: "The One With All the Cheesecakes")

107. His hot cousin, Cassie (Denise Richards). (Episode 165: "The One With Ross and Monica's Cousin")

108. The cheesecake they swiped from outside their neighbor's door. (Episode 157: "The One With All the Cheesccakes")

109. Slap her in the face. (Episode 161: "The One With Joey's New Brain")

110. Taking a Polaroid of him. (Episode 150: "The One With Rachel's Assistant")

111. Janice, referring to his and Monica's marriage. (Episode 153: "The One With Ross's Library Book")

112. Porsche (Episode 159: "The One Where Rosita Dies")

113. Chandler's savings. (Episode 148: "The One With Rachel's Book")

114. A Soapie. (Episode 164: "The One With Joey's Award")

115. maid of honor (Episode 152: "The One With the Nap Partners")

☆ Even More Star Sightings ☆

+ Robin Williams [uncredited] (Tomas) "The One With the Ultimate Fighting Champion"

+ Christine Taylor (Bonnie) "The One With the Ultimate Fighting Champion"

+ Teri Garr (Phoebe Sr.) "The One at the Beach"

+ Penn Jillette (encyclopedia salesman) "The One With the Cuffs"

+ Rebecca Romijn-Stamos (Cheryl) "The One With the Dirty Girl"

+ Michael Vartan (Dr. Tim Burke) "The One With Chandler in a Box"

+ Tate Donovan (Joshua) "The One With Rachel's Crush"

+ Charlton Heston (himself) "The One With Joey's Dirty Day"

+ Helen Baxendale (Emily) "The One With Joey's Dirty Day"

+ Sarah Ferguson [aka Fergie] (herself) "The One With Ross's Wedding, Part 1"

+ Tom Conti (Stephen Waltham) "The One With Ross's Wedding"

- Jennifer Saunders (Andrea Waltham) "The One With Ross's Wedding"

- Gary Collins (himself) "The One Where Phoebe Hates PBS"

- George Newbern (Danny) "The One With the Yeti"

- Bob Balaban (Frank Sr.) "The One With Joey's Bag"

- Soleil Moon Frye (Katie) "The One With the Girl Who Hits Joey"

- Willie Garson (from NYPD Blue and Sex and the City) (Steve, president of the Tenant's Committee) "The One With the Girl Who Hits Joey"

- Michael Rapaport (Gary) "The One With the Cop"

- Joanna Gleason (Kim) "The One Where Rachel Smokes"

- Ron Glass (Ross's attorney) "The One Where Ross Hugs Rachel"

- Conchata Ferrell (Judge) "The One With Joey's Porsche"

- Elle Macpherson (Janine) "The One Where Phoebe Runs"

- Ralph Lauren (himself) "The One With Ross's Teeth"

- Patrick Bristow (stage manager) "The One With The Routine"

- Reese Witherspoon (Jill) "The One With Rachel's Sister"

116. World War I (Episodes 169 and 170: "The One With Monica and Chandler's Wedding—Parts 1 and 2")

117. That Chandler sat on Jack's lap in the steam room. (Episode 149: "The One With Phoebe's Cookies")

118. He was covering for Rachel after her boss read the performance evaluation she'd written for Tag's eyes only. (Episode 155: "The One With All the Candy")

119. Kissing Chandler. (Episode 162: "The One With the Truth About London")

120. Tag, whom she decided to hire as her assistant after already hiring Hilda. (Episode 150: "The One With Rachel's Assistant")

121. ministers (Episode 162: "The One With the Truth About London")

122. The smoke detector that was beeping all night. (Episode 158: "The One Where They're Up All Night")

123. maid of honor. Later, Phoebe defers to Rachel, saying, "Because I think it means more to you." (Episode 152: "The One With the Nap Partners")

124. drums. Chandler quips during the episode: "Hey, Pheebs, the next time you want to get Joey a Christmas present that disrupts the entire building, why not get him something more subtle, like a wrecking ball or a vial of smallpox to release in the hallway?" (Episode 156: "The One With the Holiday Armadillo")

125. Naming all fifty states. When having difficulty, Ross later said, "Okay, maybe this is so hard because there aren't fifty states!" (Episode 154: "The One Where Chandler Doesn't Like Dogs")

126. He bought a little red sports car. (Episode 160: "The One Where They All Turn Thirty")

127. dog (Episode 154: "The One Where Chandler Doesn't Like Dogs")

128. Tag, the hot guy with no experience who interviewed to be her assistant. (Episode 150: "The One With Rachel's Assistant")

129. Chandler, whom he was supposed to be keeping an eye on before his wedding. (Episodes 169 and 170: "The One With Monica and Chandler's Wedding—Parts 1 and 2")

130. leather pants (Episode 163: "The One With the Cheap Wedding Dress")

131. Mexican (Episode 161: "The One With Joey's New Brain")

132. deposit (Episode 147: "The One With Monica's Thunder")

133. His wedding day. (Episodes 169 and 170: "The One With Monica and Chandler's Wedding—Parts 1 and 2")

134. Joey trying to figure out a way to be uncircumcised after telling a casting director he wasn't circumcised. (Episode 165: "The One With Ross and Monica's Cousin")

135. The little red sports car he'd bought himself on his birthday, which had been tightly wedged between two other cars. (Episode 160: "The One Where They All Turn Thirty")

136. What Ross was playing on the bagpipes. (Episode 161: "The One With Joey's New Brain")

137. Ross wearing the tux Val Kilmer had supposedly worn in *Batman* to Monica and Chandler's wedding. (Episode 166: "The One With Rachel's Big Kiss")

138. Silly Putty. His homemade penis fell off during the audition when he pulled his pants down. (Episode 165: "The One With Ross and Monica's Cousin")

139. win (Episode 168: "The One With Chandler's Dad")

140. Melissa (Winona Ryder), her old sorority sister. (Episode 166: "The One With Rachel's Big Kiss")

141. The little baby outfit he bought for Monica on their wedding day when he thought she was pregnant. (Episodes 169 and 170: "The One With Monica and Chandler's Wedding—Parts 1 and 2")

Season Eight

1. The tennis outfit he wore to her wedding reception. (Episode 171: "The One After 'I Do' ")

2. Putting her head between her legs and looking at her crotch. (Episode 177: "The One With the Stain")

3. She found out Rachel had moved in with Ross. (Episode 185: "The One With the Birthing Video")

4. Mento (Episode 189: "The One With Joey's Interview")

5. Chandler told him that he and Monica were having problems as an excuse to not have to socialize with him. (Episode 181: "The One With Ross's Step Forward")

6. baby shower (Episode 190: "The One With the Baby Shower")

7. Jack, who was at the hospital while Rachel was having her baby. (Episodes 193 and 194: "The One Where Rachel Has a Baby— Parts 1 and 2")

8. The father of her imaginary baby. (Episode 171: "The One After 'I Do'")

9. Eric (Sean Penn), Ursula's fiancé, who mistook Phoebe for Ursula. (Episode 176: "The One With the Halloween Party")

10. The rumor back in high school that Rachel had a hint of a penis. (Episode 179: "The One With the Rumor")

11. Monica's expensive new boots. (Episode 180: "The One With Monica's Boots")

12. Her hiring a stripper to dance for Chandler. (Episode 178: "The One With the Strip- per")

13. toast (Episode 188: "The One in Massapequa")

14. Indiana Jones (Episode 191: "The One With the Cook- ing Class")

15. She was trying to reconnect with Joey after he began avoid- ing her after telling her he loved her. (Episode 187: "The One With the Tea Leaves")

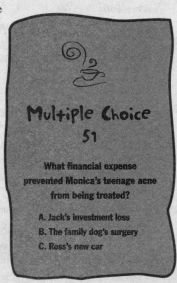

Multiple Choice
51

What financial expense prevented Monica's teenage acne from being treated?

A. Jack's investment loss
B. The family dog's surgery
C. Ross's new car

16. Rachel. (Episode 186: "The One Where Joey Tells Rachel")

17. Phoebo (Episode 183: "The One Where Chandler Takes a Bath")

18. The winner's initials for Ms. Pac-Man. (Episode 182: "The One Where Joey Dates Rachel")

19. Phoebe's explanation that being so hormonal during pregnancy was why she was so horny. (Episode 181: "The One With Ross's Step Forward")

20. Will (Brad Pitt), Monica and Ross's old high school friend who came for Thanksgiving dinner. (Episode 179: "The One With the Rumor")

21. Blursula (Episode 177: "The One With the Stain")

22. Mona, Ross's girlfriend. (Episode 176: "The One With the Halloween Party")

23. Trying to encourage Rachel not to show everyone the tape of the two of them having sex. (Episode 174: "The One With the Videotape")

24. The disposable cameras from their wedding reception. (Episode 172: "The One With the Red Sweater")

25. Phoebe. She initially said that Rachel wasn't pregnant just to see how Rachel really felt about it. (Episode 171: "The One After 'I Do' ")

26. Her baby on the sonogram picture. (Episode 173: "The One Where Rachel Tells Ross")

27. Breaking up with Monica's sous-chef, whom she was dating and Monica was about to fire. (Episode 175: "The One With Rachel's Date")

28. The hooker Monica mistakenly hired for Chandler's fake bachelor party. (Episode 178: "The One With the Stripper")

29. Joey's little sister, who asked him to introduce her to Rachel under the pretext of wanting to get into fashion. (Episode 180: "The One With Monica's Boots")

30. Getting to his new class on time. (Episode 182: "The One Where Joey Dates Rachel")

31. suicide (Episode 185: "The One With the Birthing Video")

32. baby (Episode 187: "The One With the Tea Leaves")

33. Bamboozle. (Episode 190: "The One With the Baby Shower")

34. Ross having sex with her to induce labor. (Episode 192: "The One Where Rachel Is Late")

35. deaf (Episodes 193 and 194: "The One Where Rachel Has a Baby—Parts 1 and 2")

36. Speedo; Speedo (Episode 173: "The One Where Rachel Tells Ross")

37. The Swing Kings. (Episode 171: "The One After 'I Do' ")

38. Greg and Jenny, the couple Monica and Chandler met while on their honeymoon. (Episode 174: "The One With the Videotape")

39. Charlie Brown. (Episode 176: "The One With the Halloween Party")

40. hermaphrodite (Episode 179: "The One With the Rumor")

41. The name Sandrine, which Rachel suggested naming their baby. (Episode 183: "The One Where Chandler Takes a Bath")

42. The birthing videotape titled *Candy and Cookie* he mistook for girl-on-girl porn. (Episode 185: "The One With the Birthing Video")

43. Parker (Alec Baldwin), Phoebe's zesty boyfriend. (Episode 188: "The One in Massapequa")

44. baby (Episode 190: "The One With the Baby Shower")

45. Her and Ross having sex to induce labor. (Episode 192: "The One Where Rachel Is Late")

Bits of Trivia

In "The One With Chandler's Dad," the snippy waiter at the drag show is played by Courteney Cox's brother-in-law, Alexis Arquette.

46. Ms. Pac-Man. (Episode 182: "The One Where Joey Dates Rachel")

47. His getting Rachel pregnant. (Episode 178: "The One With the Stripper")

48. The cleaning woman Chandler had hired. (Episode 177: "The One With the Stain")

49. Rachel, referring to the story she used to get Ross to sleep with her. (Episode 174: "The One With the Videotape")

50. Phoebe's maternity pants. (Episode 179: "The One With the Rumor")

51. Trudie Styler, whose son was not getting along with Ben at school. (Episode 180: "The One With Monica's Boots")

52. Taking a bubble bath. (Episode 183: "The One Where Chandler Takes a Bath")

53. Phoebe was enjoying them too much. (Episode 184: "The One With the Secret Closet")

54. Toby (Episode 175: "The One With Rachel's Date")

55. number (Episode 174: "The One With the Videotape")

56. Rachel, who planned to tell the father of her baby that he was going to be a father. (Episode 172: "The One With the Red Sweater")

57. The hooker Monica mistakenly hired for Chandler's fake bachelor party. (Episode 178: "The One With the Stripper")

58. What life would be like without Monica, after his boss took him out to a strip club. (Episode 181: "The One With Ross's Step Forward")

59. cheese (Episode 186: "The One Where Joey Tells Rachel")

60. The breast pump she got as a shower gift. (Episode 190: "The One With the Baby Shower")

61. The disgustingly happy couple who were waiting in the labor room with Rachel. (Episodes 193 and 194: "The One Where Rachel Has a Baby—Parts 1 and 2")

62. Thinking she wasn't really pregnant. (Episode 171: "The One After 'I Do' ")

63. Pottery Barn (Episode 173: "The One Where Rachel Tells Ross")

64. fire (Episode 175: "The One With Rachel's Date")

65. Brenda, the cleaning woman, who thought both Chandler and Monica had made passes at her. (Episode 177: "The One With the Stain")

66. The really expensive new boots she'd bought. (Episode 180: "The One With Monica's Boots")

67. bath (Episode 183: "The One Where Chandler Takes a Bath")

68. Ross's favorite pink shirt. (Episode 187: "The One With the Tea Leaves")

Multiple Choice 52

Why does Phoebe pretend to be Ben's mother?

A. To obtain tickets for a concert
B. To impress her new boyfriend
C. To fulfill an inner need

69. Monica and Joey. (Episode 191: "The One With the Cooking Class")

70. How the woman she shared her labor room with got to have her baby first. (Episodes 193 and 194: "The One Where Rachel Has a Baby—Parts 1 and 2")

71. Giving Mona his apartment key to get out of having to talk about where their relationship was going. (Episode 181: "The One With Ross's Step Forward")

72. Ross's talking to the baby. (Episode 180: "The One With Monica's Boots")

73. In the hospital, while Rachel was having her baby. (Episodes 193 and 194: "The One Where Rachel Has a Baby—Parts 1 and 2")

74. meat (Episode 179: "The One With the Rumor")

75. Arm wrestling Ross. (Episode 176: "The One With the Halloween Party")

76. Rachel's sonogram picture. (Episode 174: "The One With the Videotape")

77. Janice appeared in Rachel's labor room. (Episodes 193 and 194: "The One Where Rachel Has a Baby—Parts 1 and 2")

78. testicles (Episode 188: "The One in Massapequa")

79. dog (Episode 185: "The One With the Birthing Video")

80. hooker (Episode 178: "The One With the Stripper")

81. The tape of Ross and Rachel having sex. (Episode 174: "The One With the Videotape")

82. Muriel (Episode 175: "The One With Rachel's Date")

83. Eric (Sean Penn), Ursula's ex-fiancé, who was taking out his contact lenses so he wouldn't be reminded of Ursula when he looked at Phoebe. (Episode 177: "The One With the Stain")

84. Its clawlike appearance after he played Ms. Pac-Man for eight hours. (Episode 182: "The One Where Joey Dates Rachel")

85. In Monica and Chandler's bathroom while Chandler was taking a bath. (Episode 183: "The One Where Chandler Takes a Bath")

86. massage (Episode 184: "The One With the Secret Closet")

87. trots (Episode 187: "The One With the Tea Leaves")

88. Baby Girl Green, whom Ross wanted to name Delilah. (Episodes 193 and 194: "The One Where Rachel Has a Baby—Parts 1 and 2")

89. Sting (Episode 180: "The One With Monica's Boots")

90. doody (Episode 176: "The One With the Halloween Party")

91. She didn't like his suggestion to name their baby Ruth. (Episode 183: "The One Where Chandler Takes a Bath")

92. Fred Sanford (Episode 184: "The One With the Secret Closet")

93. She laughed. She thought he was kidding. (Episode 186: "The One Where Joey Tells Rachel")

94. gal pal (Episode 189: "The One With Joey's Interview")

95. How she was doing while in labor. (Episodes 193 and 194: "The One Where Rachel Has a Baby—Parts 1 and 2")

96. Ross, referring to the game show game the two played to help Joey prepare for an audition. (Episode 190: "The One With the Baby Shower")

97. Rachel's boss, whom Rachel lied about wanting to buy her baby so Joey would talk to her. (Episode 187: "The One With the Tea Leaves")

98. Eric (Sean Penn), Ursula's fiancé, whom Ursula lied to about being in the Peace Corps. (Episode 176: "The One With the Halloween Party")

99. Joey. He uses that fake name when he doesn't want to give people his real name. (Episode 174: "The One With the Videotape")

100. had sex (Episodes 193 and 194: "The One Where Rachel Has a Baby—Parts 1 and 2")

101. pure evil (Episode 192: "The One Where Rachel Is Late")

102. closet (Episode 184: "The One With the Secret Closet")

103. condom (Episode 173: "The One Where Rachel Tells Ross")

104. Phoebe saying that Monica was pregnant. (Episode 171: "The One After 'I Do' ")

105. Greg and Jenny, the couple Monica and Chandler had met on their honeymoon, had given them a fake phone number. (Episode 174: "The One With the Videotape")

106. Monica's wanting to prove that the cleaning woman had stolen her jeans. (Episode 177: "The One With the Stain")

Bits of Trivia

In "The One Where Rachel Tells Ross," originally shot before 9/11, Chandler and Monica couldn't get on their flight for their honeymoon because Chandler said the word "bomb" in the airport. After 9/11, the story was rewritten and re-shot.

107. The joint holiday card with their photo she planned to order. (Episode 181: "The One With Ross's Step Forward")

108. What she wanted the doctor to do to get her baby out. (Episodes 193 and 194: "The One Where Rachel Has a Baby—Parts 1 and 2")

109. toast (Episode 188: "The One in Massapequa")

110. The Ms. Pac-Man machine she bought for Monica and Chandler. (Episode 182: "The One Where Joey Dates Rachel")

111. bastard (Episode 178: "The One With the Stripper")

112. Chandler, whose coworker thinks his name is Toby. (Episode 175: "The One With Rachel's Date")

113. key (Episode 173: "The One Where Rachel Tells Ross")

114. Tag, who she thought was the father of Rachel's baby. (Episode 172: "The One With the Red Sweater")

115. Rachel. (Episode 186: "The One Where Joey Tells Rachel")

116. kangaroo (Episode 192: "The One Where Rachel Is Late")

117. That she makes sex noises during massages. (Episode 184: "The One With the Secret Closet")

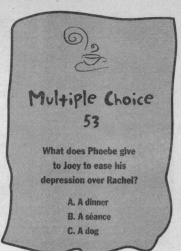

Multiple Choice 53

What does Phoebe give to Joey to ease his depression over Rachel?

A. A dinner
B. A séance
C. A dog

118. Phoebo (Episode 183: "The One Where Chandler Takes a Bath")

119. The color of his favorite pink shirt. (Episode 187: "The One With the Tea Leaves")

120. Joey, who was practicing for his game show host audition with Ross and Chandler. (Episode 190: "The One With the Baby Shower")

121. The reliability of condoms. (Episode 173: "The One Where Rachel Tells Ross")

122. Ross (Episode 176: "The One With the Halloween Party")

123. peed (Episode 171: "The One After 'I Do' ")

124. That Rachel had both male and female reproductive parts. (Episode 179: "The One With the Rumor")

125. Joey, whose name was in a crossword puzzle in *Soap Opera Digest*. (Episode 189: "The One With Joey's Interview")

126. Baby names Monica had picked out since she was fourteen. (Episodes 193 and 194: "The One Where Rachel Has a Baby—Parts 1 and 2")

127. Ross, referring to the red sweater he'd left behind after sleeping with Rachel and getting her pregnant. (Episode 172: "The One With the Red Sweater")

Season Nine

1. Her father seeing the two of them having sex in a broom closet at the hospital. (Episode 195: "The One Where No One Proposes")

2. That Monica was going to eat him. (Episode 197: "The One With the Pediatrician")

3. He wanted her to stay away from him because he'd smoked. (Episode 199: "The One With Phoebe's Birthday Dinner")

4. The videotape he found in Richard's apartment with Monica's name on it. (Episode 201: "The One With Ross's Inappropriate Song")

5. Going back into Ross's apartment, after spending the most boring evening of his life. (Episode 203: "The One With Rachel's Phone Number")

6. Oklahoma (Episode 204: "The One With Christmas in Tulsa")

7. pediatrician (Episode 197: "The One With the Pediatrician")

8. muffin (Episode 196: "The One Where Emma Cries")

9. sharks (Episode 198: "The One With the Sharks")

10. Sandy (Freddie Prinze Jr.), the male nanny who cried easily. (Episode 200: "The One With the Male Nanny")

11. sushi (Episode 202: "The One With Rachel's Other Sister")

12. The dude he thought Monica was having an affair with. (Episode 203: "The One With Rachel's Phone Number")

13. Mike, the guy Joey met at the last minute to set up with Phoebe. (Episode 197: "The One With the Pediatrician")

14. Ross's making air quotes. (Episode 196: "The One Where Emma Cries")

15. danglers (Episode 198: "The One With the Sharks")

16. A nanny interviewee, who requested at least three days' notice if they did. (Episode 200: "The One With the Male Nanny")

17. Mike (Paul Rudd), her boyfriend, whose snooty parents she was trying to impress. (Episode 201: "The One With Ross's Inappropriate Song")

18. baby (Episode 202: "The One With Rachel's Other Sister")

19. ham (Episode 204: "The One With Christmas in Tulsa")

20. Ross firing Sandy, their male nanny. (Episode 200: "The One With the Male Nanny")

21. The painting on the wall of his date's apartment, which he'd realized he'd been in before. (Episode 198: "The One With the Sharks")

22. Paris (Episode 196: "The One Where Emma Cries")

23. Sandy, the male nanny she and Ross had just interviewed. (Episode 200: "The One With the Male Nanny")

24. boobies (Episode 202: "The One With Rachel's Other Sister")

25. His suitcase, which he didn't want Joey to see. (Episode 203: "The One With Rachel's Phone Number")

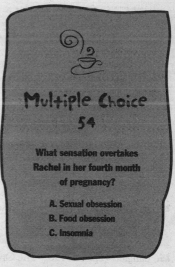

Multiple Choice 54

What sensation overtakes Rachel in her fourth month of pregnancy?

A. Sexual obsession

B. Food obsession

C. Insomnia

26. Ross's childhood pediatrician, whom Ross still saw as an adult. (Episode 197: "The One With the Pediatrician")

27. Ross, who saw Rachel wearing his grandmother's ring. (Episode 195: "The One Where No One Proposes")

28. Mike (Paul Rudd), Phoebe's blind date. (Episode 197: "The One With the Pediatrician")

29. Vikram, the imaginary long-term boyfriend Ross came up with after telling Mike, Phoebe's new boyfriend, that she'd never been in a long-term relationship. (Episode 198: "The One With the Sharks")

30. manny (Episode 200: "The One With the Male Nanny")

31. Queen of England (Episode 202: "The One With Rachel's Other Sister")

32. Her grandmother, who lived in the same building as Bill did. (Episode 203: "The One With Rachel's Phone Number")

33. Ding Dongs (Episode 199: "The One With Phoebe's Birthday Dinner")

34. Magic Marker (Episode 198: "The One With the Sharks")

35. Ross. (Episode 199: "The One With Phoebe's Birthday Dinner")

36. He rapped the Sir Mix-A-Lot song "Baby Got Back." (Episode 201: "The One With Ross's Inappropriate Song")

37. syphilis (Episode 202: "The One With Rachel's Other Sister")

38. protection (Episode 203: "The One With Rachel's Phone Number")

39. Wendy, his beautiful colleague who made a pass at him. (Episode 204: "The One With Christmas in Tulsa")

40. Richard, (Episode 201: "The One With Ross's Inappropriate Song")

41. Emma (Episode 199: "The One With Phoebe's Birthday Dinner")

42. Dr. Weiner. (Episode 197: "The One With the Pediatrician")

43. propose (Episode 195: "The One Where. No One Proposes")

44. He shouted the name "Mike" in the middle of Central Perk. (Episode 197: "The One With the Pediatrician")

45. Sharks, which Monica walked in on him watching in his Tulsa hotel room while Chandler was "getting himself off." (Episode 198: "The One With the Sharks")

46. penis model (Episode 200: "The One With the Male Nanny")

47. Phoebe, who was trying to impress her boyfriend's snooty parents. (Episode 201: "The One With Ross's Inappropriate Song")

48. strings (Episode 202: "The One With Rachel's Other Sister")

Bits of Trivia

During the theme song of season five's opener, rather than the usual montage of clips of episodes past, the producers took the opportunity to recount what happened in the season four finale through a montage of clips from that episode alone. Clever.

49. His divorce, which Ross was trying to use as a conversation starter. (Episode 203: "The One With Rachel's Phone Number")

50. sock; sock; sock (Episode 199: "The One With Phoebe's Birthday Dinner")

51. Her calling the pediatrician because Emma had the hiccups. (Episode 197: "The One With the Pediatrician")

52. David the Scientist Guy, who was in town and stopped by to see Phoebe. (Episode 200: "The One With the Male Nanny")

53. Mike (Paul Rudd), her boyfriend, whose father she was trying to impress by complimenting his physique. (Episode 201: "The One With Ross's Inappropriate Song")

54. condom (Episode 202: "The One With Rachel's Other Sister")

55. He thought Monica was cheating on him while he was in Tulsa. (Episode 203: "The One With Rachel's Phone Number")

56. Wendy, his hot colleague, who made a pass at him. (Episode 204: "The One With Christmas in Tulsa")

57. He agreed unknowingly after falling asleep during a meeting at work. (Episode 196: "The One Where Emma Cries")

58. Phoebe's imaginary long-term boyfriend Ross came up with after telling Mike, her new boyfriend, that she'd never been in a long-term relationship. (Episode 198: "The One With the Sharks")

59. The maitre d' at her new restaurant. (Episode 200: "The One With the Male Nanny")

60. She was about to rap "Baby Got Back" to make Emma laugh. (Episode 201: "The One With Ross's Inappropriate Song")

61. The last time he looked at her breasts, Emma was conceived. (Episode 203: "The One With Rachel's Phone Number")

62. Monica's paranoia about Chandler and his beautiful colleague working alone together, right after she made a pass at him. (Episode 204: "The One With Christmas in Tulsa")

63. already slept with her (Episode 198: "The One With the Sharks")

64. gay (Episode 196: "The One Where Emma Cries")

65. propose (Episode 195: "The One Where No One Proposes")

66. peach (Episode 199: "The One With Phoebe's Birthday Dinner")

67. Forgetting he was supposed to be in the Thanksgiving Day parade with the other stars of *Days of Our Lives*. (Episode 202: "The One With Rachel's Other Sister")

68. ring (Episode 195: "The One Where No One Proposes")

69. A sex video with Monica. (Episode 201: "The One With Ross's Inappropriate Song")

70. Oklahoma (Episode 204: "The One With Christmas in Tulsa")

71. rubella (Episode 197: "The One With the Pediatrician")

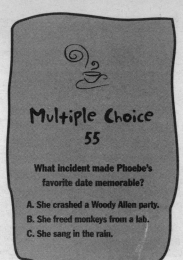

Multiple Choice
55

What incident made Phoebe's favorite date memorable?

A. She crashed a Woody Allen party.
B. She freed monkeys from a lab.
C. She sang in the rain.

72. His dad's gas. (Episode 195: "The One Where No One Proposes")

73. She was offered a head chef job in New York. (Episode 196: "The One Where Emma Cries")

74. helium (Episode 206: "The One With Phoebe's Rats")

75. scarf (Episode 207: "The One Where Monica Sings")

76. Amy, Rachel's sister, who expected to become Emma's godmother. (Episode 202: "The One With Rachel's Other Sister")

77. Richard Dreyfuss (Episode 205: "The One Where Rachel Goes Back to Work")

78. Monica was ovulating, they wanted to have sex, and Emma kept crying every time they left the room. (Episode 208: "The One With the Blind Date")

79. fake it (Episode 205: "The One Where Rachel Goes Back to Work")

80. He drank a lot of fluids beforehand so he would have to pee really bad. (Episode 209: "The One With the Mugging")

81. Bob. (Episode 206: "The One With Phoebe's Rats")

82. "Delta Dawn." (Episode 207: "The One Where Monica Sings")

83. His leaving for Tulsa. (Episode 197: "The One With the Pediatrician")

84. boy (Episode 205: "The One Where Rachel Goes Back to Work")

85. Molly, Ross and Rachel's hot new nanny. (Episode 206: "The One With Phoebe's Rats")

86. He plucked his father's and his father's "business associates' " eyebrows. (Episode 207: "The One Where Monica Sings")

87. He didn't ever want to get married again and she did. (Episode 210: "The One With the Boob Job")

88. Huggsy. (Episode 211: "The One With the Memorial Service")

89. Chandler, who was thinking about a career in advertising (Episode 205: "The One Where Rachel Goes Back to Work")

90. Rodeo clown. (Episode 207: "The One Where Monica Sings")

91. Gavin Mitchell. (Episode 206: "The One With Phoebe's Rats")

92. They tried to set each of them up on bad blind dates so they'd realize how good they had it with each other. (Episode 208: "The One With the Blind Date")

93. He told Chandler she borrowed the money for a boob job. (Episode 210: "The One With the Boob Job")

94. He wanted to see how many of his old college classmates would show up after Chandler posted Ross's sudden death on their alumni Web site. (Episode 211: "The One With the Memorial Service")

95. Joey's one plucked eyebrow. (Episode 207: "The One Where Monica Sings")

96. To come up with an ad campaign for a pair of sneakers. (Episode 209: "The One With the Mugging")

97. She was playing a nurse on *Days of Our Lives*, where he was used to hitting on the extras. (Episode 205: "The One Where Rachel Goes Back to Work")

98. Sandy, their male nanny. (Episode 200: "The One With the Male Nanny")

99. fossil brush (Episode 207: "The One Where Monica Sings")

100. She mugged him. (Episode 209: "The One With the Mugging")

101. puppy; puppy; puppy (Episode 205: "The One Where Rachel Goes Back to Work")

102. burned alive (Episode 207: "The One Where Monica Sings")

103. divorced (Episode 203: "The One With Rachel's Phone Number")

104. A scarf. (Episode 206: "The One With Phoebe's Rats")

105. Richard's apartment (Episode 201: "The One With Ross's Inappropriate Song")

106. "We Are the Champions." (Episode 207: "The One Where Monica Sings")

107. Giving birth to her brother's triplets. (Episode 206: "The One With Phoebe's Rats")

Bits of Trivia

In "The One With Rachel's Crush," Tate Donovan plays the object of Rachel's affection; he was actually Jennifer Aniston's boyfriend in real life at the time of the taping.

108. He was trying to convince his boss that he wasn't too mature for an assistant position. (Episode 212: "The One With the Lottery")

109. *Days of Our Lives* (Episode 214: "The One With the Soap Opera Party")

110. uterus (Episode 216: "The One With the Donor")

111. Curious George (Episodes 217 and 218: "The One in Barbados—Parts 1 and 2")

112. Zack, a friend from work whom he thought would make a great sperm donor. (Episode 216: "The One With the Donor")

113. Ross. (Episode 212: "The One With the Lottery")

114. laugh (Episode 208: "The One With the Blind Date")

115. Gliba. (Episode 212: "The One with the Lottery")

116. She recognized Phoebe's new shoes. (Episode 215: "The One With the Fertility Test")

117. Javu. (Episode 213: "The One With Rachel's Dream")

118. David the Scientist Guy. (Episode 216: "The One With the Donor")

119. He'd tell Rachel they were having sex while they were supposed to be watching Emma. (Episode 208: "The One With the Blind Date")

120. carcasses (Episode 212: "The One With the Lottery")

121. Her gift certificate for a massage at a corporate massage chain. (Episode 215: "The One With the Fertility Test")

122. A virus wiped out everything on his computer while Chandler was checking his e-mail. (Episodes 217 and 218: "The One in Barbados—Parts 1 and 2")

123. Professor Charlie Wheeler (Aisha Tyler). (Episode 214: "The One With the Soap Opera Party")

124. maple candy (Episode 213: "The One With Rachel's Dream")

125. Steve, the blind date with whom Phoebe set her up so she'd see how good she had it with Ross. (Episode 208: "The One With the Blind Date")

126. The extra lottery tickets she secretly bought for Chandler and herself in case the gang didn't win the pool. (Episode 212: "The One With the Lottery")

127. Joey, who told everyone he had to go to bed early that night so he could host a *Days of Our Lives* party while the others were at a play. (Episode 214: "The One With the Soap Opera Party")

128. Eight years. (Episode 216: "The One With the Donor")

129. Chandler, who took over for Monica after she whacked her hand. (Episodes 217 and 218: "The One in Barbados—Parts 1 and 2")

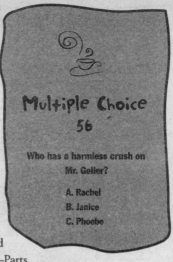

Multiple Choice
56

Who has a harmless crush on Mr. Geller?

A. Rachel
B. Janice
C. Phoebe

130. hair (Episodes 217 and 218: "The One in Barbados—Parts 1 and 2")

131. Charlie, his new girlfriend, who chose him over Ross. (Episode 215: "The One With the Fertility Test")

132. Her sudden attraction to Joey. (Episode 213: "The One With Rachel's Dream")

133. lips (Episode 212: "The One With the Lottery")

134. Ross, whom Chandler and Phoebe wanted to set up on a bad date so he'd see how good he had it with Rachel. (Episode 208: "The One With the Blind Date")

135. His secret *Days of Our Lives* Party. (Episode 214: "The One With the Soap Opera Party")

136. sperm donor (Episode 216: "The One With the Donor")

137. advice (Episodes 217 and 218: "The One in Barbados—Parts 1 and 2")

138. Mike, who flew down to ask Phoebe to marry him. (Episodes 217 and 218: "The One in Barbados—Parts 1 and 2")

Bits of Trivia

Jon Lovitz makes two appearances on *Friends* as Steve, once during the first season in "The One With the Stoned Guy" and then in the ninth season in "The One With the Blind Date." Interestingly enough, Rachel doesn't seem to remember him being at their apartment stoned years before being set up on a blind date with him by Phoebe.

Season Ten

1. Atkins (Episodes 235 and 236: "The Last One—Parts 1 and 2")

2. They're warm, nice people with big hearts. (Episode 223: "The One Where Rachel's Sister Babysits")

3. shmooprint (Episode 229: "The One Where the Stripper Cries")

4. She had an awful French accent. (Episodes 235 and 236: "The Last One—Parts 1 and 2")

5. Mississippily (Episode 221: "The One With Ross's Tan")

6. They went to a Rangers game. (Episode 226: "The One With the Late Thanksgiving")

7. my family dog, Chappy (Episode 230: "The One With Phoebe's Wedding")

8. To rescue the chick and duck, who got stuck in there. (Episodes 235 and 236: "The Last One—Parts 1 and 2")

9. interview (Episode 224: "The One With Ross's Grant")

10. Monica's new cornrows with shells on the ends. (Episode 219: "The One After Joey and Rachel Kiss")

11. The conclusion of *Melrose Place*. (Episode 234: "The One With Rachel's Going Away Party")

12. poop (Episode 231: "The One Where Joey Speaks French")

13. balls (Episode 223: "The One Where Rachel's Sister Babysits")

14. The recommendation letter that he wrote on Monica and Chandler's behalf to the adoption agency. (Episode 223: "The One Where Rachel's Sister Babysits")

15. swings (Episode 225: "The One With the Home Study")

16. Erica the birth mother, who was explaining why she wasn't absolutely certain who the father was. (Episode 231: "The One Where Joey Speaks French")

17. special place (Episode 230: "The One With Phoebe's Wedding")

18. Steel drums. (Episode 230: "The One With Phoebe's Wedding")

19. Westchester. (Episode 228: "The One Where Chandler Gets Caught")

20. One of his triplets. (Episode 220: "The One Where Ross Is Fine")

21. She ate his French fries. (Episode 227: "The One With the Birth Mother")

22. People using air quotes to describe his band. (Episode 229: "The One Where the Stripper Cries")

23. Sex with Rachel. (Episode 231: "The One Where Joey Speaks French")

24. The possible father of her baby. (Episode 231: "The One Where Joey Speaks French")

25. The stripper (Danny Devito) at Phoebe's bachelorette party. (Episode 229: "The One Where the Stripper Cries")

26. latex (Episode 224: "The One With Ross's Grant")

27. A baby to adopt. (Episode 220: "The One Where Ross Is Fine")

28. Charlie, whom she (along with Chandler and Monica) overheard kissing Ross when she was supposed to be with Joey. (Episode 219: "The One After Joey and Rachel Kiss")

29. Her father, who had just had a heart attack. (Episode 231: "The One Where Joey Speaks French")

30. pec (Episode 223: "The One Where Rachel's Sister Babysits")

31. They took Emma to a beauty pageant. (Episode 226: "The One With the Late Thanksgiving")

32. The ice sculpture for Mike and Phoebe's wedding. (Episode 230: "The One With Phoebe's Wedding")

33. She got Emma's ears pierced. (Episode 223: "The One Where Rachel's Sister Baby-sits")

34. Brussels sprouts. (Episode 226: "The One With the Late Thanksgiving")

Bits of Trivia

In the final episode of *Friends*, the extras in the airport, on the plane, and in the apartment were members of the crew and family and friends of the cast and producers.

35. penis (Episode 222: "The One With the Cake")

36. Donny Osmond (Episode 229: "The One Where the Stripper Cries")

37. He forgot to buy Emma a birthday gift. (Episode 222: "The One With the Cake")

38. cakes (Episode 222: "The One With the Cake")

39. hair (Episode 225: "The One With the Home Study")

40. Charlie (Episode 219: "The One After Joey and Rachel Kiss")

41. To get back together with her ex-boyfriend Benjamin Hobart. (Episode 224: "The One With Ross's Grant")

42. sex (Episode 221: "The One With Ross's Tan")

43. ice sculpture (Episode 230: "The One With Phoebe's Wedding")

44. Ross promised to take Rachel's boss's son to the Museum of Natural History after hours. (Episode 233: "The One Where Estelle Dies")

45. Mike, to Phoebe, referring to his girlfriend, with whom he was about to break up. (Episode 219: "The One After Joey and Rachel Kiss")

46. Her not asking Ross and Chandler to be in her and Mike's wedding. (Episode 230: "The One With Phoebe's Wedding")

47. 32C. (Episodes 235 and 236: "The Last One—Parts 1 and 2")

48. Janice. (Episode 233: "The One Where Estelle Dies")

49. She caught her hair in the swings. (Episode 225: "The One With the Home Study")

50. Which is worse: going through labor or getting kicked in the nuts? (Episodes 235 and 236: "The Last One—Parts 1 and 2")

51. MacKenzie. (Episode 232: "The One With Princess Consuela")

52. The DustBuster she was using to clean up her vacuum cleaner. (Episode 228: "The One Where Chandler Gets Caught")

53. peepees (Episode 229: "The One Where the Stripper Cries")

54. Ichiban lipstick for men. (Episode 224: "The One With Ross's Grant")

55. Ross, who really wasn't fine after he walked in on Joey and Rachel kissing. (Episode 220: "The One Where Ross Is Fine")

56. adopted (Episode 220: "The One Where Ross Is Fine")

57. Rachel's father. (Episode 231: "The One Where Joey Speaks French")

58. Jack and Erica. (Episodes 235 and 236: "The Last One—Parts 1 and 2")

59. Monica to Chandler, after discovering their potential birth mother mistook her for a reverend. (Episode 227: "The One With the Birth Mother")

60. purple (Episodes 235 and 236: "The Last One—Parts 1 and 2")

61. British (Episode 221: "The One With Ross's Tan")

62. He told her he still loved her and wanted to pick up where they had left off. (Episode 233: "The One Where Estelle Dies")

63. vagina (Episodes 235 and 236: "The Last One—Parts 1 and 2")

64. Way, No Way. (Episode 229: "The One Where the Stripper Cries")

65. A chick and a duck. (Episodes 235 and 236: "The Last One—Parts 1 and 2")

66. Her sculpture of a woman coming out of a frame, which Mike wouldn't let her keep after he moved in. (Episode 224: "The One With Ross's Grant")

67. Rachel related Phoebe's fear to the guy sitting next to her that there was something wrong with the left phalange. (Episodes 235 and 236: "The Last One—Parts 1 and 2")

68. Chandler found compromising pictures of Nana using fur-lined handcuffs. (Episode 234: "The One With Rachel's Going Away Party")

69. six (Episode 220: "The One Where Ross Is Fine")

70. Her father, who was in the hospital after having a heart attack. (Episode 231: "The One Where Joey Speaks French")

71. She took it off Joey's Cabbage Patch Kid. (Episode 226: "The One With the Late Thanksgiving")

72. Emma's birthday cake. (Episode 222: "The One With the Cake")

73. Mike's idea to propose to her on the big screen at a Knicks game. (Episode 223: "The One Where Rachel's Sister Babysits")

74. Erica. (Episode 227: "The One With the Birth Mother")

75. The decision whether to give up sex or dinosaurs. (Episode 228: "The One Where Chandler Gets Caught")

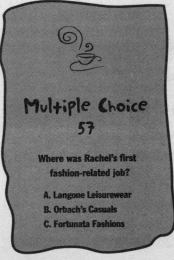

Multiple Choice 57

Where was Rachel's first fashion-related job?

A. Langone Leisurewear
B. Orbach's Casuals
C. Fortunata Fashions

76. "Ebony and Ivory" (Episode 221: "The One With Ross's Tan")

77. *Pyramid*. (Episode 229: "The One Where the Stripper Cries")

78. spelling bee (Episode 226: "The One With the Late Thanksgiving")

79. Crap Bag. (Episode 232: "The One With Princess Consuela")

80. Emma (Episode 222: "The One With the Cake")

81. birthday (Episode 219: "The One After Joey and Rachel Kiss")

82. The guy at the children's center, where the two of them returned to get back the donation they'd made earlier. (Episode 225: "The One With the Home Study")

83. Mike's girlfriend, whom he was still dating when he and Phoebe got back together. (Episode 219: "The One After Joey and Rachel Kiss")

84. Her boss was sitting at the next table during her lunch interview with Gucci. (Episode 232: "The One With Princess Consuela")

85. Mark. (Episode 232: "The One With Princess Consuela")

86. Ross. (Episodes 235 and 236: "The Last One—Parts 1 and 2")

87. 1991. (Episode 229: "The One Where the Stripper Cries")

88. Princess Consuela Bananahammock. (Episode 232: "The One With Princess Counsuela")

89. Fajitas. (Episode 220: "The One Where Ross Is Fine")

90. Rachel, to Ross, who wouldn't sleep with her because he knew she was feeling vulnerable after her father had had a heart attack. (Episode 231: "The One Where Joey Speaks French")

91. cornrows (Episode 219: "The One After Joey and Rachel Kiss")

92. Erica, the potential birth mother Monica and Chandler were meeting, who got the wrong information after a paperwork mix-up. (Episode 227: "The One With the Birth Mother")

93. falafel (Episode 223: "The One Where Rachel's Sister Babysits")

94. Gladys, the ugly woman coming out of the frame that Phoebe made. (Episode 224: "The One With Ross's Grant")

Bits of Trivia

While Phoebe was pregnant with Frank Jr.'s triplets during season four, Lisa Kudrow was pregnant in real life.

95. Realtor (Episode 228: "The One Where Chandler Gets Caught")

96. Alicia May Emmery. (Episode 226: "The One With the Late Thanksgiving")

97. Rachel's mother, who kept Emma while Ross and Rachel were in Barbados. (Episode 219: "The One After Joey and Rachel Kiss")

98. olives (Episode 234: "The One With Rachel's Going Away Party")

99. food (Episode 227: "The One With the Birth Mother")

100. *Sex For Dummies.* (Episodes 235 and 236: "The Last One—Parts 1 and 2")

101. He was having a hard time deciding whether to give up food or sex. (Episode 228: "The One Where Chandler Gets Caught")

102. Styrofoam peanuts (Episode 234: "The One With Rachel's Going Away Party")

103. *Dr. Phil* (Episode 226: "The One With the Late Thanksgiving")

104. A cotton swab with her spit on it, in case the French perfected the cloning process while Rachel was in France. (Episode 234: "The One With Rachel's Going Away Party")

105. Joey's reel of commercial work. (Episode 224: "The One With Ross's Grant")

106. testicles (Episode 222: "The One With the Cake")

107. Fur-lined handcuffs. (Episode 234: "The One With Rachel's Going Away Party")

MULTIPLE CHOICE ANSWERS

1. A	**16.** C	**31.** C	**46.** B
2. A	**17.** A	**32.** B	**47.** C
3. C	**18.** C	**33.** A	**48.** A
4. A	**19.** C	**34.** C	**49.** C
5. B	**20.** B	**35.** A	**50.** A
6. C	**21.** A	**36.** A	**51.** B
7. B	**22.** B	**37.** C	**52.** A
8. C	**23.** C	**38.** B	**53.** C
9. A	**24.** A	**39.** A	**54.** A
10. C	**25.** A	**40.** A	**55.** B
11. A	**26.** C	**41.** B	**56.** C
12. A	**27.** A	**42.** A	**57.** C
13. C	**28.** B	**43.** C	
14. B	**29.** A	**44.** C	
15. B	**30.** A	**45.** A	

The Part
WITH THE
Episode Guide

Season One

EPISODE 1: "THE PILOT"

This is the one where it all began. . . . Rachel leaves Barry at the altar, meets the gang, and moves in with Monica. Monica, meanwhile, sleeps with Paul the Wine Guy.

Original airdate: September 22, 1994

EPISODE 2: "THE ONE WITH THE SONOGRAM AT THE END"

This is the one where Ross finds out Carol's pregnant, Monica nearly has a breakdown when her parents come for dinner, and Rachel finds out that Barry and maid of honor Mindy went on *her* honeymoon.

Original airdate: September 29, 1994

EPISODE 3: "THE ONE WITH THE THUMB"

This is the one where everyone likes Monica's new boyfriend way more than she does, Chandler starts smoking again, and Phoebe finds a thumb in a can of soda.

Original airdate: October 6, 1994

EPISODE 4: "THE ONE WITH GEORGE STEPHANOPOULOS"

This is the one where Ross mourns the anniversary of losing his virginity to Carol, Rachel gets her first paycheck, the girls have a slumber party, and George Stephanopoulos's pizza is delivered to Monica by mistake.

Original airdate: October 13, 1994

EPISODE 5: "THE ONE WITH THE EAST GERMAN LAUNDRY DETERGENT"

This is the one where Joey tries to make an old girlfriend jealous and tricks Monica into posing as his new girlfriend, Ross teaches Rachel how to do laundry, and Chandler recruits Phoebe to break up with Janice for him.

Original airdate: October 20, 1994

EPISODE 6: "THE ONE WITH THE BUTT"

Joey's hired to be Al Pacino's butt double, Chandler becomes a boy-toy, and Monica tries to convince everyone she's not anal.

Original airdate: October 27, 1994

EPISODE 7: "THE ONE WITH THE BLACKOUT"

There's a blackout in the city, Chandler gets stuck in an ATM vestibule with Jill Goodacre, and Ross almost tells Rachel how he feels about her, but not before Paolo enters their lives.

Original airdate: November 3, 1994

EPISODE 8: "THE ONE WHERE NANA DIES TWICE"

Nana dies twice, Monica and her mother come to an understanding, Ross falls into an empty grave, and everyone at Chandler's office thinks he's gay.

Original airdate: November 10, 1994

EPISODE 9: "THE ONE WHERE UNDERDOG GETS AWAY"

Monica burns her first Thanksgiving dinner as the Underdog balloon gets away, Joey becomes a poster boy for VD, and Ross sings to his unborn child.

Original airdate: November 17, 1994

EPISODE 10: "THE ONE WITH THE MONKEY"

Everyone breaks their pact to celebrate New Year's Eve without dates, Ross gets a monkey who throws feces, and Phoebe meets David the Scientist Guy.

Original airdate: December 15, 1994

EPISODE 11: "THE ONE WITH MRS. BING"

Chandler's romance novelist mother comes to town, Ross kisses her, and Monica and Phoebe fight over Coma Guy.

Original airdate: January 5, 1995

EPISODE 12: "THE ONE WITH THE DOZEN LASAGNAS"

Ross finds out he's having a boy, Paolo hits on Phoebe, and Chandler and Joey buy a foosball table.

Original airdate: January 12, 1995

EPISODE 13: "THE ONE WITH THE BOOBIES"

Chandler sees Rachel's boobies, Rachel sees Joey's pee-pee, Joey sees Monica's boobies, Monica sees Joey's dad's pee-pee, Joey meets his dad's mistress, and everyone hates Phoebe's new psychiatrist boyfriend.

Original airdate: January 19, 1995

EPISODE 14: "THE ONE WITH THE CANDY HEARTS"

Ross's first date in nine years is on Valentine's Day, Susan and Carol have dinner at the same restaurant, Joey sets Chandler up with a blind date who turns out to be Janice, and the girls have a boyfriend bonfire.

Original airdate: February 9, 1995

EPISODE 15: "THE ONE WITH THE STONED GUY"

Monica cooks for a stoned restaurateur, Chandler quits his job, Ross's date wants him to talk dirty to her, and Chandler gets hired back with a promotion.

Original airdate: February 16, 1995

EPISODE 16: "THE ONE WITH TWO PARTS—PART 1"

Joey dates Ursula (Phoebe's identical twin), Phoebe feels neglected, Chandler is told to fire a colleague he's attracted to but dates her instead, and Ross goes to Lamaze class.

Original airdate: February 23, 1995

EPISODE 17: "THE ONE WITH TWO PARTS—PART 2"

Rachel persuades Monica to switch identities so she can use her health insurance, Phoebe kisses Joey after Ursula breaks his heart, and two cute ER doctors ask Rachel and Monica out, but the girls can't keep their identities straight.

Original airdate: February 23, 1995

EPISODE 18: "THE ONE WITH ALL THE POKER"

Rachel has an interview at Saks Fifth Avenue, the girls learn to play poker, and Ross lets Rachel win after she doesn't get the job.

Original airdate: March 2, 1995

EPISODE 19: "THE ONE WHERE THE MONKEY GETS AWAY"

Marcel gets away while Rachel is supposed to be watching him, Animal Control shoots Phoebe in the ass with a dart, and Barry tells Rachel he's still in love with her.

Original airdate: March 9, 1995

EPISODE 20: "THE ONE WITH THE EVIL ORTHODONTIST"

Rachel starts sleeping with Barry again, Mindy asks Rachel to be her maid of honor, Rachel comes clean with Mindy, and Chandler waits by the phone.

Original airdate: April 6, 1995

EPISODE 21: "THE ONE WITH FAKE MONICA"

Monica's credit card is stolen and she then befriends Fake Monica, Joey tries out a new stage name with Chandler's help, Marcel reaches sexual maturity, and Ross tries to find him a zoo.

Original airdate: April 27, 1995

EPISODE 22: "THE ONE WITH THE ICK FACTOR"

Monica finds out she's just slept with a seventeen-year-old, Rachel has sex dreams about Joey and Chandler, and Phoebe temps for Chandler and finds out that no one at work likes him anymore.

Original airdate: May 4, 1995

EPISODE 23: "THE ONE WITH THE BIRTH"

Ross, Phoebe, and Susan get locked in a broom closet while Carol is in labor, Monica's biological clock begins to tick, Joey helps a stranger have a baby, and Rachel flirts with Carol's doctor.

Original airdate: May 11, 1995

EPISODE 24: "THE ONE WHERE RACHEL FINDS OUT"

Joey starts dating a woman while participating in a fertility study in which he can't have sex, Ross goes to China, Chandler lets it slip that Ross is in love with Rachel, and Ross returns from China with Julie while Rachel waits at the gate.

Original airdate: May 18, 1995

Season Two

EPISODE 25: "THE ONE WITH ROSS'S NEW GIRLFRIEND"

Rachel meets Julie, Phoebe gives Monica a bad haircut, and Joey learns his tailor is a very, very bad man.

Original airdate: September 21, 1995

EPISODE 26: "THE ONE WITH THE BREAST MILK"

Ross freaks out at the thought of drinking Carol's breast milk, Rachel gets mad that Monica and Julie are shopping together, and Joey has a showdown with the Hombré Man.

Original airdate: September 28, 1995

EPISODE 27: "THE ONE WHERE HECKLES DIES"

Mr. Heckles dies and leaves everything to Monica and Rachel, Chandler freaks out when he discovers how similar he and Mr. Heckles were, and Ross is astounded when Phoebe tells him she thinks evolution is a load of crap.

Original airdate: October 5, 1995

EPISODE 28: "THE ONE WITH PHOEBE'S HUSBAND"

Phoebe reveals she's married to a Canadian ice dancer, and Ross confides to Rachel that he and Julie haven't yet slept together and asks for her advice.

Original airdate: October 12, 1995

EPISODE 29: "THE ONE WITH FIVE STEAKS AND AN EGGPLANT"

Chandler takes advantage of a beautiful woman who got stood up by "Bob" (Chandler), and income issues divide the Friends until Monica gets fired from her job.

Original airdate: October 19, 1995

EPISODE 30: "THE ONE WITH THE BABY ON THE BUS"

Ross has an allergic reaction to kiwi, Chandler and Joey leave Ben on a bus, and Phoebe is replaced by a professional singer at Central Perk.

Original airdate: November 2, 1995

EPISODE 31: "THE ONE WHERE ROSS FINDS OUT"

Rachel leaves Ross a drunken message telling him she's over him, Monica appoints herself Chandler's personal trainer, and Phoebe's boyfriend won't sleep with her.

Original airdate: November 8, 1995

EPISODE 32: "THE ONE WITH THE LIST"

Monica gets a job creating recipes out of Mockolate, and Ross asks Joey and Chandler to help him decide between Rachel and Julie.

Original airdate: November 16, 1995

EPISODE 33: "THE ONE WITH PHOEBE'S DAD"

Phoebe finds out where her father lives and takes Joey and Chandler along for the ride, Monica and Rachel give homemade cookies for Christmas tips, and the girls' heater breaks just in time for their Christmas party.

Original airdate: December 14, 1995

EPISODE 34: "THE ONE WITH RUSS"

Monica gets back together with Fun Bobby and encourages him to stop drinking, Joey gets a part on *Days of Our Lives*, and Rachel dates a guy named Russ, who looks and sounds just like Ross.

Original airdate: January 4, 1996

EPISODE 35: "THE ONE WITH THE LESBIAN WEDDING"

Carol and Susan get married, Phoebe is inhabited by the spirit of an eighty-two-year-old woman, and Rachel's mom announces she's getting divorced from Rachel's father.

Original airdate: January 18, 1996

EPISODE 36: "THE ONE AFTER THE SUPER BOWL—PART 1"

Ross finds out Marcel is working in commercials, Joey goes out with a crazed fan, and Phoebe sings for children in a library.

Original airdate: January 28, 1996

EPISODE 37: "THE ONE AFTER THE SUPER BOWL—PART 2"

Monica and Rachel compete for Jean-Claude Van Damme, Chandler goes out with an old schoolmate who has revenge on her mind, and Ross is reunited with Marcel.

Original airdate: January 28, 1996

EPISODE 38: "THE ONE WITH THE PROM VIDEO"

Joey buys Chandler a friendship bracelet, the friends watch Monica and Rachel's old prom video, and Rachel forgives Ross.

Original airdate: February 1, 1996

EPISODE 39: "THE ONE WHERE ROSS AND RACHEL . . . YOU KNOW"

Monica gets a job catering for Richard Burke and winds up kissing him, and Ross and Rachel have sex.

Original airdate: February 8, 1996

EPISODE 40: "THE ONE WHERE JOEY MOVES OUT"

Joey moves out, Rachel gets a tattoo, and the Gellers find out Monica is dating Richard.

Original airdate: February 15, 1996

EPISODE 41: "THE ONE WHERE EDDIE MOVES IN"

Joey decides he wants to move back but Chandler already has a new roommate, Phoebe makes a "Smelly Cat" video, and Monica is oddly bothered by Ross and Rachel dating.

Original airdate: February 22, 1996

EPISODE 42: "THE ONE WHERE DR. RAMORAY DIES"

Dr. Drake Ramoray falls down an elevator shaft and Joey loses his job, Phoebe helps Chandler bond with Eddie, and Rachel and Monica discuss their sexual histories with Ross and Richard.

Original airdate: March 21, 1996

EPISODE 43: "THE ONE WHERE EDDIE WON'T GO"

Chandler tells Eddie to move out but Eddie won't go, Joey has to get rid of his cool new toys, and the girls read a book on female empowerment.

Original airdate: March 28, 1996

EPISODE 44: "THE ONE WHERE OLD YELLER DIES"

Phoebe finally sees the end of *Old Yeller*, Richard hangs out with Joey and Chandler, and Rachel flips out after learning Ross is planning their future and already knows the names of their kids.

Original airdate: April 4, 1996

EPISODE 45: "THE ONE WITH THE BULLIES"

Chandler and Ross are picked on by two bullies at Central Perk, Monica takes a job at a '50s diner, and Phoebe meets Frank Jr.

Original airdate: April 25, 1996

EPISODE 46: "THE ONE WITH TWO PARTIES"

The gang throw Rachel a surprise party and realize they have to have two, one for each of her feuding parents.

Original airdate: May 2, 1996

EPISODE 47: "THE ONE WITH THE CHICKEN POX"

Phoebe gets chicken pox, Joey takes a job at Chandler's office, and Monica's upset that Richard doesn't have a "thing."

Original airdate: May 9, 1996

Rachel is Mindy's maid of honor, Chandler's cybergirlfriend turns out to be Janice, and Monica and Richard break up.

Original airdate: May 16, 1996

Season Three

EPISODE 49: "THE ONE WITH THE PRINCESS LEIA FANTASY"

Ross tells Rachel about his Princess Leia fantasy, Monica has insomnia after her breakup with Richard, and Chandler wants Joey to bond with Janice.

Original airdate: September 19, 1996

EPISODE 50: "THE ONE WHERE NO ONE'S READY"

Ross flips out when no one is ready for his banquet, Joey and Chandler fight over Monica's chair, Rachel can't figure out what to wear, and Monica listens to Richard's answering machine after leaving an embarrassing message.

Original airdate: September 26, 1996

EPISODE 51: "THE ONE WITH THE JAM"

Phoebe dates the guy who is stalking Ursula, Ross and Rachel give Chandler lessons on how to be a good boyfriend, and Monica makes jam to take her mind off Richard, then instead considers artificial insemination.

Original airdate: October 3, 1996

EPISODE 52: "THE ONE WITH THE METAPHORICAL TUNNEL"

Phoebe pretends to be Joey's agent, Ben plays with Barbie dolls, and Chandler decides to face his fear of commitment by going overboard.

Original airdate: October 10, 1996

EPISODE 53: "THE ONE WITH FRANK JR."

Phoebe and Frank Jr. bond, Joey builds an entertainment center, and Ross laminates his list only hours before Rachel gives him permission to sleep with Isabella Rossellini.

Original airdate: October 17, 1996

EPISODE 54: "THE ONE WITH THE FLASHBACK"

Janice asks who all have slept with (or almost slept with) each other and we find out Ross and Phoebe, Joey and Monica, and Rachel and Chandler almost had.

Original airdate: October 31, 1996

EPISODE 55: "THE ONE WITH THE RACE CAR BED"

Monica buys a new bed and the wrong one is delivered, Joey teaches soap acting class, Rachel tries to get her father and Ross to bond, and Joey discovers Janice is back with her husband.

Original airdate: November 7, 1996

EPISODE 56: "THE ONE WITH THE GIANT POKING DEVICE"

Joey tells Chandler he saw Janice kissing her estranged husband, Ben bumps his head while Rachel is baby-sitting, Chandler lets Janice go, and everyone thinks Ugly Naked Guy is dead because someone always dies when Phoebe goes to the dentist.

Original airdate: November 14, 1996

EPISODE 57: "THE ONE WITH THE FOOTBALL"

Monica and Ross show their true colors while the gang play football on Thanksgiving day, and Ross and Chandler compete for a Nordic beauty.

Original airdate: November 21, 1996

EPISODE 58: "THE ONE WHERE RACHEL QUITS"

Rachel quits Central Perk, Joey sells Christmas trees, and Ross sells cookies for the little Brown Bird girl whose leg he accidentally broke.

Original airdate: December 12, 1996

EPISODE 59: "THE ONE WHERE CHANDLER CAN'T REMEMBER WHICH SISTER"

Rachel meets Mark, who gets her a job at Bloomingdale's, Ross is suspicious of Mark's motives, and Chandler gets drunk and fools around with one of Joey's sisters.

Original airdate: January 9, 1997

EPISODE 60: "THE ONE WITH ALL THE JEALOUSY"

Ross is jealous of Mark, Joey has to teach a dance to his Broadway cast after lying on his résumé, and Monica dates a busboy who hates American women.

Original airdate: January 16, 1997

EPISODE 61: "THE ONE WHERE MONICA AND RICHARD ARE JUST FRIENDS"

Monica and Richard decide to try being friends who sleep together, Joey reads *Little Women* while Rachel reads *The Shining*, and Phoebe's boyfriend lets it all hang out.

Original airdate: January 30, 1997

EPISODE 62: "THE ONE WITH PHOEBE'S EX-PARTNER"

Phoebe's ex-partner wants to get back together, Ross's jealousy is starting to wear on his relationship with Rachel, and Chandler dates a girl with a fake leg.

Original airdate: February 6, 1997

EPISODE 63: "THE ONE WHERE ROSS AND RACHEL TAKE A BREAK"

Rachel tells Ross she wants to take a break, Ross sleeps with Chloe the copy girl, and Phoebe dates a diplomat who doesn't speak English.

Original airdate: February 13, 1997

EPISODE 64: "THE ONE WITH THE MORNING AFTER"

Rachel finds out that Ross slept with Chloe, the two go back to her apartment and break up, while everyone else is trapped in Monica's bedroom, listening in.

Original airdate: February 20, 1997

EPISODE 65: "THE ONE WITHOUT THE SKI TRIP"

Rachel invites everyone except Ross to go skiing, Chandler starts smoking again, and Phoebe's cab runs out of gas and Ross has to come to their rescue.

Original airdate: March 6, 1997

EPISODE 66: "THE ONE WITH THE HYPNOSIS TAPE"

Monica dates a millionaire, Chandler tries to quit smoking with a hypnosis tape for women, and Frank Jr. announces he's getting married.

Original airdate: March 13, 1997

EPISODE 67: "THE ONE WITH THE TINY T-SHIRT"

Rachel goes out with Mark, Monica continues to date the millionaire even though she's not attracted to him, and Joey develops a crush on his costar.

Original airdate: March 27, 1997

EPISODE 68: "THE ONE WITH THE DOLLHOUSE"

Chandler dates Rachel's boss, Joey sleeps with his costar, and Monica inherits a dollhouse but won't let Phoebe play with it.

Original airdate: April 10, 1997

EPISODE 69: "THE ONE WITH A CHICK AND A DUCK"

Monica's millionaire buys a restaurant and offers Monica a job, Joey and Chandler buy a chick and a duck, and Ross misses participating in a panel discussion on the Discovery Channel to take Rachel to the ER.

Original airdate: April 17, 1997

EPISODE 70: "THE ONE WITH THE SCREAMER"

Rachel dates a guy who screams at everyone, Ross is the only one who seems to know this, Phoebe's on hold forever, and Joey falls in love with his costar, who winds up taking a job in L.A.

Original airdate: April 24, 1997

EPISODE 71: "THE ONE WITH ROSS'S THING"

Ross finds a "thing" on his butt, Phoebe dates a hot fireman and a hot schoolteacher and can't decide between them, and Monica thinks her millionaire is about to propose.

Original airdate: May 1, 1997

EPISODE 72: "THE ONE WITH THE ULTIMATE FIGHTING CHAMPION"

Monica's millionaire wants to become the Ultimate Fighting Champion, Monica breaks up with him after he loses, Phoebe sets Ross up with her used-to-be-bald friend, and Chandler's boss can't keep his hands off Chandler's ass.

Original airdate: May 8, 1997

EPISODE 73: "THE ONE AT THE BEACH"

The gang goes to the beach so Phoebe can meet her dead mother's best friend, Rachel convinces Ross's new girlfriend to shave her head, and Ross discovers Rachel is still in love with him.

Original airdate: May 15, 1997

Season Four

EPISODE 74: "THE ONE WITH THE JELLYFISH"

Phoebe finds out her dead mother's best friend is really her mother, Monica steps on a jellyfish, Chandler pees on Monica's foot, and Ross chooses Rachel and breaks up with his bald girlfriend.

Original airdate: September 25, 1997

EPISODE 75: "THE ONE WITH THE CAT"

Phoebe finds a cat and thinks it's her dead mother, Monica dates Rachel's ex-boyfriend from high school, and Joey gets locked in the entertainment center while the apartment is cleaned out.

Original airdate: October 2, 1997

EPISODE 76: "THE ONE WITH THE CUFFS"

Rachel's boss handcuffs a half-naked Chandler to her file cabinet, Monica caters her mother's party, and Joey buys an encyclopedia.

Original airdate: October 9, 1997

EPISODE 77: "THE ONE WITH THE BALLROOM DANCING"

Monica's building super threatens to evict her unless Joey teaches him ballroom dancing, Phoebe is attracted to one of her massage clients, and Chandler's gym won't let him quit.

Original airdate: October 16, 1997

EPISODE 78: "THE ONE WITH JOEY'S NEW GIRLFRIEND"

Chandler falls in love with Joey's new girlfriend, Kathy, Ross and Rachel try to make each other jealous, and Phoebe catches a cold.

Original airdate: October 30, 1997

EPISODE 79: "THE ONE WITH THE DIRTY GIRL"

Ross dates a hot girl living in squalor, Chandler buys Kathy (Joey's girlfriend) a birthday present, and Phoebe helps Monica cater a funeral.

Original airdate: November 6, 1997

EPISODE 80: "THE ONE WHERE CHANDLER CROSSES THE LINE"

Chandler kisses Kathy (Joey's girlfriend), Joey finds out, and Ross plays the keyboard.

Original airdate: November 13, 1997

EPISODE 81: "THE ONE WITH CHANDLER IN A BOX"

Monica invites Richard's son to Thanksgiving dinner after seeing him about an eye problem, and Chandler tries to prove to Joey how sorry he is by sitting in a box during Thanksgiving dinner.

Original airdate: November 20, 1997

EPISODE 82: "THE ONE WHERE THEY ARE GOING TO PARTY!"

Ross and Chandler plan to party all night with an old friend who winds up canceling, Rachel's boss promotes her but dies before putting through the paperwork, and Monica gets a job as head chef at Allesandro's.

Original airdate: December 11, 1997

EPISODE 83: "THE ONE WITH THE GIRL FROM POUGHKEEPSIE"

Ross dates a girl from Poughkeepsie, Chandler sets Rachel up with a couple of coworkers, and Monica hires Joey so she can fire him in front of her coworkers, who all hate her.

Original airdate: December 18, 1997

EPISODE 84: "THE ONE WITH PHOEBE'S UTERUS"

Frank Jr. asks Phoebe to carry his baby, Joey takes a job at the museum with Ross, and Chandler fears he won't be able to satisfy his new girlfriend, Kathy, since she used to date Joey.

Original airdate: January 8, 1998

EPISODE 85: "THE ONE WITH THE EMBRYOS"

The girls lose their apartment to the boys on a bet, and Phoebe finds out she's pregnant.

Original airdate: January 15, 1998

EPISODE 86: "THE ONE WITH RACHEL'S CRUSH"

Chandler accuses Kathy of having an affair with her costar, Monica gives her new apartment a makeover, and Rachel is demoted to personal shopper, then falls for Joshua, her first big client.

Original airdate: January 29, 1998

EPISODE 87: "THE ONE WITH JOEY'S DIRTY DAY"

Joey goes to work smelling really bad, the girls take Chandler to a strip club after Kathy breaks up with him, and Rachel convinces Ross to take out her boss's niece, Emily, so she can go to Joshua's club opening.

Original airdate: February 5, 1998

EPISODE 88: "THE ONE WITH ALL THE RUGBY"

Ross plays rugby with some of Emily's friends from back home, Monica tries to figure out what the light switch in her new apartment is for, and Chandler sleeps with Janice, then tells her he's moving to Yemen.

Original airdate: February 26, 1998

EPISODE 89: "THE ONE WITH THE FAKE PARTY"

Rachel throws Emily a surprise going-away party so Rachel can see Joshua socially, and Phoebe craves meat and gives up vegetarianism while she's pregnant.

Original airdate: March 19, 1998

☆ What's in a Name? ☆

+ Mr. Suity Man—Phoebe's name for Chandler, who was dressed for a job interview

+ Dr. Skeptismo—Phoebe's nickname for Ross, who didn't believe her cat was really her dead mother

+ Mental Geller—What they called Ross at work after he left a threatening note on his lunch

+ Clifford Alvarez and Rolland Chang—The names on Ross's and Chandler's fake IDs back in college

+ Sir Limpsalot—The nickname Ross gave Chandler after he lost the tip of his toe

+ Street Phoebe—Phoebe before she met the other Friends

+ Mondler—What Ross called Chandler because he was starting to look like Monica after moving in with her

+ Humswhilehepees—The cute coffeehouse guy Phoebe dated

+ Skidmark—What Chandler's old camp girlfriend called him

+ Ray-Ray Green—Rachel's nickname in college

+ Pervie Perverson—What Monica called Chandler after he almost pounced on her hot cousin

EPISODE 90: "THE ONE WITH THE FREE PORN"

Phoebe finds out she's carrying triplets, Monica convinces Ross to tell Emily he loves her, and Joey and Chandler get free porn.

Original airdate: March 26, 1998

EPISODE 91: "THE ONE WITH RACHEL'S NEW DRESS"

Ross thinks Emily is going to turn into a lesbian after she offers to show Susan around London, Phoebe decides to name one of the babies Chandler, and Rachel gets caught in her lingerie by Joshua's parents.

Original airdate: April 2, 1998

EPISODE 92: "THE ONE WITH ALL THE HASTE"

Ross proposes to Emily, and the girls get their apartment back after kissing for Joey and Chandler.

Original airdate: April 9, 1998

EPISODE 93: "THE ONE WITH ALL THE WEDDING DRESSES"

Joey goes to a sleep clinic, Rachel's upset over Ross's engagement and asks Joshua to marry her, and the girls all put on wedding dresses and drink beer.

Original airdate: April 16, 1998

EPISODE 94: "THE ONE WITH THE INVITATION"

Ross and Emily send out their wedding invitations and the gang remi-nisce about Ross and Rachel's relationship, Rachel says she's not going to the wedding, and Phoebe finds out she can't because she's pregnant.

Original airdate: April 23, 1998

EPISODE 95: "THE ONE WITH THE WORST BEST MAN EVER"

Ross asks Joey to be his best man, Phoebe has major mood swings, and Monica and Rachel throw Phoebe a baby shower.

Original airdate: April 30, 1998

EPISODE 96: "THE ONE WITH ROSS'S WEDDING—PART 1"

Ross, Monica, Joey, and Chandler go to London, Phoebe helps Rachel to see she's still in love with Ross, and Rachel decides to go to London to tell Ross she still loves him.

Original airdate: May 7, 1998

EPISODE 97: "THE ONE WITH ROSS'S WEDDING—PART 2"

Phoebe tries to warn everyone that Rachel's coming to break up the wedding, Monica and Chandler sleep together, Rachel arrives but decides not to say anything, and during the wedding vows, Ross says Rachel's name instead of Emily's.

Original airdate: May 7, 1998

Season Five

EPISODE 98: "THE ONE AFTER ROSS SAYS RACHEL"

Emily leaves Ross right after the ceremony, Ross invites Rachel on his honeymoon, and Monica and Chandler make a pact that they can sleep together only in London, but change their minds once they return home.

Original airdate: September 24, 1998

EPISODE 99: "THE ONE WITH ALL THE KISSING"

Monica and Chandler hide their relationship, Rachel returns from Greece, Chandler has to kiss everyone after absentmindedly kissing Monica, and Phoebe's water breaks.

Original airdate: October 1, 1998

EPISODE 100: "THE ONE HUNDREDTH"

Phoebe has her babies, her obstetrician is obsessed with Fonzie, Joey is admitted to the hospital for kidney stones, and Monica and Chandler have their first fight.

Original airdate: October 8, 1998

EPISODE 101: "THE ONE WHERE PHOEBE HATES PBS"

Emily tells Ross she'll work on the marriage if he stops seeing Rachel, Joey thinks he's the host of a PBS telethon, and Phoebe tries proving to Joey that she can do a selfless good deed.

Original airdate: October 15, 1998

EPISODE 102: "THE ONE WITH THE KIPS"

Monica and Chandler go away for the weekend and end up fighting, Ross tells Rachel he can't see her anymore if he's going to work things out with Emily, and Joey finds out about Monica and Chandler.

Original airdate: October 29, 1998

EPISODE 103: "THE ONE WITH THE YETI"

Emily demands Ross get rid of anything with Rachel germs, including his apartment, Monica and Rachel hit Danny with a bug bomb, Phoebe wears fur, and Emily finds out Ross is still hanging out with Rachel and tells him it's over.

Original airdate: November 5, 1998

EPISODE 104: "THE ONE WHERE ROSS MOVES IN"

Ross moves in with Joey and Chandler, Phoebe dates a health inspector, and Rachel thinks she and Danny are playing cat and mouse.

Original airdate: November 12, 1998

EPISODE 105: "THE ONE WITH ALL THE THANKSGIVINGS"

The gang reminisce about Thanksgivings past: Monica cuts off Chandler's toe with a kitchen knife while trying to seduce him and Joey gets a turkey stuck on his head. After all the reminiscing, Chandler tells Monica he loves her.

Original airdate: November 19, 1998

EPISODE 106: "THE ONE WITH ROSS'S SANDWICH"

Someone steals Ross's leftover Thanksgiving turkey sandwich at work and then he gets suspended for going off on his boss, Joey covers for Monica and Chandler even though he looks like a pervert, and Phoebe and Rachel take a literature class.

Original airdate: December 10, 1998

EPISODE 107: "THE ONE WITH THE INAPPROPRIATE SISTER"

Phoebe volunteers for the Salvation Army, Rachel goes out with Danny, but can't handle his close relationship with his sister, and Ross encourages Joey to write a screenplay.

Original airdate: December 17, 1998

EPISODE 108: "THE ONE WITH ALL THE RESOLUTIONS"

Ross gets stuck in a pair of leather pants, Chandler tries not to make fun of anyone, Phoebe teaches Joey to play the guitar, and Rachel tries to stop gossiping, but has a hard time after discovering that Monica and Chandler are sleeping together.

Original airdate: January 7, 1999

EPISODE 109: "THE ONE WITH CHANDLER'S WORK LAUGH"

Ross finds out Emily is getting married, Monica discovers Chandler's work laugh, and Rachel tries to get Monica to spill the beans about her relationship with Chandler.

Original airdate: January 21, 1999

EPISODE 110: "THE ONE WITH JOEY'S BAG"

Joey wears a man purse, Phoebe's grandma dies, and Phoebe finally meets her father.

Original airdate: February 4, 1999

EPISODE 111: "THE ONE WHERE EVERYBODY FINDS OUT"

Phoebe hits on Chandler to try to get him to admit to his relationship with Monica, Chandler and Monica figure out what she's up to, and Ugly Naked Guy moves out and Ross gets his apartment, from which he spots Monica and Chandler kissing.

Original airdate: February 11, 1999

EPISODE 112: "THE ONE WITH THE GIRL WHO HITS JOEY"

Joey's new girlfriend likes to hit him, Ross's new neighbors don't like him because he won't donate $100 to the retiring handyman, and Chandler proposes to Monica after having a fight.

Original airdate: February 18, 1999

EPISODE 113: "THE ONE WITH THE COP"

Phoebe dates a cop named Gary, Ross buys a new sofa, and Joey dreams about Monica.

Original airdate: February 25, 1999

EPISODE 114: "THE ONE WITH RACHEL'S INADVERTENT KISS"

Rachel accidentally kisses her new boss, Monica worries she and Chandler aren't as hot as Phoebe and Gary, and Joey can't find the attractive girl who lives in Ross's building.

Original airdate: March 18, 1999

EPISODE 115: "THE ONE WHERE RACHEL SMOKES"

Ben and Joey audition for the same commercial, Rachel takes up smoking to fit in at work, and Monica and Phoebe plan a surprise birthday party for Rachel.

Original airdate: April 8, 1999

EPISODE 116: "THE ONE WHERE ROSS CAN'T FLIRT"

Ross tries to flirt with the pizza delivery girl, Joey's grandma comes over to watch Joey appear on *Law and Order*, and Joey tries to cover when he realizes his part was cut from the show.

Original airdate: April 22, 1999

EPISODE 117: "THE ONE WITH THE RIDE-ALONG"

Gary takes the guys on a ride-along, Ross thinks Joey saved his life, and Emily calls the night before her wedding to tell Ross she might still love him.

Original airdate: April 29, 1999

EPISODE 118: "THE ONE WITH THE BALL"

Gary asks Phoebe to move in with him, Rachel buys a Sphynx cat, Phoebe breaks up with Gary after he shoots a bird, and the others toss a ball around for hours without dropping it.

Original airdate: May 6, 1999

EPISODE 119: "THE ONE WITH JOEY'S BIG BREAK"

Rachel goes to the eye doctor, Joey goes to Vegas to star in an independent film but discovers his film has been shut down, and afterward he gets a job at Caesar's Palace.

Original airdate: May 13, 1999

EPISODE 120: "THE ONE IN VEGAS—PART 1"

Monica and Chandler decide to go to Vegas for their anniversary, Phoebe invites herself, Ross, and Rachel along, Ross draws on Rachel's face, and Joey meets his identical hand twin.

Original airdate: May 20, 1999

EPISODE 121: "THE ONE IN VEGAS—PART 2"

Rachel draws on Ross's face, Monica and Chandler decide to get married, but Ross and Rachel beat them to the altar.

Original airdate: May 20, 1999

Season Six

EPISODE 122: "THE ONE AFTER VEGAS"

Ross and Rachel find out they got married, Monica and Chandler decide not to get married but to live together, Phoebe drives back from Vegas with Joey, and Ross tells Rachel he got an annulment, even though he didn't.

Original airdate: September 23, 1999

EPISODE 123: "THE ONE WHERE ROSS HUGS RACHEL"

Ross realizes he's still in love with Rachel, Chandler tells Joey he's moving out, and Monica is upset that Rachel isn't more upset that she has to move out.

Original airdate: September 30, 1999

EPISODE 124: "THE ONE WITH ROSS'S DENIAL"

Joey advertises for a new roommate, Monica and Chandler fight over what to do with Rachel's room, and Phoebe gives Ross a hard time about his being in love with Rachel.

Original airdate: October 7, 1999

EPISODE 125: "THE ONE WHERE JOEY LOSES HIS INSURANCE"

Joey loses his health insurance, Ross speaks in a British accent while giving a lecture, Phoebe's psychic tells her she's going to die within the week, and Rachel finds out she's still married to Ross.

Original airdate: October 14, 1999

EPISODE 126: "THE ONE WITH JOEY'S PORSCHE"

Joey finds the keys to someone's Porsche, Monica and Chandler help Phoebe baby-sit the triplets, and Ross and Rachel can't get an annulment, so they get a divorce.

Original airdate: October 21, 1999

EPISODE 127: "THE ONE ON THE LAST NIGHT"

Monica and Rachel fight on their last night as roommates, Chandler wants to give Joey money, so he teaches him to play Cups, and Ross pretends he's got Ben for the night to get out of helping Rachel pack.

Original airdate: November 4, 1999

EPISODE 128: "THE ONE WHERE PHOEBE RUNS"

Rachel and Phoebe go running together, Joey finds a hot new roommate named Janine, and Chandler tries to surprise Monica by cleaning the apartment.

Original airdate: November 11, 1999

EPISODE 129: "THE ONE WITH ROSS'S TEETH"

Ross bleaches his teeth, Phoebe thinks she made out with Ralph Lauren in the copy room, and Rachel's boss thinks Rachel did.

Original airdate: November 18, 1999

EPISODE 130: "THE ONE WHERE ROSS GOT HIGH"

Ross and Monica's parents come for Thanksgiving dinner, Rachel makes dessert, Phoebe thinks Jack Geller is hot after having a dream about him, and Ross admits to lying to his parents about Chandler smoking pot in his bedroom to cover his own ass.

Original airdate: November 25, 1999

EPISODE 131: "THE ONE WITH THE ROUTINE"

Janine invites Joey, Monica, and Ross to *Dick Clark's New Year's Rockin' Eve*, Ross and Monica do "the routine," and Joey kisses Janine.

Original airdate: December 16, 1999

EPISODE 132: "THE ONE WITH THE APOTHECARY TABLE"

Rachel tells Phoebe that their new apothecary table came from a flea market, since Phoebe hates Pottery Barn, Janine tells Joey that Monica and Chandler are loud and boring, Ross buys an apothecary table, and Joey breaks up with Janine.

Original airdate: January 6, 2000

EPISODE 133: "THE ONE WITH THE JOKE"

Ross gets a joke published in *Playboy*, Chandler claims it's *his* joke, Joey starts working at Central Perk, and Phoebe tells Monica that, if she had to date either her or Rachel, she'd pick Rachel.

Original airdate: January 13, 2000

EPISODE 134: "THE ONE WITH RACHEL'S SISTER"

Rachel's younger sister, Jill, comes to town, Monica gets a cold, but won't admit it, and Ross dates Jill and Rachel flips out.

Original airdate: February 3, 2000

EPISODE 135: "THE ONE WHERE CHANDLER CAN'T CRY"

Chandler can't cry, Rachel convinces Ross that Jill is just using him, and Phoebe finds out her twin, Ursula, is a porn star and is using Phoebe's name.

Original airdate: February 10, 2000

EPISODE 136: "THE ONE THAT COULD HAVE BEEN—PART 1"

The gang fantasizes about what could have been: Ross is still married to Carol, Rachel is married to Barry, but wants to have an affair with Joey the soap star, Monica is still fat and a virgin, Chandler is an aspiring writer who takes a job as Joey's personal assistant, and Phoebe is a stockbroker and has a heart attack.

Original airdate: February 17, 2000

EPISODE 137: "THE ONE THAT COULD HAVE BEEN—PART 2"

Ross and Carol have a threesome with Susan, Rachel tries to sleep with Joey, but throws up instead, Monica loses her virginity to Chandler, and Phoebe gets fired from her job.

Original airdate: February 17, 2000

EPISODE 138: "THE ONE WITH *UNAGI*"

Ross tries to teach Rachel and Phoebe about *Unagi*, Chandler and Monica decide to give each other homemade Valentine's Day gifts, and Joey tries to participate in an identical-twin research study.

Original airdate: February 24, 2000

EPISODE 139: "THE ONE WHERE ROSS DATES A STUDENT"

Ross begins dating a student named Elizabeth, Joey convinces Chandler to ask an old girlfriend to get Joey an audition for her new movie, and Phoebe and Rachel's apartment catches fire and they have to move out.

Original airdate: March 9, 2000

EPISODE 140: "THE ONE WITH JOEY'S FRIDGE"

Joey's refrigerator breaks, Elizabeth tells Ross she's going to Daytona for spring break, and Rachel needs a date for a charity bash.

Original airdate: March 23, 2000

EPISODE 141: "THE ONE WITH MAC AND C.H.E.E.S.E."

Joey auditions for the lead role in a new series, Chandler forgets to give him the message that he has a callback, so another actor gets the part, but Joey winds up getting it after the first actor is mauled by a dog.

Original airdate: April 13, 2000

EPISODE 142: "THE ONE WHERE ROSS MEETS ELIZABETH'S DAD"

Ross meets Elizabeth's dad, Paul, who hates Ross but likes Rachel, and Joey gets off on the wrong foot at his new TV gig.

Original airdate: April 27, 2000

EPISODE 143: "THE ONE WHERE PAUL'S THE MAN"

Elizabeth takes Ross to her father's cabin, Paul takes Rachel at the same time, Joey tries to get his picture back up on the dry cleaner's wall, and Chandler confides to Phoebe that he's going to propose to Monica.

Original airdate: May 4, 2000

EPISODE 144: "THE ONE WITH THE RING"

Chandler and Phoebe go ring shopping, Ross and Joey are feeling "dissed" by Chandler and Phoebe makes matters worse by telling them Chandler is really mad at them, and Rachel tries to get Paul to open up.

Original airdate: May 11, 2000

EPISODE 145: "THE ONE WITH THE PROPOSAL—PART 1"

Ross breaks up with Elizabeth, Joey buys a boat, and Chandler tries to propose to Monica at dinner, but can't after Richard shows up. Chandler then tries to throw her off by telling her he's not interested in marriage, and Richard tells Monica he wants to marry her.

Original airdate: May 18, 2000

EPISODE 146: "THE ONE WITH THE PROPOSAL—PART 2"

Monica contemplates Richard's marriage proposal, Chandler confronts Richard, Joey tells Monica what's really going on, and Chandler finally proposes—though Monica is the one who asks.

Original airdate: May 18, 2000

Season Seven

EPISODE 147: "THE ONE WITH MONICA'S THUNDER"

On the night of Monica and Chandler's engagement, Rachel kisses Ross and Monica thinks she's trying to steal her thunder, Joey prepares for an audition as a nineteen-year-old, and in all the excitement, Chandler can't get it up.

Original airdate: October 12, 2000

EPISODE 148: "THE ONE WITH RACHEL'S BOOK"

Joey finds Rachel's trashy novel and gives her a hard time, Monica discovers her parents spent the "Monica Wedding Fund," and Phoebe moves in with Ross, bringing her massage clients with her.

Original airdate: October 12, 2000

EPISODE 149: "THE ONE WITH PHOEBE'S COOKIES"

Monica wants Phoebe's grandmother's chocolate chip cookie recipe, Rachel tries to teach Joey to sail, and Chandler sits on Monica's father's lap in the steam room.

Original airdate: October 19, 2000

EPISODE 150: "THE ONE WITH RACHEL'S ASSISTANT"

Rachel hires Tag as her new assistant, Mac and C.H.E.E.S.E is canceled, and Monica and Chandler share secrets.

Original airdate: October 26, 2000

EPISODE 151: "THE ONE WITH THE ENGAGEMENT PICTURE"

Monica and Chandler try taking an engagement picture, but Chandler can't smile, Phoebe and Ross date a couple in the midst of a messy divorce, and Joey bonds with Tag.

Original airdate: November 2, 2000

EPISODE 152: "THE ONE WITH THE NAP PARTNERS"

Ross and Joey nap together, Rachel and Phoebe compete to be Monica's maid of honor, and Monica encourages Chandler to apologize to an old girlfriend for dumping her when she got fat.

Original airdate: November 9, 2000

EPISODE 153: "THE ONE WITH ROSS'S LIBRARY BOOK"

Ross discovers students fooling around in front of his library book, Joey's new girlfriend dumps him by using one of his excuses, and Monica unintentionally invites Janice to her wedding.

Original airdate: November 16, 2000

EPISODE 154: "THE ONE WHERE CHANDLER DOESN'T LIKE DOGS"

Ross has to name all fifty states before he can eat Thanksgiving dinner, Phoebe looks after a friend's dog but doesn't tell Chandler or Monica she's got it in the apartment, and Rachel tells Tag how she feels about him.

Original airdate: November 23, 2000

EPISODE 155: "THE ONE WITH ALL THE CANDY"

Monica makes candy for her neighbors, Ross buys Phoebe her first bike, and Rachel writes an evaluation for Tag's eyes only, which Tag unwittingly sends to human resources.

Original airdate: December 7, 2000

EPISODE 156: "THE ONE WITH THE HOLIDAY ARMADILLO"

Ross tries to teach Ben about Hanukkah, but all Ben wants to hear about is Santa, Phoebe's apartment is ready and she's worried that Rachel won't want to move back in with her, and Chandler tries to master the art of tipping discreetly.

Original airdate: December 14, 2000

EPISODE 157: "THE ONE WITH ALL THE CHEESECAKES"

Chandler and Rachel eat stolen cheesecake, Monica finds out why she wasn't invited to her cousin's wedding after she goes as Ross's guest, and Phoebe is reunited with David the Scientist Guy, who's about to return to Minsk.

Original airdate: January 4, 2001

EPISODE 158: "THE ONE WHERE THEY'RE UP ALL NIGHT"

Ross and Joey get locked out on the roof, Monica can't sleep and keeps Chandler up all night, Tag and Rachel argue over a FedEx envelope, and Phoebe's fire alarm won't stop beeping.

Original airdate: January 11, 2001

EPISODE 159: "THE ONE WHERE ROSITA DIES"

Phoebe takes a job as a telemarketer and convinces her first customer not to kill himself, Rachel breaks Joey's favorite chair, and Monica's dad gives her his Porsche after he lets all her memory boxes get ruined in a flood.

Original airdate: February 1, 2001

EPISODE 160: "THE ONE WHERE THEY ALL TURN THIRTY"

When Rachel turns thirty, the gang all reminisce about their thirtieth birthdays: Ross buys a red sports car, Monica gets drunk, Phoebe finds out she's really a year older, and after her own celebration, Rachel breaks up with Tag.

Original airdate: February 8, 2001

EPISODE 161: "THE ONE WITH JOEY'S NEW BRAIN"

Dr. Drake Ramoray comes out of his coma and gets a new brain, Rachel and Phoebe fight over a lost cell phone, and Ross wants to play the bagpipes at Monica and Chandler's wedding.

Original airdate: February 15, 2001

EPISODE 162: "THE ONE WITH THE TRUTH ABOUT LONDON"

Chandler finds out Monica really intended to sleep with Joey that night in London, Phoebe worries about the side effects of Monica's headache medicine, Joey becomes ordained as a minister over the Internet, and Rachel teaches Ben a few tricks.

Original airdate: February 22, 2001

EPISODE 163: "THE ONE WITH THE CHEAP WEDDING DRESS"

Monica fights with another woman over a wedding dress, and Joey and Ross date the same girl.

Original airdate: March 15, 2001

EPISODE 164: "THE ONE WITH JOEY'S AWARD"

Joey is nominated for a Soapie, one of Ross's male students tells him he failed his midterm because he was in love with Ross, and Monica realizes that once she marries Chandler she'll never get to be with another man again.

Original airdate: March 29, 2001

EPISODE 165: "THE ONE WITH ROSS AND MONICA'S COUSIN"

Monica and Ross's hot cousin comes to town, Monica helps Joey with an audition in which he must be uncircumcised, and Rachel and Phoebe throw an impromptu wedding shower for Monica.

Original airdate: April 19, 2001

EPISODE 166: "THE ONE WITH RACHEL'S BIG KISS"

Rachel runs into an old sorority sister at Central Perk, Phoebe doesn't believe Rachel when she says she made out with her old sorority sister back in college, Monica is upset when Joey invites his parents to her wedding, and Chandler and Ross argue over Batman's tux.

Original airdate: April 26, 2001

EPISODE 167: "THE ONE WITH THE VOWS"

Monica and Chandler reminisce as they struggle to write their wedding vows.

Original airdate: May 3, 2001

EPISODE 168: "THE ONE WITH CHANDLER'S DAD"

Monica and Chandler go to Vegas to invite Chandler's dad to their wedding, Rachel gets pulled over for speeding while driving Monica's Porsche, and Joey wears Rachel's underwear.

Original airdate: May 10, 2001

EPISODE 169: "THE ONE WITH MONICA AND CHANDLER'S WEDDING—PART 1"

Chandler flips out the night before the wedding and disappears, and Joey works with a famous actor who spits.

Original airdate: May 17, 2001

EPISODE 170: "THE ONE WITH MONICA AND CHANDLER'S WEDDING—PART 2"

Phoebe finds a pregnancy test in Monica's bathroom and assumes Monica's pregnant, Phoebe and Ross find Chandler and bring him back, Joey almost misses the wedding, and Monica and Chandler finally get married.

Original airdate: May 17, 2001

☆ Yet More Star Sightings ☆

- Cole Mitchell Sprouse (Ben) "The One That Could Have Been"

- Alexandra Holden (Elizabeth) "The One Where Ross Dates a Student"

- Bruce Willis (Elizabeth's father, Paul) "The One Where Ross Meets Elizabeth's Dad"

- Eddie Cahill (Tag) "The One With Rachel's Assistant"

- Kristin Davis (Erin) "The One With Ross's Library Book"

- Jason Alexander (Earl) "The One Where Rosita Dies"

- Susan Sarandon (Cecilia) "The One With Joey's New Brain"

- Andrea Bendewald (bride-to-be) "The One With the Cheap Wedding Dress"

- Denise Richards (Cousin Cassie) "The One With Ross and Monica's Cousin"

- Winona Ryder (Melissa) "The One With Rachel's Big Kiss"

- Kathleen Turner (Chandler's dad) "The One With Chandler's Dad"

- Mark Consuelos, aka Mr. Kelly Ripa (Officer Hanson) "The One With Chandler's Dad"

- Gary Oldman (Richard Crosby) "The One With Monica and Chandler's Wedding"

- Sean Penn (Eric) "The One With the Halloween Party"

- Trudie Styler (herself) "The One With Monica's Boots"

- Marla Sokoloff (Dina) "The One With Monica's Boots"

- James Le Gros (Jim) "The One With the Tea Leaves"

- Alec Baldwin (Parker) "The One in Massapequa"

- Rena Sofer (Katie) "The One With the Cooking Class"

- Paul Rudd (Mike) "The One With the Pediatrician"

- Freddie Prinze Jr. (Sandy) "The One With the Male Nanny"

- Christina Applegate (Amy) "The One With Rachel's Other Sister"

- Selma Blair (Wendy) "The One With Christmas in Tulsa"

- Evan Handler (director) in "The One Where Rachel Goes Back to Work"

- Dermot Mulrony (Gavin) in "The One Where Rachel Goes Back To Work"

- Jeff Goldblum (Leonard) in "The One With the Mugging"

- Jon Lovitz (Steve) in "The One With the Blind Date"

Season Eight

EPISODE 171: "THE ONE AFTER 'I DO'"

Ross meets Mona at Monica and Chandler's reception, Phoebe tells everyone she's pregnant to cover for Rachel, Monica figures out that it's really Rachel and encourages her to take another test to confirm it.

Original airdate: September 27, 2001

EPISODE 172: "THE ONE WITH THE RED SWEATER"

Chandler loses the disposable cameras from the wedding, Rachel still won't give up who the father is, Joey produces a red sweater that was left behind the night Rachel was with someone, and Ross is relieved to find his lost sweater.

Original airdate: October 4, 2001

EPISODE 173: "THE ONE WHERE RACHEL TELLS ROSS"

Monica and Chandler leave for their honeymoon, Phoebe and Joey break into Monica and Chandler's apartment, and Rachel tells Ross about the baby.

Original airdate: October 11, 2001

EPISODE 174: "THE ONE WITH THE VIDEOTAPE"

Monica and Chandler return from their honeymoon, Ross and Rachel each recount their versions of what happened the night they slept together, and Ross comes up with a videotape of the event.

Original airdate: October 18, 2001

EPISODE 175: "THE ONE WITH RACHEL'S DATE"

Phoebe starts dating a guy from Monica's restaurant, Monica plans to fire him the same day Phoebe wants to dump him, Ross discovers Chandler's coworker has been calling him Toby for the last five years, and Rachel goes on her first date since finding out she was pregnant.

Original airdate: October 25, 2001

EPISODE 176: "THE ONE WITH THE HALLOWEEN PARTY"

Monica and Chandler throw a Halloween party, Phoebe invites Ursula and her fiancé, Eric, Rachel worries she'll suck as a mother, and Phoebe tells Eric the truth about Ursula.

Original airdate: November 1, 2001

EPISODE 177: "THE ONE WITH THE STAIN"

Chandler hires a cleaning woman who Monica is convinced has stolen her bra and blue jeans, Ross tries to get Rachel an apartment in his building, and Eric breaks it off with Ursula and starts dating Phoebe . . . until he sleeps with Ursula by mistake.

Original airdate: November 8, 2001

EPISODE 178: "THE ONE WITH THE STRIPPER"

Monica hires Chandler a stripper since he didn't have one at his bachelor party, the stripper turns out to be a hooker, Mona finds out that Ross got Rachel pregnant, and Rachel tells her dad she's pregnant.

Original airdate: November 15, 2001

EPISODE 179: "THE ONE WITH THE RUMOR"

Monica invites Will, an old high school friend, to Thanksgiving dinner, Rachel finds out he and Ross started the I Hate Rachel club, and Joey vows to eat an entire turkey by himself.

Original airdate: November 22, 2001

EPISODE 180: "THE ONE WITH MONICA'S BOOTS"

Monica's expensive new boots hurt her feet, Phoebe tries to score concert tickets after finding out that Sting's son goes to the same school as Ben, and Joey's little sister tells him she's pregnant.

Original airdate: December 6, 2001

EPISODE 181: "THE ONE WITH ROSS'S STEP FORWARD"

Ross freaks out when Mona asks if he wants to do holiday cards, Chandler's boss takes him to a strip club, and Rachel propositions Joey while hormonal.

Original airdate: December 13, 2001

EPISODE 182: "THE ONE WHERE JOEY DATES RACHEL"

Phoebe buys Monica and Chandler a Ms. Pac-Man game for a belated wedding gift, Ross teaches a class that he can never get to on time, and Joey develops feelings for Rachel.

Original airdate: January 10, 2002

EPISODE 183: "THE ONE WHERE CHANDLER TAKES A BATH"

Monica teaches Chandler the art of the bubble bath, Joey's crush on Rachel intensifies, and Ross and Rachel talk about baby names.

Original airdate: January 17, 2002

EPISODE 184: "THE ONE WITH THE SECRET CLOSET"

Chandler discovers Monica's really a closet slob, Phoebe gives Monica a massage, and Joey suggests Rachel move in with Ross so Ross can be more involved in Rachel's pregnancy.

Original airdate: January 31, 2002

EPISODE 185: "THE ONE WITH THE BIRTHING VIDEO"

Ross tells Mona that Rachel's living with him and she dumps him, Joey tells Ross he's in love with Rachel, and Chandler thinks Monica got him porn for Valentine's Day but it turns out to be a stomach-turning birthing video.

Original airdate: February 7, 2002

EPISODE 186: "THE ONE WHERE JOEY TELLS RACHEL"

Phoebe thinks she's met Monica's soul mate, Joey tells Rachel how he feels about her, and Rachel breaks his heart.

Original airdate: February 28, 2002

EPISODE 187: "THE ONE WITH THE TEA LEAVES"

Joey avoids Rachel, Ross breaks into Mona's to retrieve his favorite pink shirt, and Phoebe meets a hot guy who turns out to be a loser.

Original airdate: March 7, 2002

EPISODE 188: "THE ONE IN MASSAPEQUA"

Jealous over Ross's tearjerking toasts, Monica writes her own toast for her parents' thirty-fifth wedding anniversary party, Jack and Judy tell everyone Ross and Rachel are married, and Phoebe brings her zesty new boyfriend to the party.

Original airdate: March 28, 2002

EPISODE 189: "THE ONE WITH JOEY'S INTERVIEW"

Joey is interviewed by *Soap Opera Digest* and reminisces about his acting career.

Original airdate: April 4, 2002

EPISODE 190: "THE ONE WITH THE BABY SHOWER"

Monica throws Rachel a baby shower but forgets to invite Rachel's mother until the last minute, Rachel flips out about becoming a mom, and Joey auditions for a job as a game show host.

Original airdate: April 25, 2002

EPISODE 191: "THE ONE WITH THE COOKING CLASS"

Monica takes a cooking class after a critic slams her restaurant, Phoebe helps Chandler prepare for a job interview, and Rachel gets jealous when Ross takes out the clerk from the baby store.

Original airdate: May 2, 2002

EPISODE 192: "THE ONE WHERE RACHEL IS LATE"

The highly irritable and very pregnant Rachel is way past her due date, Chandler falls asleep during the premiere of Joey's movie, Rachel's doctor tells her that sex might speed things up a bit, but her water breaks just before she and Ross do it.

Original airdate: May 9, 2002

EPISODE 193: "THE ONE WHERE RACHEL HAS A BABY—PART 1"

Rachel's upset because everyone else seems to be having babies but her, Judy gives Ross her mother's engagement ring, Monica and Chandler try to get pregnant, and Janice shows up to have a baby, too.

Original airdate: May 16, 2002

EPISODE 194: "THE ONE WHERE RACHEL HAS A BABY—PART 2"

Rachel has her baby, Monica and Chandler keep trying to get pregnant, and Rachel thinks Joey is proposing after he bends down to pick up Ross's ring.

Original airdate: May 16, 2002

Season Nine

EPISODE 195: "THE ONE WHERE NO ONE PROPOSES"

Rachel accepts Joey's nonproposal, Phoebe thinks Ross proposed, and no one quite knows what's going on until they all realize no one intended to propose.

Original airdate: September 26, 2002

EPISODE 196: "THE ONE WHERE EMMA CRIES"

Chandler falls asleep in a business meeting and inadvertently agrees to move to Tulsa, Emma can't stop crying, and Ross hits Joey.

Original airdate: October 3, 2002

EPISODE 197: "THE ONE WITH THE PEDIATRICIAN"

Rachel discovers Ross still sees his childhood pediatrician, Joey forgets to find Phoebe a blind date and sets her up with a random "Mike," and Monica decides to stay in New York.

Original airdate: October 10, 2002

EPISODE 198: "THE ONE WITH THE SHARKS"

Monica thinks Chandler watches "shark porn," Joey dates a girl he thinks he's already slept with, and Ross interferes with Phoebe's relationship with Mike.

Original airdate: October 17, 2002

EPISODE 199: "THE ONE WITH PHOEBE'S BIRTHDAY DINNER"

Phoebe plans a birthday dinner for herself and everyone's late, Monica tricks Chandler into having sex while having a fight, and Rachel doesn't want to leave Emma.

Original airdate: October 31, 2002

EPISODE 200: "THE ONE WITH THE MALE NANNY"

Ross and Rachel hire a male nanny, Monica tells Chandler the maitre d' in her new restaurant is the funniest guy in the world, and David the Scientist Guy comes back to see Phoebe.

Original airdate: November 7, 2002

EPISODE 201: "THE ONE WITH ROSS'S INAPPROPRIATE SONG"

Ross and Rachel rap the Sir Mix-A-Lot song "Baby's Got Back" for Emma, Phoebe meets Mike's parents, and Chandler finds a videotape in Richard's apartment with Monica's name on it.

Original airdate: November 14, 2002

EPISODE 202: "THE ONE WITH RACHEL'S OTHER SISTER"

Rachel's sister Amy comes for Thanksgiving dinner, Ross and Rachel announce they'd like Monica and Chandler to be Emma's godparents, and Joey forgets to show up for the Macy's Thanksgiving parade.

Original airdate: November 21, 2002

EPISODE 203: "THE ONE WITH RACHEL'S PHONE NUMBER"

Rachel gives her number out to a guy and then has second thoughts, Ross and Mike have their "first date," and Joey thinks Monica is cheating on Chandler.

Original airdate: December 5, 2002

EPISODE 204: "THE ONE WITH CHRISTMAS IN TULSA"

Chandler spends Christmas in Tulsa, a colleague hits on him, then Chandler quits his job and returns to New York.

Original airdate: December 12, 2002

EPISODE 205: "THE ONE WHERE RACHEL GOES BACK TO WORK"

Rachel returns to work and meets Gavin, Joey gets Phoebe a part on *Days of Our Lives*, and Chandler questions whether or not he and Monica are ready to get pregnant.

Original airdate: January 9, 2003

EPISODE 206: "THE ONE WITH PHOEBE'S RATS"

Phoebe and Mike parent seven orphaned baby rats, Joey has the hots for Ross and Rachel's new nanny, Monica throws Rachel a birthday party, and Rachel kisses Gavin.

Original airdate: January 16, 2003

EPISODE 207: "THE ONE WHERE MONICA SINGS"

Joey gets his eyebrows waxed, Phoebe encourages Monica to sing at Mike's piano bar, and Ross and Rachel decide not to live together anymore.

Original airdate: January 30, 2003

EPISODE 208: "THE ONE WITH THE BLIND DATE"

Phoebe and Joey make a plan to get Ross and Rachel back together by setting them up on horrible blind dates, and Monica and Chandler baby-sit Emma while Monica's ovulating.

Original airdate: February 6, 2003

EPISODE 209: "THE ONE WITH THE MUGGING"

Phoebe realizes she mugged Ross when they were kids, Joey has to pee while auditioning for a play, and Chandler gets an internship at an advertising agency.

Original airdate: February 13, 2003

EPISODE 210: "THE ONE WITH THE BOOB JOB"

Chandler thinks Monica's about to get a boob job, Monica thinks Chandler is worried she'll get fat when she gets pregnant, and Phoebe and Mike break up.

Original airdate: February 20, 2003

EPISODE 211: "THE ONE WITH THE MEMORIAL SERVICE"

Ross jokingly posts news of Chandler's "coming out" on their alumni Web site, Ross has Monica and Chandler throw him a memorial service after Chandler posts news of Ross's sudden death, and Monica tries to keep Phoebe away from Mike.

Original airdate: March 13, 2003

EPISODE 212: "THE ONE WITH THE LOTTERY"

The gang pools their money and purchases a bunch of Powerball tickets, Ross initially resists, and Phoebe drops the tickets over the balcony when a pigeon swoops by.

Original airdate: April 3, 2003

EPISODE 213: "THE ONE WITH RACHEL'S DREAM"

Chandler takes Ross to a Vermont inn when Monica tells him she can't go, Ross and Chandler steal as much stuff from the room as they can, and Rachel has a kissing dream about Joey.

Original airdate: April 17, 2003

EPISODE 214: "THE ONE WITH THE SOAP OPERA PARTY"

Joey tries to send everyone to a play so he can have a secret *Days of Our Lives* party. Rachel finds out about the party and soon everyone but Chandler knows and decides to attend. Meanwhile Chandler is stuck at the play alone. Ross meets Charlie, a hot professor, and Rachel makes up her mind that she wants to kiss Joey but finds Joey kissing Charlie instead.

Original airdate: April 24, 2003

EPISODE 215: "THE ONE WITH THE FERTILITY TEST"

Ross helps Joey prepare for his intellectual date with Charlie, Rachel discovers that Phoebe is working in a corporate massage chain, and Monica and Chandler find out they won't be able to have children.

Original airdate: May 1, 2003

EPISODE 216: "THE ONE WITH THE DONOR"

Chandler invites to dinner a coworker he thinks would make a great sperm donor, Phoebe and Rachel take Charlie shopping, and Phoebe and David the Scientist Guy reunite.

Original airdate: May 8, 2003

EPISODE 217: "THE ONE IN BARBADOS—PART 1"

The gang goes to Barbados for Ross's convention and Phoebe brings along her ex-boyfriend, David. Chandler accidentally deletes Ross's speech, so Charlie helps Ross rewrite it, leaving Rachel and Joey to get drunk together. Mike plans to ask Phoebe to marry him, and he shows up at the last minute to ask her, interrupting David's proposal with his own.

Original airdate: May 15, 2003

EPISODE 218: "THE ONE IN BARBADOS—PART 2"

Phoebe rejects Mike's proposal but tells him she still wants to be with him, Charlie and Joey break up, and Rachel finally tells Joey about her crush on him. Joey decides nothing can happen because of his friendship with Ross, but after seeing Ross and Charlie kissing, he and Rachel do kiss. Meanwhile Monica and Mike compete at a game of Ping-Pong.

Original airdate: May 15, 2003

Season Ten

EPISODE 219: "THE ONE AFTER JOEY AND RACHEL KISS"

Ross and Charlie hold off on going any further until Ross talks with Joey, Rachel and Joey decide to do the same, Monica gets cornrows, and Mike breaks up with Precious for Phoebe.

Original airdate: September 25, 2003

EPISODE 220: "THE ONE WHERE ROSS IS FINE"

Ross walks in on Joey and Rachel kissing and says he's fine, Chandler and Monica visit with a couple whose adopted child didn't know he was adopted until Chandler told him, and a stressed-out Frank Jr. contemplates giving Phoebe one of his triplets.

Original airdate: October 2, 2003

EPISODE 221: "THE ONE WITH ROSS'S TAN"

Ross decides to get a spray-on tan, Joey and Rachel try but can't have sex, and Monica finds out that Phoebe once tried to cut her out.

Original airdate: October 9, 2003

EPISODE 222: "THE ONE WITH THE CAKE"

Emma turns one, and Rachel throws her a birthday party, but won't let the party start until Emma wakes up from her nap. Meanwhile everyone has somewhere they need to be, and Emma's cake turns out to be a penis instead of a bunny.

Original airdate: October 23, 2003

EPISODE 223: "THE ONE WHERE RACHEL'S SISTER BABYSITS"

Rachel's sister Amy visits and Rachel finally agrees to let her babysit Emma, which she regrets when Emma comes home with pierced ears, Joey writes a letter of recommendation to the adoption agency on Monica and Chandler's behalf, and Phoebe spoils Mike's plans to propose, but after several attempts, they get engaged.

Original airdate: October 30, 2003

EPISODE 224: "THE ONE WITH ROSS'S GRANT"

Ross applies for a paleontology grant to be awarded by Dr. Hobart, Charlie's ex-boyfriend, Monica and Rachel fight over who *doesn't* get Phoebe's artwork, Chandler lies to Joey about recommending him to his boss for a commercial part, and Charlie breaks up with Ross after learning of Dr. Hobart's feelings for her.

Original airdate: November 6, 2003

EPISODE 225: "THE ONE WITH THE HOME STUDY"

A social worker from the adoption agency visits Monica and Chandler, but learns that the guy who never called after a one-night stand is their friend Joey. Ross and Rachel take Emma to the park after Ross discovers Rachel's fear of swings, and Phoebe and Mike can't decide what to do with their wedding money.

Original airdate: November 13, 2003

EPISODE 226: "THE ONE WITH THE LATE THANKSGIVING"

Rachel and Phoebe take Emma to a beauty pageant, Joey and Ross go to a Rangers home game, and they are all late for Monica and Chandler's Thanksgiving dinner, so Monica and Chandler lock them all out. After they all beg for forgiveness, they are finally reunited when Monica and Chandler get a call from the adoption agency.

Original airdate: November 20, 2003

EPISODE 227: "THE ONE WITH THE BIRTH MOTHER"

Monica and Chandler meet the woman, Erica, who will serve as a birth mother for them but Erica thinks they are a reverend and a doctor, Joey dates one of Phoebe's friends who eats off his plate, and Rachel shops for Ross but Ross accidentally wears Rachel's new shirt on his date.

Original airdate: January 8, 2004

EPISODE 228: "THE ONE WHERE CHANDLER GETS CAUGHT"

Monica and Chandler find a house in the suburbs and have a hard time telling the gang, who mistakenly think their real estate agent is Chandler's mistress. The friends reminisce about their memories of Monica and Chandler's apartment.

Original airdate: January 15, 2004

EPISODE 229: "THE ONE WHERE THE STRIPPER CRIES"

Rachel and Monica find a last-minute stripper for Phoebe's bachelorette party, Joey guest stars on *Pyramid*, and Ross learns that Chandler and Rachel made out back in college.

Original airdate: February 5, 2004

EPISODE 230: "THE ONE WITH PHOEBE'S WEDDING"

Phoebe fires Monica as her wedding planner, a snowstorm nearly puts the wedding on hold, and Phoebe and Mike decide to go ahead with the wedding despite the bad weather.

Original airdate: February 12, 2004

EPISODE 231: "THE ONE WHERE JOEY SPEAKS FRENCH"

Joey tries to learn French, Rachel's father has a heart attack, and Erica, birth mother for Monica and Chandler, visits New York.

Original airdate: February 19, 2004

EPISODE 232: "THE ONE WITH PRINCESS CONSUELA"

Phoebe changes her name, Rachel gets fired from Ralph Lauren, and Joey reluctantly goes to see Monica and Chandler's new house in the suburbs.

Original airdate: February 26, 2004

EPISODE 233: "THE ONE WHERE ESTELLE DIES"

Rachel takes a job in Paris, Estelle dies, Ross tries to get back Rachel's job at Ralph Lauren, and Janice almost buys the house next to Monica and Chandler's new home.

Original airdate: April 22, 2004

EPISODE 234: "THE ONE WITH RACHEL'S GOING AWAY PARTY"

Monica learns that Nana liked it rough after finding a pair of handcuffs in the closet, Rachel says her farewells to everyone but Ross, Erica goes into

☆Still More Star Sightings☆

- Aisha Tyler (Professor Charlie Wheeler) "The One With the Soap Opera Party"

- John Stamos (Zack) "The One With the Donor"

- Jennifer Coolidge (Amanda) "The One With Ross's Tan"

- Greg Kinnear (Dr. Benjamin Hobart) "The One With Ross's Grant"

- Anna Faris (Erica) "The One With the Birth Mother"

- Danny DeVito (Officer Goodbody) "The One Where the Stripper Cries"

- Donny Osmond (himself) "The One Where the Stripper Cries"

- Leslie Charleson (herself) "The One Where the Stripper Cries"

- Dakota Fanning (MacKenzie) "The One With Princess Consuela"

- Jane Lynch (Ellen) "The One Where Estelle Dies"

labor, and Ross and Rachel finally get together.

Original airdate: April 29, 2004

EPISODE 235: "THE LAST ONE—PART 1"

Joey buys Monica and Chandler a baby chick and duck as a gift, Ross and Rachel sleep together, Monica and Chandler become proud parents of twins, and Rachel leaves for Paris.

Original airdate: May 6, 2004

EPISODE 236: "THE LAST ONE—PART 2"

Monica destroys the foosball table to free the duck and chick, Ross catches up to Rachel at the airport, Rachel decides to stay, and the gang spends their final moments together in Monica and Chandler's apartment.

Original airdate: May 6, 2004